# THE CURRENT ECONOMY

# THE CURRENT

# ECONOMY

ELECTRICITY MARKETS

AND TECHNO-ECONOMICS

## CANAY ÖZDEN-SCHILLING

STANFORD UNIVERSITY PRESS

STANFORD, CALIFORNIA

Stanford University Press
Stanford, California

Printed in the United States of America on acid-free, archival-quality paper

Library of Congress Cataloging-in-Publication Data

Names: Özden-Schilling, Canay, author.
Title: The current economy : electricity markets and techno-economics /
    Canay Özden-Schilling.
Description: Stanford, California : Stanford University Press, 2021. |
    Includes bibliographical references and index.
Identifiers: LCCN 2020047026 (print) | LCCN 2020047027 (ebook) | ISBN
    9781503612273 (cloth) | ISBN 9781503628212 (paperback) | ISBN
    9781503628229 (ebook)
Subjects: LCSH: Electric utilities—United States. | Electric
    utilities—Social aspects—United States. | Markets—Social
    aspects—United States. | Expertise—Economic aspects—United States. |
    Technology—Economic aspects—United States. | Economic
    anthropology—United States.
Classification: LCC HD9685.U5 O85 2021 (print) | LCC HD9685.U5 (ebook) |
    DDC 333.793/20973—dc23
LC record available at https://lccn.loc.gov/2020047026
LC ebook record available at https://lccn.loc.gov/2020047027

Cover design: Andrew Brozyna

FOR TOM

# CONTENTS

# ACKNOWLEDGMENTS

I began to explore the ideas that would become *The Current Economy* at the Massachusetts Institute of Technology in the Program in History, Anthropology, and Science, Technology and Society, where I was a doctoral student. During my time at what is affectionately known as HASTS, I had the opportunity to work with exceptional mentors. Over the years, Mike Fischer's mentorship has broadened my horizons in countless ways and given me models of scholarly thinking that I can only hope to emulate. I am endlessly grateful to Stefan Helmreich for tirelessly sharpening my ruminations into arguments and encouraging me to be a better thinker. From Susan Silbey, I have learned the methods of scholarly pursuit. Finally, since my first days in graduate school at New York University, Tim Mitchell has inspired me to feed my curiosity into the questions that matter. Among the affiliates of HASTS, I have been grateful to the reading, support, and encouragement of David Kaiser, Heather Paxson, Harriet Ritvo, Chris Walley, and Susann Wilkinson. Karen Gardner's friendship was as indispensable as her guidance in navigating administrative waters.

At MIT and in greater Cambridge, I had the distinction of having the loveliest friends one could hope to have in graduate school. Shreeharsh Kelkar manages to bring fun and joy to every day. Shira Shmuely will forever be my sister. Ashawari Chaudhuri and Lucas Müller have been steady sources of understanding and kindness. Amah Edoh and Marie Burks know how much I relied on them during my Cambridge years. A larger group of fellow graduate students knew when my research needed one more citation and/or one more beer. In HASTS past and present, they include Orkideh Behrouzan, Renée Blackburn, Kieran Downes, Xaq Frohlich, Amy Johnson, Clare Kim, Grace Kim, Nicole Labruto, Crystal Lee, Jia Hui Lee, Lan Li, Xi Emily Lin, Lisa Messeri, Teasel Muir-Harmony, Peter Oviatt, Luisa Reis Castro, Beth Semel, David Singerman, Ellan Spero, Mitali Thakor, Michaela Thompson, Nate Deshmukh Towery, and Ben Wilson. Beyond HASTS, Aslı Arpak, Ekin Kurtiç, Andy Rosing and Stephen Tapscott, Aytuğ Şaşmaz, and Mengqi Wang made Cambridge a better place.

The research that went into this book was made possible thanks to many generous people. I thank the market analysts, traders, engineers, market participants, and citizen activists who brought markets to life for me in long conversations. I would like to particularly thank Marija Ilić and her team for hosting and humoring me in Pittsburgh. My activist friends in West Virginia and Illinois gave me new critical thinking skills and taught me to have fun along the way. I am endlessly excited about future conversations with them. Financial support for the research was provided by the Wenner-Gren Foundation for Anthropological Research.

Over the years, I have been fortunate to be able to develop and share the key arguments of this book with excellent audiences by way of invited lectures, workshops, and journal pages. I am especially grateful to Simone Abram, Hayal Akarsu, Andrea Ballestero, Dominic Boyer, Stephen Collier, Elizabeth Ferry, Stephanie Friede, Gökçe Günel, Sheila Jasanoff, Leksa Lee, Miriam Posner, Antina von Schnitzler, Brit Ross Winthereik, and Caitlin Zaloom. Among the audiences to which I had the chance to present my research, I would like to particularly acknowledge the Department of Sociology at the National University of Singapore, which I am thrilled to join soon as faculty. At Stanford University Press, it was a privilege to work with Michelle Lipinski and Margo Irvin. I am humbled by the incredibly productive and generous reviews by the anonymous reviewers. Needless to say, all of this book's errors are mine.

Chapter 2 draws on the following, previously published article: "The Infrastructure of Markets: From Electric Power to Electronic Data." *Economic Anthropology* 3 (1): 68–80. Published Wiley-Blackwell, © 2016 American Anthropological Association. Parts of the following article are reproduced in the Introduction: "Economy Electric." *Cultural Anthropology* 30 (4): 578–588. Published Wiley-Blackwell, © 2015 American Anthropological Association.

This book was written in Baltimore during a postdoctoral fellowship at Johns Hopkins University. At Hopkins, I had the invaluable opportunity to work with three outstanding scholars as part of an invigorating Sawyer Seminar, "Precision and Uncertainty in a World of Data." Naveeda Khan's intellectual strength, enthusiasm, and much-appreciated humor continue to be irreplaceable. I will forever cherish the modes of responsible and caring scholarship I have learned from Veena Das, as well as her support and warmth. Jeremy

Greene, in addition to inspiring me with his prolific scholarship (and prolific running), has gifted me the title of this book. All four of us and the Seminar were kept afloat by Sam Gomes's expert administrative assistance. For making the Anthropology Department a welcoming place, I would like to also extend my gratitude to Alessandro Angelini, Michael Degani, Niloofar Haeri, Clara Han, Nicole Labruto, Anand Pandian, Deborah Poole, and Valeria Procupez. During the final stage of revisions, writing sessions with Hayal Akarsu and Shreeharsh Kelkar were a critical source of camaraderie and sustenance.

In Baltimore, many friends have tremendously contributed to this book by letting me drone on about academic minutiae and giving me plenty of reasons to look forward to breaks. In particular, I am grateful to Maggie Epps, Nicole Aranda, and their families, for making Baltimore home. I can't wait to raise our families together and support each other through the good, the bad, and the pandemic.

My parents, Aytül and Ercan Özden, have always had the unwarranted conviction that I knew what I was doing with my life. I have always relied on their unconditional trust, and for that, I am thankful. Over the years, my nuclear family grew to include wonderful new people. I thank the extended Schilling clan for being so fun to hang out with and so reassuring a presence. My gratitude goes particularly to Gail Schilling, who taught my son about flowers while I was racing this book to the finish line.

I am still in awe of the good fortune that has put me on the same path as my favorite person, my center and my destination, my partner in all things, Tom Özden-Schilling. It beats me how he can be as supportive, loving, and caring as he is, but he always finds a way, no exceptions. This book wouldn't have come to fruition without his unwavering, stubborn encouragement, and for that, it is dedicated to him. Finally, Leo cheered me on from inside my belly when this book was still in its early stages. His entire life overlapped with the book's writing and revisions. No matter how many books I write, words will always fail me when I try to describe how much his love sustains me. Together we grow each day and there is nothing more important. The next book is for you, *benim güzel oğluşum*.

# THE CURRENT ECONOMY

# INTRODUCTION

## The Current Economy

Electricity is ordinary. The denizens of the fully electrified world tend to take its continued presence for granted and are startled by moments of its interruption, like blackouts or brownouts.[1] But electricity is also extraordinary, and not only because, over the course of less than a century and a half within its introduction, it has had a transformative effect on how social life is experienced in urban spaces (Nye 1992) and households (Cowan 1983). Electricity is an extraordinary *commodity*—not one to be used in economics textbooks to demonstrate the purported laws of supply and demand.

First, electricity is very difficult to store. It cannot wait in a warehouse, like clothes or even perishable foods can to varying degrees, while consumers make up their minds or wait for the right price. Many industrialists are currently racing to produce, and produce cheaply, the first grid-level batteries big enough to hold power plants' worth of electricity; in the meantime, most electricity produced in power plants needs to be consumed almost immediately, lest extra supply or sudden loss hurt the wires through which electricity moves. (That is when blackouts may occur.) Second, electricity's transportation is peculiar. Many commodities lend themselves to alternative modes of transportation. Buyers and sellers may switch from air to sea to land, and from shipper to shipper within each mode, in search of lower costs. Electricity, on the other hand, is married to its transportation infrastructure—the electric grid—until the day it can be stored, boxed, and loaded up onto trucks. Furthermore, demand for electricity is what economists often consider "inelastic," which means it barely changes based on changes in prices. Consumers, after all, struggle to conceive of substitutes for electricity when the power goes out.

For at least the second half of the twentieth century, electricity served as a literal textbook example of how there simply could not be markets in certain commodities (Ulbrich 1991). In discussing electricity, textbooks held that "competition is impractical, inconvenient, or simply unworkable" (McConnell 1960, quoted in Ulbrich 1991, 179) and "obviously uneconomical" (Samuelson 1958, quoted in Ulbrich 1991, 179). The initial investment in infrastructure was simply too high for many competitors to undertake, just like in other businesses considered public utilities—water, natural gas, and mail delivery. According to these textbooks, each of these situations called for a "natural monopoly"—a single firm licensed and regulated by a state or government to serve a demarcated territory. That the electricity industry was the archetypal natural monopoly was received wisdom in economics in the early 1980s, when Richard Schmalensee, an economist from the Massachusetts Institute of Technology (MIT) who studied the regulation of electric utilities, was having a chat with officials from the Ronald Reagan administration along with his colleague Paul Joskow. During the chat, the officials, to Schmalensee and Joskow's shock, casually floated the idea of "deregulation" in the electricity industry—the idea to break up the monopolies and initiate market competition. Could there be many producers competing to sell their electricity in the same territory instead of one vertically integrated company producing, transmitting, and delivering it all by itself?

In a conversation that I shared with Schmalensee in his office in 2013, the economist remembered himself and Joskow struggling to contain their incredulity: "'Wait, what? Uh, no! They're natural monopolies! I mean, there's only one set of wires. You can't have competing wires!'" To that, he remembered the officials responding, "You sure? It works everywhere else."[2] Other infrastructural systems across the US, Reagan's officials reminded the economists, were being or had been deregulated at a record pace. Airlines. Trucking. Telecommunications. Within a year or two of that chat, Joskow and Schmalensee wrote one of the first works in the world that addressed the possibility of deregulation in electricity in depth and advised, albeit cautiously, a path toward allowing competition in the generation of electricity (1983).

Less than a decade later, in 1992, the Energy Policy Act passed in the US with clauses that allowed states to break up electricity monopolies. Today, in sixteen states, electricity can be produced, transmitted, and retailed by different entities. In 1996 and 1998, the Federal Energy Regulatory Commission (FERC) took further measures to make competition in electricity a reality. FERC required all transmission operators to open the use of the grid on a nondiscriminate basis to the newly minted buyers and sellers. It also defined rules for transmission operators to run markets for electricity. "Market" specifically meant a commodity exchange, like other commodity exchanges in cotton, wheat, or crude oil, where prices are established periodically by processing a multitude of bids and offers for each megawatt of electricity. Seven electricity markets in the US have come online since. The combined footprint of electricity markets amounts to some two-thirds of the contiguous US. Territorial monopolies, in other words, now make up the minority of the American electricity business. What is more, consumers are taking on more active roles in these markets as our everyday electronics, from electric vehicles to air conditioners, begin to interface with these markets. Once a prime example of economic impossibility, electricity markets have become an unambiguous reality.

What happened? If electricity is so incongruent with our existing ideas of markets, what does it take to build markets in electricity—what kinds of work and expertise are involved in making, maintaining, and inhabiting them? What can we learn from this about the locus of market-building ambition and authority in our contemporary moment in capitalism? In the twenty-first century US, how are domains of social life previously governed by nonmarket reasonings turned into markets—who creates and maintains new markets where none existed before? How do different actors, from traders to everyday consumers, inhabit these new markets? This book sets out to answer these questions.

Electricity's quirks as a commodity come up rather quickly when one starts to talk to people familiar with the business. When I first became interested in electricity markets as a doctoral student in anthropology, I sat in a graduate-level class about electricity regulation offered by MIT's Engineering Systems Division. There, almost every lecture was built around a unique issue related to electricity's physics that made it a business unlike most others. Electricity traveled through the electric grid, for instance, following the path of least resistance. "There is no such thing as, say, blue electricity," said the instructor, an electrical engineer who had become a market regulator. "You can't say, I want my electricity to come from X power plant." Then I began to meet electricity traders and market analysts at "happy hours" in Boston. I noticed how often they, too, brought up electricity's quirks and its essential roles in everyday life— always with smiles on their faces, broadcasting their own fascination with the object of their trade. They spoke, for instance, of how they needed to calibrate their price models every year right before the Super Bowl in anticipation of a massive simultaneous surge in electricity demand to run televisions across the country. From electricity physics to data science to optimization, these experts each had different areas of focus, but for all of them, their expertise was informed by electricity's particular exigencies. Gradually, I also became aware of everyday electricity consumers who protested the infrastructure expansion projects encouraged by electricity markets. They spoke of their sense of property ownership, again, in a way that was informed by the layout of the electric grid, like the farmers who described to me how close the transmission wires hung to their crops.

This book reports on ethnographic work with several kinds of groups that design, maintain, and critique markets in electricity. Each chapter is a building block in examining the puzzle that animates this book—how a market is made, maintained, and inhabited in an unlikely commodity like electricity. Throughout this endeavor, I document several different kinds of practice, expert and otherwise, which all take electricity as its object. These include the work of engineer-economist teams who theorized the mathematics of price-making formulas for markets that would honor electricity's physics; data workers who create computational representations of electricity that enable remote trade by far-flung actors; optimization and behavioral research experts who invent better ways to balance the supply and demand of electricity; and citizen activists whose experiences with the electric grid lead them to demand more just mechanisms for the exchange of electricity. To explore how the *natural* monopoly days are being left behind, this book takes us to the *cultural* settings of a variety of electricity-focused groups. These cultures, I argue, are what give electricity its markets today—in forms that are diverse, contested, yet unambiguously real.

The title of this book, *The Current Economy*, works in two ways. One is specific to the markets of electricity; at the ethnographic level, the book shows a robust, humming economy built around the fleeting current of electricity in the contemporary US. The other points at a larger phenomenon in contemporary capitalism, one about which electricity's markets have much to teach us. The book sketches the contours of the economies in which we currently live—economies built and maintained, technologically, by specific groups of workers. I seek to show that novel economic reasonings, market-making ambition, and expertise originate in heterogenous technological domains. Only rarely, furthermore, do these critical facets of contemporary markets develop from the explicit borrowing or trickling down of explicit ideologies. We live, in other words, with the products of the economic imaginations of electrical engineers, data experts, optimization experts, among others—and not merely the imaginations of policymakers or economists whose expertise receives vastly more attention in popular and scholarly critiques of contemporary economic orders. By way of an economic ethnography of electricity in the US, *The Current Economy* seeks to explore the heterogenous and technologically informed nature of economic expertise, imaginations, and aspirations today.

## Work Cultures

It is nine in the morning on a Monday. I enter the ballroom of an upscale hotel in Northampton, Massachusetts, arranged like a classroom with long desks facing a projector screen. At the check-in desk, a smiling woman hands me my name tag, a thick binder full of printouts, and a calculator. Like the few dozen people around me, I find a seat that I will wind up keeping over the course of a densely scheduled week. Soon, representatives from the Independent System Operator of New England (ISO-NE) will take the stage one after the other to explain how they run their electricity market. Theirs is one of the seven markets in the United States and nine in North America for the exchange of electricity, and still a new creation (about two decades-old at the time of this writing). We go around the room to introduce ourselves; with the exception of me and another researcher (a graduate student in economics), every participant is here because their employment entails doing business with New England's electricity market.

There are electricity traders who are switching to New England's market after having traded in different electricity markets. There are regulators from state regulation agencies. There are engineers from electric utilities, who will, over the course of the week, grow most interested when an occasional piece of electric grid equipment is passed around. There are accountants, one of whom during our lunch break together will sheepishly admit to struggling to follow the "technical discussions": "I just want to match the numbers." The twenty-something trader sitting to my right listens to the instructor while his eyes are glued to his phone. In whispered remarks throughout the sessions, a disgruntled power plant engineer sitting to my left waxes nostalgic to me about premarket days. We each have come to this room with different kinds of expertise, priorities, and beliefs; we will feel out of place or at home accordingly as instructors bring up the different slices of the phenomenon that is markets in electricity.

Perhaps one manager from an electricity generation company comes closest to articulating our shared goal: "I'm here to understand how we make money." We are here to understand how electricity and money are made to move alongside each other in the twenty-first century, in the US, in a complex new economy.

But we don't always understand so well. Many of us endure and even enjoy solving the simplistic price calculation exercises we are given. The accountants are particularly good at this. But, through their comments at different sessions throughout the week, it becomes clear that many attendees continue to be nagged by simple yet existential questions about how markets in electricity can even exist in the first place—a service, we intuitively know, is so subconsciously and spontaneously consumed. One participant shouts, "My fridge doesn't want to only work when the price is low." Another, in a dramatic gesture, walks to the light switch in the room and turns the lights off to ask, somewhat daringly, how the market will account for this minute but unexpected change in demand. The trader to my left, still comfortably glued to his phone, is unfazed by these protests; he thinks there can be a market in anything. When he has heard something he truly does not understand, like how power plants' fuel type sets a price window, he finally puts down his phone, sits up, and raises his hand. The power plant engineers in the room brush him off; it is *just* about the physics of electricity production. Later, it is time for those engineers to be vexed by the matter of why and how virtual trading (buying and selling on paper for profit) is allowed in electricity markets. Isn't the entire point of the business, they ask, *actually* producing and consuming electricity?

This scene demonstrates the heterogeneity of priorities and expertise in electricity markets. It reflects the many kinds of work required to put an electricity market in place. As the following chapters show, this work may be more or less harmonious. The policymaking effort in the 1990s, like the legal acts that removed the obstacles in the way of competition in electricity, was but a small part of this collective process. To this day, Schmalensee remembers those officials from the Reagan administration as "wide-eyed ideologues," people who merely liked the sound of deregulation and free markets, who naively assumed that markets could be generic, and that competition could be copied from business to business, from airlines, to trucks, to telecommunications, to electricity. But copying would not do the job; several groups, whose work cultures coalesced around electricity and specific toolkits developed to address its properties, have eased electricity into market circulation and continue to give shape to its economy.

Figure I-1. Independent System Operators (ISOs) or Regional Transmission Organizations (RTOs) in the United States and Canada. Each one of these entities operates an electricity market. Source: *ferc.gov*.

To trace the origins and trajectories of the expertise that animates these markets, I suggest that researchers enter the laboratories, offices, and classrooms, where such expertise is produced and passed on. Only there, I argue, can scholars discern whether the knowledge and practices that make markets work are direct imports from policymaking or economics circles. When such an exercise is conducted in the field of electricity, we come across original economic modes of reasoning, which resist straightforward alignment with broader ideologies. We see experts at work, removed from sustained government funding or expertise, enacting their economic reasonings in everyday life and work by designing and maintaining markets with a wide reach. I suspect this originality is not unique to experts of electricity and the making of markets in electricity.

I suggest, in other words, delving deep into a variety of "work cultures" for answers about contemporary market building and maintenance practice. I define these as cultures of sustained work with materials and their associated properties, assisted by particular toolkits, be it electric meters, spreadsheets, or applied mathematics. These toolkits predispose experts to diagnose particular kinds of problems in the social world and, over time, generate and uphold corresponding kinds of actions to treat those perceived problems. Work cultures are technological; they come to being as actors respond to the properties of certain materials and design interventions into these materials' social lives. Sometimes, these interventions have an *economic* character—the character of having the potential to distribute and redistribute resources or wealth at a societal level.

In anthropology and Science and Technology Studies (STS), interest has exploded in recent decades in the figure of the "expert," an actor whose skill and epistemic authority have societal ramifications (for a review, see Carr 2010). I use "work cultures" in this book instead of "cultures of expertise" (Boyer 2008, 44), not to signal a categorical difference between work and expertise, but to accentuate the sense of modesty and ordinariness with which many of my interlocutors approach their work. For the purposes of this book, the concept includes other forms of technological labor that are often accorded less epistemic authority in critical studies of expertise: labor like that of electricity trade's database workers or those workers whom Lilly Irani calls "data janitors" (2015). This work can also include so-called domestic work—the household, land, and property management work that many of my citizen activist interlocutors bring to their understanding of electricity markets. Perhaps even more so than defining who these workers are and in what their work consists, however—empirical questions that I take on in each chapter of this book—I find it important to develop here the "culture" component of "work culture" (or "cultures of expertise" for that matter), which tends to be less problematized in the scholarship on experts. What do we mean when we say experts or workers have a culture of their own?

There is value in holding on to "culture," especially after anthropology's twentieth-century self-reflections have definitively alerted us to the term's potential instrumentality in upholding the colonial power dynamics into which anthropology was born (Clifford 1988; Fischer 2007). Through those self-reflections came newer working definitions for culture, like one from Marilyn Strathern, who, while considering how we rethink kinship through new reproductive technologies, wrote, "Culture consists in the images which make imagination possible, in the media with which we mediate experience" (1992, 33). Many of those images and media through which people generate beliefs about what is acceptable, good, or important in the shared social field come to life and thicken with practice in work environments.

I refer to those images and media as the experts' *toolkits* in this book.

Toolkits, by definition, are diverse. They might include anything from a spreadsheet meant to represent the world in individually distinguishable bits to a specific mathematical formula to which an expert grows attached over time. Partly generic (i.e., transferred from context to context, as in the case of the spreadsheet) and partly unique to specific materials (e.g., electric meters), toolkits predispose their users to identify problems in the world in specific ways—ways that can be addressed by those very toolkits to which they have access and over which they have mastery. In forwarding this conceptualization of culture informed by toolkits, I am heavily influenced by sociologist Ann Swidler, who writes, "Culture influences action not by providing the ultimate values toward which action is oriented, but by shaping a repertoire or 'tool kit' of habits, skills, and styles from which people construct 'strategies of action'" (1986, 273). When Swidler refers to a toolkit, she has in mind "symbols, stories, rituals, and world-views, which people may use in varying configurations to solve different kinds of problems" (1986, 273). While the work of Max Weber and the Parsonian sociology that followed in Weber's footsteps typically focus on a group's presumed collective values and wants, Swidler argues that the toolkit a particular group has at its disposal is what explains the range of actions to which its members typically resort. Similarly, in this book, I depict electric meters, the spreadsheet, and variants of applied mathematics as parts of toolkits. Through these, my interlocutors build spoken and unspoken consensus around questions like the nature of social problems and what can be done to address them—questions shot through with the images and media that make sense to people populating a culture. Throughout the following chapters, I treat this process as the emergence and reproduction of a culture, of work or otherwise.

Holding onto culture is also holding onto ethnographic fieldwork and anthropology. In his meditation on methods for an anthropology of expertise, Dominic Boyer suggests that we form connections with experts beyond their physical spaces of expertise—that we spend time with them as they relax and socialize outside their offices, so as to avoid painting them merely as rationalist followers of a logic of expertise—simply put, that we "humanize" them (2008, 45). It was while spending this kind of unscripted time with my interlocutors that I came to gradually note that in today's US, market-building motivation and expertise is routinely removed from explicit ideological dedication to markets as a social good. It was during conversations at "happy hours" in Pittsburgh and Boston that my interlocutors, whom I consider expert market builders and maintainers, would casually express support for politicians who themselves had expressed hesitation toward forms of market-based governance, without seeming to register a paradox. We could interpret this behavior as cognitive dissonance, only if the range of political acts we consider remains limited to ideological alignment. In that way, my argument in this book also emerges from my observations of "silences" (Das 2006, 9) and omittances as much as utterances—the kind of observations that were only possible to make if sustained engagement, beyond interviews, gave me reason to expect certain utterances. Seeing a culture through not only its acts and utterances but also its silences and omittances may allow us a "descent," to use Veena Das's term (2006, 15), into a range of the political ordinary, where it is possible to be a market builder who does not necessarily believe in markets as solutions to social ills.

## Techno-economics

Electricity's quirks might be unusual. But every commodity, after all, has unique properties: properties with which people work in their attempts to build and transform new economies. In that vein, we can chart a field of activity, key to the making of contemporary economies, that the study of electricity might illuminate. I propose an approach that understands commodities—whether they are inorganic processes like electricity or living nonhumans like livestock (Blanchette 2020), plants (Besky 2014), or microscopic organisms (Paxson 2008)—as more than passive receptacles of human design. My approach instead locates humans within their efforts to commoditize and marketize materials, even somewhat quirky ones like electricity. This approach compels us to take agency as a "matter of intra-acting" or an "enactment," as opposed to "something that someone or something has" (Barad 2007, 214). Considered this way, agency concerns not only humans but also nonhumans, especially in scientific and technological fields, where the object with which one works is often a nonhuman force like electricity. In these fields, "there is a sense in which 'the world kicks back'" in Karen Barad's words (2007, 215). Drawing on Timothy Mitchell's concept of "techno-politics"—"an amalgam of both human and nonhuman, things and ideas" and a combination of open-ended, "intentional" and "unintended" interactions (2002, 42–43)—I call this field of study "techno-economics."

Electricity, indeed, might compel us to reconsider how we think about materiality and agency in social theory. The "material" is often considered to be operating in the "world of atoms" (Boucher et al. 2019, 11), both for those who develop a binary between the digital and the material (Negroponte 1995) and those who critique that binary (Boucher et al. 2019). Electricity, strictly speaking, is not matter but a flow. As a flow (of electrons), it does not unambiguously belong to the realm of atoms. Those who debate the character of agency regularly speak of materials as "things" (Callon 2005; Miller 2005a) and use materials with more straightforward relationships with atoms, like cars, in their argumentation (Miller 2005b). In this book, I do take electricity to be material (in its adjective form) and a material (in its noun form) because it is a physical nonhuman presence with which humans are coterminous in their economic endeavors. In the techno-economic field I chart, materiality is perhaps not a question of atoms but of agency. Electricity is a material that "kicks back" in its "intra-acting" with humans (Barad 2007, 214–15).

Techno-economics responds to a long conversation in economic anthropology and its troubles with the technological field. As Bill Maurer (2006a) notes, economic anthropologists have long reproduced the "great transformation" paradigm put forward by Karl Polanyi (1944). Assuming that markets became disembedded from social relations in Western market societies and that state-backed Western money commensurated otherwise incommensurable objects and activities (Simmel 1907), economic anthropologists following Polanyi of the so-called substantivist school have turned their attention to exchange systems thought to be outside market relations, including systems based on reciprocity, redistribution, and subsistence (Bohannan 1959; Dalton 1965; Halperin 1977; Polanyi 1947; Taussig 1980). Economic sociologists, on the other hand, notably Marc Granovetter (1985) and other proponents of the "new economic sociology," attempted to reclaim market studies by positing the continued embeddedness of economic actions in social relationships in the West, as elsewhere (see also Krippner 2001). Interestingly, Granovetter, with coauthor Patrick McGuire (1998), singled out the electricity industry specifically to illustrate their point. Its continuous dependence on the mobilization of social networks was proof, they argued, that Western industries did not always exclusively follow technical dictates of rationality, and that these industries were, instead, socially constructed. This formulation, however, has only reaffirmed an opposition between social and technical ways of organizing the economic field, and preserved the "great transformation" paradigm by according it a gradient from lesser to greater embeddedness (for a critique, see Mitchell 2008).

Polanyi's yoke is now thrown off and scholars of economic life study market structures, from financial markets (Beunza and Stark 2004; Zaloom 2003) to investment banking (Ho 2009) across the globe, with no worry for distinguishing the social aspects of economic life from technological ones. Part of the credit for this goes to STS scholars, and to their invitation to study sciences and technological milieus as cultures, and scientists as makers, rather than mere reporters, of reality. The implication for economic expertise is that it, too, plays a role in building the reality it purports to simply describe. Drawing on J. L. Austin's work in the philosophy of language (1962), Michel Callon notably singles out the role of economists in building markets, which he dubs the "performativity of economics" (1998). His invitation has generated close and potent investigations of the relationship between textbook economics and financial markets (Callon and Çalışkan 2010; Lépinay 2011; MacKenzie 2006). The performativity approach effectively refutes once and for all the view of markets as self-evident and spontaneous, and opens up the technical nitty-gritty of the economic field to unapologetic social study.

In charting the field of techno-economics, I build on this body of theory that bridges the social and the technological fields in studies of markets, but with a different emphasis. The "performativity of economics" (Callon 1998) paradigm has led scholars to investigate primarily those experts with a claim to economic theory, like economists (MacKenzie, Muniesa, and Siu 2008). In this book, I aim to shift attention away from those with explicit claims and intentions regarding economic theory and toward economic reasonings that emerge in the thick of interactions with a technological commodity like electricity. I seek to explore the economic work of those actors who express little interest in the production of economic knowledge or market building as a political goal, when the roles that they play in economic design and maintenance are perhaps more significant than the roles played by economic experts or policymakers. I believe Austin's nuanced theory makes room for recognizing incongruities between actions and utterances, as well as the fragility of the link between them (Das 2006, 178).

A techno-economic approach would carry forward the current concerns of the economically inflected anthropologies of the US. Rich in depictions of both the receiving and the inflicting parties of capitalistic processes, the anthropology of the US has documented the effects of deindustrialization on individual lives in the Rust Belt (Walley 2013), the burdens faced by laborers adapting to the loss of manufacturing jobs since the 1980s (Martin 1994), and the racialized economies that either trap groups in poverty or deny them their autonomy (Cattelino 2008). What we know about the many experts involved in these processes suggests that they are often socialized into accepting capitalistic wealth growth as a norm. We know that the ultra-rich pass on to new generations an understanding of well-deserved wealth and distinction via educational institutions (Khan 2012). We know that investment bankers and other privileged, yet not-quite-ultra-rich, maintainers of financial systems believe in the talent-producing merits of the high employee turnover culture in finance, which they then propagate across US industries (Ho 2009).

But what other milieus of socialization exist for the makers and maintainers of US markets? Where might they be learning to design markets as solutions to social ills, even when they do not necessarily articulate such aspirations? I believe we can study technological cultures where individuals learn to operate specific tools, develop corresponding "economic imaginations" (Appel 2014), and come to engage in market building and maintaining activity, without necessarily developing or articulating that activity's political implications. We can also study how everyday consumption sites and encounters with public infrastructures prime people to develop certain economic imaginations. The unarticulated and covert nature of a pro-market attitude in the cultures I study might go a long way toward explaining the wide sway of market-building and maintenance activity in the US—an activity devotedly pursued by even those who do not endorse it politically. There is, perhaps, a techno-economic consensus within work cultures that propagate market formations, even when the meanings at stake—of markets, of technologies, and of capitalism writ large—are open-ended and diverse.

I envision techno-economics to contribute to the recent attempts to theorize energy flows, especially the roles that energy flows have played in the making of modernity. Much of this scholarship has been prompted by the catastrophic progress of anthropogenic climate change. Andreas Malm, for instance, reconsiders modern capitalism as the mobilization of "fossil capital," or the energy extracted from fossils, which allowed the ruling classes to subordinate laborers more extensively than in earlier modes of production (2016). Malm's argument has helped stimulate some scholars to rethink all modes of production as modes of harnessing energy, including human energy in the entangled histories of slavery and capitalism (D. Hughes 2017). In the same spirit, Dominic Boyer has proposed a new genealogy for modern power, coterminous with Michel Foucault's biopower, that accounts for the use of immense amounts of electricity and fuel in managing life in the Anthropocene (2014).

I agree that energy and political economy have an intertwined trajectory primed for theorization—the way Timothy Mitchell has theorized crude oil and its role in the dismantlement of labor organization and the emergence of condensed urban living and mass democracies in the twentieth century (2011). Electricity is particularly befitting of that task, having received much less attention in energy scholarship than crude oil, despite the latter's comparatively modest share in global consumption figures (Jones 2016). But the theorization I call for is not transhistorical; I do not aim to chart out an *electric capital* since electricity has a different social life in the improvisational infrastructures of urban Tanzania (Degani 2018) than in the context of humanitarian electrification projects in rural India (Cross 2013). Even in the same country and time period, studying electricity work cultures uncovers different aspirations for economic exchange.

Studying techno-economics situates us in specific instances where the reorientation of energy flows facilitates the emergence of new economic patterns. As the following section explains, many such patterns in the US have histories closely linked to experimentation with electricity production and consumption, from natural monopolies to economies of scale. These patterns are tightly wound with activity in the techno-economic field, where people attempt to reorient electricity flows and electricity, necessarily, kicks back.

## Electric Histories

Analyzing the techno-economic field requires following the materials with which our interlocutors are entangled. Of course, there are many possible ways to chase after electricity. That is exactly what Benjamin Franklin famously did when he flew a kite in a storm in 1750. Franklin showed that a force occurs between positively and negatively charged bodies—clouds were his particular objects of interest—and proposed that electricity was a matter of the travel of opposing charges, and not a matter of fluid motion in the ether, as many natural philosophers had previously postulated (Isaacson 2004, 129–46). The electricity that this book follows is not in Franklin's clouds, though it is not completely unrelated to the sort of electricity produced by lightning, either.

While a number of different phenomena related to electrical charge are considered "electricity" in physics and electrical engineering, the kind of electricity I discuss in the pages to follow is distinguished by the infrastructure that enables its production, exchange, and use—the kind of infrastructure that anthropologists have defined as "matter that enables the movement of other matter" (Larkin 2013, 329), "delivering critical services for human communities and economies" (Carse 2012, 540). The electricity I discuss is a standardized commodity, produced by dynamos and measured in the electricity bills that US consumers receive in their mail. Among engineers, this electricity is commonly called "electric power," or, in more specific engineering terms, "electromagnetic field energy." It is priced in kilowatt/hours and delivered in alternating current (AC) at a standardized voltage and frequency.[3] Unlike Franklin's electricity, the electricity I discuss is synonymous with electric power since its desirability as a commodity is a function of its ability to power appliances. The market actors I study use "electricity" and "electric power" interchangeably; electricity markets are often also referred to as "power markets." For the sake of consistency, I use simply "electricity" in this book.

Electricity's earlier moment in the US before markets was as techno-economic as its present; it simultaneously contributed to the rise of twentieth-century US managerial capitalism and was sustained by it. In the first half of the twentieth century, electricity was organized into a "big grid" (Özden-Schilling 2019a): one that was operated through the concentration of wealth at the hands of a few producers by way of natural monopolies. The big grid depended first and foremost on turning citizens into consumers. This original grid and the relationships it called into being formed one techno-economic field, a field that electrical engineers, computer programmers, data scientists, behavioral researchers, and others are now busily disassembling. As I show throughout this book, a new techno-economic field is taking its place, one in which electricity flows have been refashioned in the image of a market, replete with calculative choice and competition at many scales.

Let us first dwell on the emergence of the big grid to understand our current moment's specificity. Urban citizens of the US, writes historian of electricity David Nye, "encountered electrification in many guises": as spectacle at fairs, as public transportation that reorganized public space, and even as a therapeutic substance to be used in medicine whose wonders waited to be unlocked (1992, 138). Interestingly, electricity *itself* was not actually the original principal commodity of the electrical industry. George Westinghouse and other original industrial players made money by selling electricity production equipment to city governments and industrial manufacturers. The commodity that changed hands was a material means of production in its own right. By the end of the nineteenth century, however, with Thomas Edison's new business plan, electricity's "many guises" (Nye 1992, 138) were narrowed down. Instead of selling production equipment, Edison built a network around his central power station with the aim of selling domestic lighting to consumers (T. Hughes 1993). Edison singled out electricity, the fleeting current, as a useful commodity that could be made to change hands, and thus ushered in the era of electricity consumption as we know it.

Electricity, as it came to be in Edison's network, was not a commodity for which contemporaneous political economists had any straightforward account. Look back to Karl Marx's *Capital*, which employed cotton to illustrate how commodities gain exchange value (1977 [1867] 293–302). Or consider *The Principles of Economics* by Alfred Marshall, the pioneer of neoclassical economics, which famously featured the first graphic representation of the supply and demand curve—for knives, in this case—in a mere footnote (1890, 432). Useful objects such as cotton and knives helped reinforce the notion that production and consumption, as well as supply and demand, were separate forces that would interact over time until equilibrium between the two could be reached. Such commodities could wait in a warehouse while producers and consumers rethought their buying and selling decisions. In the case of electricity, however—even to this day—the time window to establish equilibrium is limited to seconds; that is the temporality enacted in keeping the electric grid intact and functioning. If the removal of supply (say, as a result of a tripped power station) is too sudden, blackouts can occur near and far. Similarly, transmission lines can malfunction if they are subjected to significantly more power than their carrying limit allows.

The topic of making current into a commodity commanded the attention of electrical engineers from the very beginning of electrification. Building on Edison's earlier experience with telegraphy engineering, his engineers devised electromagnetic devices—regulators and exciters—that stabilized the grid in the event of minor deviations from standard supply (T. Hughes 1993, 43). Edison's centrally orchestrated system used only one power plant and, with a known number of light bulbs (around 10,000), forecasting demand (or "load" in electrical parlance) was not a major problem. But Edison's network was built to expand. Since the profit came from small consumers, it would become profitable only if electricity became a daily necessity for household tasks and ever more consumers were convinced to plug in. By the early twentieth century, small grids run by individual small utilities were increasingly being integrated into big grids by way of mergers and purchases, connecting different kinds of power stations and carrying AC across long distances.

Network-building efforts similar to the construction of the electric grid changed the face of capitalism beginning with the twentieth century. Companies that sold other infrastructural commodities, such as railroad service and electric telegraphy, were developing complex managerial hierarchies to organize the flows of these goods—structures and processes that other scholars have described as "managerial capitalism" (Chandler 1977). Enrolling transportation, communications, and electricity-enabled workplace technologies like the assembly line, they combined under their roofs various production and distribution tasks that had formerly been provided by small, single-purpose companies. Natural monopolies like electric utilities initiated mass production and mass distribution services, incorporating into their operations different tasks previously fulfilled through market coordination among many competitors. In the context of the electric grid, utilities to this day define their tasks under three categories: generation, transmission, and distribution. Generation is the production of electricity. Transmission is its shipping via high-voltage transmission lines—those lines that descend from tall transmission towers and occasionally go in and out of electric substations where voltage is stepped up or down. Distribution is the last step, where electricity breaks off of high-voltage lines into low-voltage tentacles that enter end-consumers' dwellings and power our appliances. A vertically integrated natural monopoly would provide all three of these tasks.

Studying the techno-economic field means that we do not take technological developments as passive receptacles of societal economic changes, or vice versa. The electricity industry was not merely an example of managerial capitalism; it contributed to its very rise in significant ways. Electricity industrialists produced economic theory and contributed to the mainstream of economics in their endeavor to advance the big grid. Samuel Insull—an Englishman who was originally a protégé of Edison and later the head of a small electric utility in Chicago—was able to build an empire, Commonwealth Edison, that swallowed all but a few competitors in the Chicago area by unearthing the idea of "natural monopoly" from old economic treatises. John Stuart Mill had ruminated in the mid-nineteenth century that, in industries with large starting costs and large demand, only one firm could meet demand in a given territory while continuing a profitable existence (Seavoy 2006, 269–71). It was not one of Mill's most eminent theorizations until Insull's strategic unearthing of it.

To legitimize his claims to monopoly, Insull created demand for electricity by investing heavily in research on electrical appliances. For instance, home economists heavily recruited by electric utilities at this time knocked on doors in urban areas all over the country to tell women that good homemaking depended on using electrical appliances (Goldstein 1997). Utility managers sought to solve a problem specific to electricity's production—uneven demand between day and night, which was hard on machinery—with the introduction of home electronics like refrigerators running around the clock (Goldstein 1997). Outside the day-to-day operations of utilities themselves, Insull mobilized Mill's argument to persuade state politicians, to whose election campaigns he had financially contributed, to grant his companies exemptions from anti-trust laws and for the right to the exclusive use of the electric grid. To the shock of other American industrialists in the lighting business supporting ideals of free enterprise and competition, he announced his advocacy for state regulations that would allow monopolistic activity (McDonald 1958). The notion of the natural monopoly made it into neoclassical economics textbooks as established fact only in the mid-twentieth century (Mosca 2008), decades after Insull had successfully if controversially introduced it as the economic justification for his network building. Economic patterns that were to become staples in American economic life were coming into being as Insull was trying to meet the challenges of profiting from the fleeting current.

Growing by way of mergers beyond measure, Insull's empire ushered in a model of "economies of scale" in the electricity industry—a situation where the increase in production correlates with the increase in cost savings and, hence, profit (T. Hughes 1993, 216). For the first few decades, vertically integrated, monopolistic corporations like Insull's Commonwealth Edison met resistance from public forces like city governments, cooperatives, and the federal government in the form of legal action concerning consumer rates. In the wake of World War II, however, as Keynesian welfarism and the social state became conventional wisdom, the US federal government made peace with large, vertically integrated corporations. In the postwar period, the government had become a customer of corporations as part of a commitment to maintain full employment and high aggregate demand (Chandler 1977). The techno-economic project of managerial capitalism seemed largely unchallenged; the concept of the natural monopoly became canon in both neoclassical economics and across the electricity industry writ large.

In short, the techno-economic field that was assembled around electricity, from the beginning of electrification until the last decade of the twentieth century, was one in which suppliers steadily grew and eventually became monopolistic, raking in profits through economies of scale. This is the techno-economic field that has been steadily disassembled in the recent decades as different economic logics—market logics of precise calculation, granular matching, and competition—have gradually taken hold.

## The Present, Chapters, Methods

Today, electricity is a function of the infrastructure through which it moves; the entirety of the hardware and software equipment that enables its movements— the infrastructure abstractly called the electric grid by providers, markets, and government offices.[4] It is made up of stronger and weaker transmission lines and the nodes where these lines intersect, like electric substations, which allow the injection or withdrawal of electricity. In that sense, the electric grid is an amalgam of multiple, overlapping grids. One can talk about grids at many different scales, without necessarily excluding one or another particular grid, depending on what economic, political, or metallic bonds one chooses to bring into focus. The grid of the continental US is made up of three grids with regard to synchrony in frequency and phase (the Western Interconnection, the Eastern Interconnection, and the Texas Interconnection), which connect to each other through weak bonds—a few direct current (DC) transmission lines to be used only in extreme emergencies. Each of these interconnects hosts several additional grids run by nonprofit transmission operators.

Each of these grids functions as economic entities because they run daily market processes within which electricity changes hands. After the 1960s, when the first major blackout of the US took place (Nye 2010), it gradually became customary for individual utilities to form alliances to share their service areas as a bulwark against localized failures. Formerly known as "power pools," these organizations were rebranded in the 1990s as Independent System Operators (ISOs) after FERC defined them as nonprofit transmission operators, which would also run *electricity markets*—commodity exchanges in electricity. In these markets, individual participants would submit bids and offers to buy and sell each megawatt of electricity for every preset interval (usually every day), and prices binding for every participant would be announced at a preset time. The first electricity market came online in California in 1998, and today there are seven across the country, each with hundreds of generators and utilities as participants.

Chapter 1, "Regulating," begins with the early moment in deregulation's history to show that the invention of rules for new markets is a techno-economic activity par excellence. The chapter relies on oral history interviews with electrical engineers and energy economists who, in the 1980s and '90s, were involved in turning electricity deregulation from a generic pro-market thought exercise into a reality. They did so by theorizing price-setting mechanisms specific to markets in electricity—mechanisms that would honor marginal cost theory as well as electricity's physics, so that supply and demand's intersections agreed with the carrying capacity of electric wires. One of the actors involved in this process described such activity of theorizing to me as the "gluing of economics and engineering." This chapter endeavors to contribute to an economic anthropology of regulation. In it, I theorize regulation (and its subcategory, deregulation) as incipient market-making activities. Because regulation invariably pertains to both humans and materials at once, I argue the regulation of voltages and the regulation of markets cannot be considered discrepant activities.

Since that moment, wholesale electricity markets have grown considerably in both their geographical footprints and in the volume of electricity traded. The unbundled generators participate to sell their electricity, and the unbundled utilities participate to buy electricity on consumers' behalf. While it is possible to buy and sell electricity through bilateral agreements without going through a market structure even in market footprints, the prices in those agreements are highly affected by market prices as well. No player in the business, in other words, can afford to ignore the markets. ISO-NE (the ISO whose training session I describe above), for instance, reported in 2019 that its market included the participation of more than 500 buyers and sellers, who together traded $7.6 billion worth of electricity at an average price of $30.67 per megawatt.[5] The entities that participate in markets usually have specific trading teams responsible for interfacing with ISOs. In addition, there is a growing number of trading firms with no assets, which buy and sell electricity on paper for arbitrage purposes. Just like in any other established market, there is now considerable research and effort in identifying good trades. Third-party firms collecting information and selling trading advice—market intelligence firms—also emerged and proliferated in the electricity industry in this process. This growing information infrastructure that has come to being around electricity trading connects far-flung actors and increasingly expands the purview of electricity markets.

Chapter 2, "Representing," reports on the thick of everyday electricity trading. Electricity markets have been electronic and remote since their inception, as opposed to open outcry pit trading where traders need to be physically present. The present century has seen information workers gradually taking over electricity trading and reshaping it into a practice of data creation, management, and analysis. These experts are concerned with capturing the world—or rather, the electric grid, with everyone and everything plugged into it—in electronic databases in as much detail as possible, so as to sharpen their price predictions. Even when whether more information will secure more profit is not easily verifiable, the information workers soldier on. In this chapter, I report from the floor of a market intelligence firm I call EnTech,[6] a firm whose primary product is electricity trading advice. This is a place populated by people who create, maintain, and tame information—data managers, computer programmers, software developers, as well as the more modest database workers. While at EnTech, I contributed to a mapping project and also completed my week-long market training at ISO-NE. This chapter shows that in electricity, the work of market actors has been redefined as the provision of granular representations of the world (as opposed to, say, each other's body language as it used to be the case in open outcry trading). This labor has had the effect of ostracizing those market actors who do not have the means to chase and make databases of such granularity; this labor, I argue, is steadily pushing other kinds of workers and experts out of electricity's economy.

The current economy is robust at the level of wholesale electricity exchange, or, the bulk exchange of electricity between the generators that produce electricity and the utilities that purchase it on behalf of end consumers. Some, though, hold alternative aspirations for the forms and functions of electricity's future markets. For instance, while consumers can choose their electric utilities in a number of "deregulated" states (sixteen at the time of writing), prices are largely static at the retail level, changing only once or twice per year. This is where a vision for a "smart grid" begins to matter. The smart grid refers to an agenda to improve the grid with advanced communication technologies. It responds to a variety of needs, including demands for advanced security features and increased physical robustness. These demands became especially urgent following the northeastern blackout of 2003, the most recent multistate blackout in the US. As a more robust version of the contemporary grid, smart-grid designers expect such a grid to act as a marketplace that enables the creation and communication of dynamically changing retail prices for everyday consumers. The smart-grid agenda is pursued by a variety of entities, including national laboratories, groups at research universities, and industry actors, all hoping to reduce waste (and hence costs) by increasing communication inside the grid.

Chapter 3, "Optimizing," is about a subset of electrical engineers who specialize in the operations and, specifically, the optimization of the electric grid. They are concerned with adorning our grids with just enough communication devices so that supply and demand match each other as closely as possible, and doing so silently, in the background of our lives. To optimization engineers, making the grid itself a market will render separate markets near obsolete. These experts are also helped by psychologists and other decision-making scientists in finding ways to enroll humans into the fold of the *grid market*. Drawing on ethnographic portraits of an optimization lab at Carnegie Mellon University in Pittsburgh, I identify what I describe as a "culture of optimization," one rooted in the mid-twentieth-century sciences of systems and uncertainty, as well as in earlier sciences of the first electric grids. Prior to conducting fieldwork at this laboratory, I also worked as a summer research assistant for the lab leader in 2011, exploring electricity consumption culture in the Azores, Portugal, for her project concerning the optimization simulations of the Azorean grid. This gave me a chance to observe the Azorean optimization project at different stages over the years, from research formulation to data collection to argumentation. This chapter is intended to chart an economic anthropology of optimization; in it, I urge readers to see the proliferation of decentralized, modular, and everyday economic formations as a function of a particular work culture of optimization, one that has emerged only recently across several domains of expertise.

Before the current period of market-based electricity exchange, the grid's infrastructure was growing monopolistically. Now it is still growing, but this time it is doing so in a way that enables long-distance trading between far-flung actors. ISOs do not add transmission themselves as non-profit transmission operators, but they have the authority to approve transmission line projects as necessary for reliability purposes—an act that then socializes the cost of the infrastructure expansion project onto the consumer base in the entire ISO's market footprint. The exponential growth of the grid remains controversial. As I show in the chapter to follow, not everyone is happy with the machinations of electricity's cultures.

Chapter 4, "Protesting," chronicles the travails of two discontented citizen groups, precursors to what has become a nationally significant anti-transmission line movement. These groups, one in West Virginia and the other in northern Illinois, first came to an electric consciousness when they learned of transmission expansion projects that were set to cut through their own neighborhoods and land. Both groups quickly moved beyond a mere disapproval of the projects' proposed location onto an elaborate critique of electricity experts' designs on public life. In public events and in court, these activists have disputed the expansion of long-distance transmission for the purpose of promoting long-distance trading. In the process, they have articulated a counter-economics grounded in citizenship and sacred private property. Here, I extend the concept of work culture to recognize the work of property owning, household management, and farming as undertaken by my interlocutors in fights mostly led by women. Techno-economics once again transcends broad-brush ideological narratives as the two groups develop a mutual electric politics despite differences in stances on other political matters. This chapter is an invitation for an economic anthropology of infrastructures; I theorize the public infrastructures we inhabit as milieus of economic socialization—milieus where we learn to generate economic reasonings, aspirations, and imaginations. I argue that it is in everyday encounters with infrastructures and moments of critique that emerge during them that change might seep into the texture of our economic lives.

Ethnographic fieldwork for *The Current Economy* was conducted in most sustained fashion in 2013, with several years before and after for prefieldwork and follow-up, and across a multitude of spaces. Much has been written about the indispensability of multisited ethnographic work when sites and cultures do not overlap or exhaust each other (Marcus and Fischer 1986). An ethnography of electric grids would have been unthinkable if multisited work was not commonly accepted in anthropology today. Even so, "methodological anxieties," in George Marcus's words (1995, 99), are not easy to leave behind. The sites that I selected in the process of conducting research for this book will always require justification if they are to be relied on to represent, or at least provide entry points into, the work cultures I mean to analyze. That justification requires that the ethnographer pass through even more sites for the sake of distinguishing exceptions. Such was the unreported work that went into the making of this book. I sat through countless presentations at other research settings, spent many "happy hours" with market analysts beyond EnTech, and tracked many new anti-transmission groups that have popped up across the US since my first period of fieldwork began. While no book can claim to be an exhaustive study of a thing as pervasive as an electric grid, I am confident that the one you are holding is a representative survey of the US electric grid as it is being refashioned in the image of a market. Most of all, this book surveys the many economic imaginations that grids host, experts and users shape, and electricity transmits. It is a map to the current economy into which we are plugged as citizens of an electric world.

$$\left(\begin{array}{c}1\end{array}\right)$$

# REGULATING

Richard Schmalensee had observed electricity markets since their appearance and helped them come alive. Many experts of electricity markets praised him to me as one of the most knowledgeable economists about electricity and its industry—quite the praise coming, especially, from those with an engineering background who like teasing economists for their bird's eye view of industries. Given his acclaimed expertise in electricity's markets, he must not be puzzled by much on that matter. Yet he was, toward the end of a long conversation we had in his MIT office in Cambridge, Massachusetts, ruminating on where markets in electricity had come from and where they were headed.[1] "I find the ideology interesting," he said, lighting up the way a researcher lights up when they appreciate a bona fide puzzle, even when they are not able to solve it. In the US, states perceived as liberal[2] had checked all the boxes of market friendliness in electricity—enacting deregulation, being in market footprints, having almost no publicly owned producer of electricity. The states lagging behind in market friendliness in most respects were also some of the most solidly conservative areas in the country.

I quickly drew up a mental map of the US with its familiar red and blue, denoting states voting Republican and Democratic respectively,[3] superimposing it on a mental map of electricity markets and states that deregulated their electricity industries. There certainly seemed to be a correlation (with the large exception of Texas—a politically conservative state with a robust electricity market). "[In] Nebraska, which is as Republican a state as you can find, there's no private electric utilities. Hawaii, which is as Democratic a state as you can find, has no public power," Schmalensee said throwing his hands in the air. "The Mountain West and the Southeast" show, to this day, no intention to "move to markets," whereas "in the liberal blue Northeast, we went to markets pretty quietly, pretty generally." The puzzle, of course, rests on a commonsensical intuition about how ideology works in the US. Liberal, left-wing policymakers are expected to show hesitation toward markets and err on the side of regulation, whereas conservative, right-wing policymakers are expected to trust markets and aim to reduce regulation. In electricity, this intuition has certainly not delivered; the first electricity market came online in the blue California (with disastrous early consequences, to which I return later in this chapter).

I jumped in and asked, "Do you have a theory to explain this?" There were many theories—maybe too many—to explain why each state had behaved the way it did. Perhaps Nebraska's agricultural history and strong cooperative tradition had diminished private producers—a prerequisite for a competitive environment? Perhaps in Wyoming, the availability of cheap coal had eliminated interest in changing things up? "Maybe just a historical accident?" Schmalensee acknowledged with a laugh that he had no theory—no overarching theory at least. "The red-blue thing is a little too simplistic," he said, wrapping up the observation.

Beginning with the 1980s, in the US and elsewhere, engineers of various stripes and economists came together to work out how competitive pricing in the electricity industry could be a reality. Some, like Schmalensee and Joskow, were aware of and motivated by policymaking attempts to that effect. Others did not see themselves or their work as connected to deregulation at all; they were chasing a more efficient way to use resources across the electric grid. They were engineers and economists who taught themselves each other's language in an effort to write rules to price electricity that would honor both textbook economics and textbook physics—rules that would keep electricity's supply within the carrying capacities of the electric grid. For instance, electricity creates congestion as it travels through the grid in high-demand areas like cities, which, the experts thought, prices should reflect. Every power plant has different physical characteristics, from fuel type to ramp-up time, which the pricing mechanism should also accommodate. One of them would call the activity to address physical and economic priorities within the same framework the "gluing of economics and engineering" in a conversation with me.

A more run-of-the-mill name for this activity would be inventing regulation. Economic regulation is legally enforceable rulemaking for economic activity, whether undertaken by governmental or nongovernmental actors. As such, regulation should include rulemaking for *competitive* economic activity as well. In line with the rest of this book, I argue that regulation may originate in the thick of scientific and technological traditions, collaborations, and agendas—during episodes of, for instance, the "gluing of economics and engineering" that this chapter discusses. Once again, ideological influence falls short of fully explaining the trajectories of market-making activity—what it entails, where it originates, and by whom it is undertaken. The "ideology [is] interesting," in Schmalensee's words, to the extent that it, in fact, fails to explain market proclivities and actions when it is expected to. A map denoting voting behavior falls short of explaining how, why, and where markets were made in a commodity like electricity. A story of specific technological constraints and scientific collaborations has better answers.

Regulation, then, is a techno-economic phenomenon for it is a function of experts' scientific agenda and technological skill set, as opposed to a direct translation of political agendas. In this chapter, I track particular experts who played important roles in the history of the US electricity markets by drafting rules for electricity's competitive pricing. Some economists, like Schmalensee and Joskow, began their work with the question of potential competition in electricity in mind, but with the proviso that such potential could be assessed only through the lens of electricity's transmission physics and industry particulars. Some engineers, like a foundational research group led by electrical engineer Fred Schweppe, did not see their efforts as related to deregulation debates until those debates took off; they had set out to advance their control theory interests to pursue a finer balance of electricity production and consumption—what they called "homeostasis" for utilities. Gradually, these engineers would adopt an economic vocabulary and team up with economists to convey their ideas to a larger public. Joining forces, these experts set onto creating new mathematical formalisms and abstractions for future competitive buyers and sellers of electricity—so they could trade the fleeting current in a way that would keep the lights on and the electric infrastructure intact. I argue that regulatory work, understood in this techno-economic light, extends beyond policy circles and into such technological sites informed by experts' disciplinary commitments and the material exigencies of the technologies with which they work.

It is perhaps counterintuitive to think of regulation as applicable to competition and markets. Scholars have successfully undermined the idea of a "free market" as a self-evident entity that organizes itself thanks to an invisible hand once certain regulatory obstacles are removed (Harcourt 2011), but it is still all too easy to fall back on a perception of regulation and markets as oppositional forces in an adversarial playing field—to perceive one's gain as the other's loss. To undermine this perception is also to recenter our anthropological interest in regulation as an activity that pertains to economic rulemaking writ large. Regulators are rulemakers who have certain ideas about fair and desirable economic activity; regulation is the course of action they see as fitting to achieve those ideas in reality.

I will borrow an example from Ignacio Pérez-Arriaga, one of the characters that this chapter introduces—an expert and master teacher of electricity regulation who served in multiple countries and taught graduate-level courses at MIT for many years. This was one of the many colorful examples to which he liked coming back over the two years of his classes I sat in. Imagine a basketball game between professional athletes and grade school students, Pérez-Arriaga would say to his students. It would make a very unequal playing field; competition would be pointless. The work that you would do for the game to be more competitive—the new rules you would introduce, the existing ones you would change—is regulation. Of course, regulation does not always achieve the intended effect. Let us say, your measure was to simply decrease the time of the game; the pros would, of course, still defeat the grade school students badly. Perhaps a better measure would be to make the pros play with one leg tied behind; that would certainly change the ratio of the score. That, Pérez-Arriaga, would say, is the difference between bad and good regulation.

To be sure, the perception of adversity between regulation and markets is not helped by a word like "deregulation"—a word that, in English, implies an elimination of regulation, commonly used to denote the emergence of competition in a previously uncompetitive line of business. Once again, scholars have successfully argued that deregulation as a "system" where "public regulation is abolished and replaced by exclusive reliance on market transactions" is simply an "inaccurate characterization of what is happening [under what is called deregulation]" (Kearney and Merrill 1998, 1324–25). Deregulation might be an unfortunately coined word, but that is no excuse not to study the phenomenon underlying the misnomer. To start on an empirical note, many experts in the electricity industry routinely use the more descriptive word "restructuring" to denote the legal changes in favor of competition that occurred in the 1990s in the US. When they do casually refer to "deregulation" or "regulated vs. deregulated states," it is rather for the sake of familiarity and not a sign of their perception of markets as uncontrollable beasts. In fact, Pérez-Arriaga once explained to me his interest in teaching regulation for many years by referring to the fact that, since deregulation/restructuring, "regulation has [had] more content."

Recentering our attention in the regulation of deregulation has theoretical value. It offers a way to rethink neoliberalism, a concept that is depicted in anthropology all too often in broad strokes—in a way that misses the technological texture of economic activities rooted in specific work cultures. Scholars often take deregulation, understood as a receding of rules and regulation, to be a telltale sign of neoliberalism—a lawlessness that leads to capitalism run amok (for a critique of this approach, see Özden-Schilling 2018). What this scholarship all too easily forgets is that injustice does not occur only as a result of a lack of rules and regulations—that rules and regulations can be written to sustain the unfairness experienced by subjected parties. I believe, however, that a critique of this broad-stroke application of neoliberalism should not content itself with a mere debunking of the concept of deregulation. Instead, the theoretical ambition of this chapter is to lay down the techno-economic terms of an economic anthropology of regulation—an anthropology that takes regulation as techniques of rulemaking that vary depending on the technologies available to a work culture, as opposed to a proxy concept for government control, fiduciary prerogative, or limitation of competition. The idea is to ask: How did Pérez-Arriaga's imaginary regulators come up with ideas of decreasing play time or moderately incapacitating the more skilled players? Why did they think a game between these two groups should occur to begin with and should do so in a way that could be regarded as competitive?

The regulation I theorize also offers a counterpoint to the "performativity of economics" paradigm (Callon 1998), which points at instances of economists bringing to life what was posited in economic theory. The story I tell often has a reverse character, where scientific research constrained by material technologies and disciplinary commitments gradually takes on an economic appearance, as in the case of Fred Schweppe's market-making activity driven primarily by "revolutionary developments occurring in the fields of communication and computation" (Schweppe et al. 1980, 1151) in his and his colleagues' words. In this story, economic agendas originate from within technical expert circles, with economists playing the role of communication facilitators and basic (micro) economics serving as a lingua franca for the different experts to communicate among themselves. Regulation does not translate economic theory into reality; it aims for humans and materials to routinely deliver results desirable to the rulemakers—results that can also be presented as beneficial to the improvement of competition and/or fairness. It is a "gluing" not to be taken for granted when humans and materials do not bend to the will and whims of ideologies all that easily.

Below, I begin with an ideological history of electricity regulation in the US to discern the limits of ideological motivation in the making of contemporary electricity markets. Then I focus on the history of the research group led by Schweppe in the 1980s—one of the first to theorize a change in electricity's business as usual—to see the play-by-play of how homeostasis-driven engineering thinking was gradually translated into an economic conversation about markets and deregulation. I then illustrate how such conversations circulate globally, noting that the circulation of market making also depends on the global movements of expert groups, as opposed to a presumed neoliberal wave that makes indiscriminate landfall across the globe. Finally, I ask what happens when the glue comes undone by dwelling on the case of an early failure in the history of electricity markets—the California electricity crisis of 2000–2001.

## What Can Regulators Regulate?

Let me begin by discerning in what ways economists have given shape to deregulation—and in what ways they have not. We saw in the introduction that Richard Schmalensee and Paul Joskow had been flabbergasted at the casual suggestion of deregulation by some unnamed officials from the early Reagan administration. What made these two otherwise pro-competition economists so aghast by the idea of deregulation in electricity was a particular kind of received wisdom in US economics, which was itself shaped by the history of electricity regulation in the US. That history goes back to the Public Utility Holding Company Act (PUHCA) of 1935—an act that passed in an era of government expansion and investment in public works in the US, well known as the New Deal. PUHCA was what the 1992 Energy Policy Act and, subsequently the 2005 Energy Policy Act, targeted; if any expert regards deregulation as an elimination of regulation, it is because these latter acts eliminated parts of PUHCA and ultimately repealed it. However, PUHCA was neither the first entity of regulation there was and nor did its end mean the end of regulation.

"You can't have competing wires!" Schmalensee thought to himself at the suggestion of deregulation, but one did, in fact, have competing wires during the first decades of electrification in the US at the turn of the twentieth century, when streets were layered with nascent electricity firms' rival wires (Nye 1992). The gradual disappearance of small firms and the emergence of big monopolistic players is often credited to one British-born American business magnate, Samuel Insull, as we saw. Insull, originally a Thomas Edison protégé, moved to Chicago in 1892 to head Chicago Edison, a small, struggling firm of electricity production and delivery—one of over one hundred such firms in the city when Insull arrived (Rudolph and Ridley 1986). Within twenty years, there was none but Insull's now-renamed Commonwealth Edison. Insull's Chicago-based empire had grown massively by way of mergers, in the meantime garnering him national fame, recognized by such feats as being featured on the cover of *Time* magazine in 1926.

Insull shall also be credited as a pioneer of regulation; his was a self-serving, anti-competitive kind. There were, in fact, few rules as to how electricity companies should operate before Insull—whether these companies that were starting to be known as "utilities," providing what had become particularly essential services, should be subject to specific rules whether or not they were private entities. Insull needed law's help to eliminate competition while making sure not to violate anti-trust regulations. His lobbying efforts ushered in an era of state-based regulatory agencies—state agencies that were to ensure fair rates and quality of service. The existence of these agencies meant that Insull could influence agency-based regulation and eventually state legislation through personal relationships; he was thus able to secure the legal recognition of his monopoly as a "natural monopoly" protected by law (McDonald 1958). Natural monopoly was thus a regulatory creation before it became a staple of economics textbooks (McDonald 1958).

The rates Commonwealth Edison charged its consumers (now across three states) swelled as competition legally shrank. In the 1920s, consumers marched in the streets to protest in what was an unprecedented act of consumer rights activism (Rudolph and Ridley 1986). Insull's empire had employed questionable methods to acquire its size and ran on too little equity. In 1933, after suffering devastating losses incurred during the Great Depression, Insull's holding company defaulted and ruined the investments of about 600,000 shareholders (Rudolph and Ridley 1986). Decades before the Enron scandal, Insull became the face of corporate greed—arguably the first in the country's economic history.

He was brought to court for charges of corruption and unjustifiably high rates and was eventually acquitted. Orson Welles noted later that he drew inspiration for his classic 1941 movie *Citizen Kane* from "his Chicago days" and Samuel Insull in particular (Welles and Bogdanovich 1998, 49).

Insull's acquittal did not sit well with a politician. For his 1932 presidential election, Franklin D. Roosevelt ran on a campaign that heavily featured his critique of the excesses of the electricity industry. He effectively mobilized the public sentiment against the industry to gain office and eventually pass PUHCA. PUHCA reflected how the Roosevelt administration understood the root cause of high electricity prices for consumers despite the supervision of state regulatory agencies. The corporations had been charging consumers rates based on the costs of subsidiary companies in different states with higher fuel costs (Rudolph and Ridley 1986). PUHCA thus included a mandate for corporations to register in one state only and not own more than one utility—a measure to be enforced by the Securities and Exchange Commission and the Federal Power Commission (a precursor of FERC). The hope was to bring corporations under more firm state supervision—ironically to extend the regulatory system Insull had helped put in place. PUHCA's limitations on buying and selling electricity across state lines are what the 1992 Energy Policy Act repealed.

PUHCA was, then, regulation put in place against not lawlessness but a certain kind of legal behavior that still called fairness into question and resulted in public resentment. In many ways, it did not change the principles of state-led regulation, which Insull himself had pioneered; it encouraged companies to grow close relationships with their state regulators—relationships that remain today, as Schmalensee remarked to me, in the large swaths of the politically conservative Mountain West region of the US, where state legislatures show no inclination to move toward competition. In the decades that followed, Insull's notion of natural monopoly persisted, became ensconced in economics textbooks, and even flourished, only to be checked by often sympathetic state regulators. Companies continued to be vertically integrated, providing all three electricity services—generation, transmission, and distribution—in mutually exclusive territories. But was PUHCA good regulation? That is, had it achieved its goal to keep costs down for the consumers? "Around 1970, people began to wonder; is regulation doing anything good?" Schmalensee said to me, citing those economists who had influenced him in his thinking of the same question.

A truly notable one among them was George Stigler, a prominent figure of the "Chicago School of Economics"—the intellectual root of American neoliberalism—and a 1982 Nobel laureate. In a 1962 article titled "What Can Regulators Regulate?" Stigler and Claire Friedland used the electricity industry as an example to illustrate the dysfunctions of regulation in general. If regulation's goal was to lower electricity rates for consumers in any way, it had failed in its goal since, Stigler and Friedland showed, no significant change had taken place in electricity rates after state regulatory agencies began emerging in the US (Stigler and Friedland 1962). Taking this observation several steps further in a 1971 article, Stigler argued that regulation was anti-democratic because it took away citizens' freedom to cast "economic votes"—their freedom and right to choose from among consumption choices (1971, 10).

Another influence was Alfred Kahn, an economist who chaired Cornell University's Department of Economics from 1947 until his death in 2010. Kahn had served as a regulator himself—first as a commissioner on the New York Public Service Commission (1974–1978) and then as the chairman of the now-defunct Civil Aeronautics Board (1978–1985), which he joined under pressure from President Jimmy Carter. During the later post, he led the deregulation of the airlines industry. Known as the "father of airlines deregulation" (Hershey Jr. 2010) Kahn is on record having responded to an invitation to speak at a dinner with airlines executives with little enthusiasm: "I don't know one airplane from another; to me, they're all just marginal costs with wings" (Dudley 2011, 10).

What does Stigler and Kahn's influence on Schmalensee and Joskow—and the book they eventually would publish in 1983—say about the role of economics and economists in electricity's deregulation? Could Stigler's influence be the smoking gun that neoliberalism is the driving intellectual force behind it all? As Stephen Collier has explored at length, George Stigler belonged to a "micro-tradition" in neoliberal thought, along with others (e.g., Richard Posner, Harold Demsetz, Sam Peltzman), which specifically problematized the achievements of regulation and eventually found itself a venue of publication with the 1970 launching of the Bell Journal of Economics and Management Science in 1970 (2011, 222–23). Crucially, what Stigler and others attacked in the pages of that journal was not necessarily regulation per se; it was an undersubstantiated and overdeployed "desire to regulate" (Stigler and Friedland 1962, 1) instantiated in a rival thought in economics—public interest theory.

Public interest theory, Stigler and others often argued, had posited regulation as a self-evident good beyond analysis or reproach. To counter this attitude, the articles that populated the Bell Journal (later the RAND Journal) often had the simple empirical goal of comparing costs and prices incurred under specific regulations with those under different regulations or none. Like other Chicago economists, Stigler and other neoliberal regulation theorists approached the state, firms, and the public as separate, calculative actors, responding variably to available incentives (Collier 2011, 218–24). However, beyond a shared toolkit, they were a "microtradition" far from representative of the Chicago School's concerns or conclusions. Collier comments that "the Chicago neoliberals contributed, thus, to the deregulation crusade, but as a political movement deregulation was not only neoliberal, nor could be it located at one given point on the political spectrum" (Collier 2011, 223).

Stigler and his colleagues did have a lasting legacy in economics that reached beyond the confines of a neoliberal microtradition. By treating regulators as calculative agents responding to incentives like anyone else, they conjured a lasting mistrust of regulators as actors to which industries could cozy up to secure favorable oversight—a phenomenon known as "regulatory capture" (Collier 2011, 221). Regulator, here, is used in the strict sense of someone sitting on a state regulatory agency board or FERC to supervise utility behavior. This observation is not so different from historians' assessment of Insull's relationship with the regulatory establishment, but Stigler's oeuvre has made it prevalent among economists as well. Schmalensee commented to me several times that the post of the regulator had not attracted talent since, perhaps, Fred Kahn. With thinly veiled condescension, I have heard many economists refer to the post of the regulator casually as "not that exciting."

Once again, that is not because rules and regulations have been thrown out the window since deregulation, but the bulk of the work of enforceable rulemaking, that is regulation itself, has shifted elsewhere. Since generation became competitive, the rules that govern generation competition have been crafted by Independent System Operators (ISOs) Although those officials who sit on ISOs' design units will not be known by the name of "regulator," they are unambiguously known to be behind the production of the legally enforceable regulations that govern much of electricity's trade. They answer to federal regulators, namely FERC, which is also in charge of the supervision of interstate transmission (since PUHCA was repealed and interstate trade is now possible). But FERC has been known to be a mostly agreeable overseer, leaving the intricacies of market design largely to ISOs and intervening only in moments of interstate disagreement. With all this, state regulators have been largely confined to the supervision of the distribution level of electricity, where price changes are much less frequent and stakes are generally lower. During my market training at ISO-NE, state regulators remained the quietest during classes—not one controversial remark came from a regulator. The figure of the state regulator has indeed been marginalized since deregulation; this often gives easy rhetorical ammunition to those critics who would like to see regulation itself as having been marginalized.

Stigler and Kahn's influence had prepared Schmalensee and Joskow to critique electricity regulation, but not to disregard it altogether as the officials from the Reagan administration seemed to suggest. Neither Stigler nor Kahn were "wide-eyed ideologues"; their work encouraged Schmalensee and Joskow to consider electricity deregulation as a serious possibility. But it was a whole other matter to imagine what shape that possibility could take based on the exigencies of a longtime running electric grid. At the end of that exchange, the officials offered Schmalensee and Joskow funds from the Department of Energy to carry out research on the potential of deregulation for the electricity industry. They accepted. *Markets for Power*, the first monograph dedicated to the subject in the US, came out in 1983 and gave the two economists a somewhat ironic reputation as deregulation advocates—attributed to them by "people who haven't read the book," as Schmalensee remarked to me. In the book, the authors adopted a circumspect attitude and advised a slow and gradual move away from the then-current state of affairs. In the preface, they explained their motivation to research the subject, possibly with that original encounter in mind: "Although we were aware of the large and growing body of literature and experience that makes clear the superiority of competition to economic regulation in most industries, it was unclear to us that one could apply lessons learned in those contexts to the electric power industry" (1983, ix).

In the book, Schmalensee and Joskow evaluated a similar question to that pursued by Stigler: whether competition would reduce costs for both the buyers and sellers of electricity service in different parts of the electricity industry. Electricity generators using different kinds of fuels—mainly nuclear, coal, and natural gas—were analyzed separately since the operating costs of those generators could depend on wildly different factors. For instance, the profitability of running a nuclear power plant may depend on the continuity of the operation, since ramping a nuclear plant up and down takes a long time. Schmalensee and Joskow, then, were unlike Fred Kahn who saw planes as marginal costs with wings; they recognized that power plants could each demand a particular treatment based on their physical characteristics. The book they wrote was circumspect yet optimistic. The authors concluded that, if done well, deregulation could reduce overall costs to electricity buyers and sellers. Alluding to his original unease with the idea of complete and unconditional deregulation, Schmalensee explained to me how their thinking evolved: "Obviously, you couldn't deregulate the wires, but you could probably deregulate the generators." His approach to electricity markets that emerged after deregulation was the same: If "you design good markets, well, it turns out it *can* work."

In what ways, then, have economists given shape to deregulation in electricity—and in what ways have they not? The particular economists discussed here have had important communicatory roles in problematizing the work of monopolistic regulation previously taken for granted by even the most competition-friendly experts. By communication, I mean several things. One is, for instance, Kahn's work of communicating—via scholarship and political activity—the achievements of deregulation in an entirely different industry to peers who might ask the same questions on matters of electricity. Another is Schmalensee and Joskow's work of communicating the specifics of the electricity industry back to policymakers filtered through their disciplinary authority. Schmalensee and Joskow continued this work by advising several electricity market boards in the present century. Investigating the widely held belief that economics is the most influential social science, sociologists Daniel Hirschman and Elizabeth Popp Berman find that "economists are most likely to be influential advisers in situations understood as technical, and in ill-defined situations where uncertainty forces policymakers to look for new solutions" (2014, 780). There is also a more mundane version of communication, where noneconomist technical experts, like the electrical engineers discussed in the next sections, borrow a simplified version of the economists' language to convey their solutions and wishes to nonengineers.

This work of communication is not to be dismissed as inessential, but it should be discerned for what it is—and not more. Hirschman and Berman identify a tendency in social science scholarship to attribute great influence to economics in the US policy circles by virtue of the fact that economists have "positions in every part of the executive and legislative branches," along with an advisory office in the White House (779). They comment that even then, "Every economist . . . knows that such influence is extraordinarily limited, when it exists at all" (779) since politicians do not necessarily heed their advisors' advice. As far as the specific influence of neoliberal economists in deregulation, Stephen Collier, as I note above, comments that deregulation could not be chalked up to the theorizations of a particular brand of economists (2011, 223). If economists do not hold the key when many critics think they do, what seat of power should we look to, then, for an answer to how regulation gets made? Hirschman and Berman, and Collier would point the proverbial finger at historically contingent coalitions of economists and policymakers. That is where my focus begins to shift away from theirs; sitting in an unsuspected seat of power, I suggest, are those material-specific experts whose place in policymaking debates is latent, roundabout, or nonexistent.

Economic rulemaking must enroll materials into cooperation as much as it must humans. The enrollment of materials may generate practice that is not readily identifiable as economic. The creation of a pricing algorithm for wholesale electricity was essential to electricity competition and wholly unachievable by economists or ideologues alone. I now turn to a group of engineers and economists that toiled for that purpose in the 1980s.

## Of Gluing Economics and Engineering

A professor of electrical engineering at MIT from 1966 until his death in 1988, Fred Schweppe specialized in control theory like many other electrical engineers—a field that focuses on feedback and synchrony in dynamic systems, like the electric grid, for purposes of stability. The four-person research group he headed at MIT from the late 1970s onwards focused on developing pricing mechanisms to be used in reorganizing the relationship between consumers and utilities. The process culminated in the publication of a 1988 book, now near legendary among market actors and highly cited, *The Spot Pricing of Electricity*, which came out a few months after Schweppe died. When they started out, the four-person group did not think of their work as part of the deregulation process; they thought they were developing a mechanism for monopolistic, regulated utilities to charge "spot prices" to consumers—prices that would change based on the cost of producing electricity in such frequent intervals as every hour.[4] By the end, their methods had inspired the organization of the flagship vehicle of deregulation: electricity markets.

What we see in this story is a market-making endeavor taking root in an engineering group, encouraged by the "[r]evolutionary developments occurring in the fields of communication and computation," much less so than contemporary political developments. We also see how their initial goal to "develop an efficient, internally-correcting control scheme" (Schweppe et al. 1980, 1151) eventually became developing a "marketplace" that spoke to the deregulation debates, after the subject had been broached in economics and policymaking circles. Their example illustrates the techno-economic environment where electricity gradually has acquired its economics. To learn about this story, in 2015, I sat down with Richard Tabors, a member of Schweppe's group, in his office in Boston, Massachusetts, where he now heads a consultancy company that works with electricity and natural gas firms.

Schweppe was an esteemed engineer by the time he met Tabors. By 1970, he had developed the "state estimator" for utilities (1969; also see Monticelli 2000)—a mathematical representation and summation of the electric grid's current conditions, to be deployed in electricity-producing utilities' control rooms. The state estimator encapsulated just enough information a producer would need to make decisions—like injecting electricity to the electric grid or adjusting voltage—without destabilizing the rest of the electric grid. It had quickly become the industry standard that improved communication for monopolistic utilities that were pooling resources to serve the same consumer base. For Schweppe, the logical next step after the state estimator was to extend these communication gains onto the relationship between utilities and consumers.

In 1978, Schweppe published an article, titled "Power Systems 2000," prophesying the state of the electric grid in year 2000. In it, he laid out the electric grid as an interconnected system of sophisticated controls jointly operated by humans and computers. "The need exists, the technology is available, and the dividends from its use will justify the expense," he wrote (Schweppe 1978, 42). The control systems were categorized into "levels," from the "direct-acting devices for automatic local control" at Level 0 to the decision-making boards at coordination centers (anticipating today's ISOs) at Level 3 (Schweppe 1978, 42). Based on superior communication and controls, this holistic system would let its components accommodate each other, as opposed to let one dictate the actions of the other. This tenet most directly concerned the future of the relationship between utilities and consumers. Schweppe lamented that, in 1978, consumers held the upper hand in that relationship, forcing the utility to provide electricity at consumers' whim, immediately and regardless of the utility's circumstances. (Feeling strongly about the subject, Schweppe even resorted to the disturbing analogy of "master/slave" to depict the power unevenness in the consumer-utility relationship.[5]) He prophesied that, "By [2000], the utilities and customers will be equals who deal with each other through the energy marketplace" (Schweppe 1978, 44). He would take up how to get to that marketplace at the next stage of his career, in a research group, after Tabors joined MIT.

Richard Tabors came to MIT's Energy Laboratory in 1976 after having received a PhD in geography and economics from Syracuse University and having served as faculty member at Harvard University's Graduate School of Design. He was recruited to work on a Department of Energy–funded project on how utilities could deploy photovoltaics—or convert solar rays to electricity. This was a time of newly ignited interest in renewable electricity sources like solar. Following the 1973 oil crisis, the department had started funding research on renewable energy at research universities, including photovoltaics research. Although a well-funded project that gave Tabors intellectual freedom over the years, it was not an intellectual priority to the management of the Energy Lab. The lab took the opportunity to introduce Tabors to Schweppe, whose ideas were "intellectually interesting and much less well organized and managed," according to Tabors.

The two started the Utility Systems Program, in which Schweppe became the academic head and Tabors the administrative head. It was to be an eclectic group, where everyone played a different role to glue engineering and economics, yet control theory prevailed as a central expertise area accompanied by flavors of economics. They were soon joined by two of Tabors's former colleagues from Harvard University: Michael Caramanis, a control theory and operations research PhD from Harvard with a minor in microeconomics, who came to the Energy Lab as a research scientist, and Roger Bohn, who had an applied mathematics undergraduate degree from Harvard and had collaborated with Tabors in developmental economics projects, and who came to MIT's Sloan Business School as a doctoral student to work with Richard Schmalensee. Tabors and his earlier collaborators were thrilled to have been introduced to Schweppe, whom they had known as the creator of the state estimator.

In Tabors's retelling, the story of their collaboration is one of academic chemistry; they pursued ideas that they felt were "cool." But what counted as cool and how it changed over the course of their collaboration is telling. Initially, they found inspiration in the familiar grounds (to an electrical engineer) of cybernetics and control theory. They called their project "homeostatic utility control," which was also the title of a 1980 article they produced. Tabors now remembers having simply "played" with the idea of homeostasis, although it seems to be no coincidence that the concept would serve as a framework for group, given the members' backgrounds. Originally a biological concept referring to the steady and stable state of an organic being, homeostasis was borrowed by Norbert Wiener to be applied to all of communication and control across machines and animals (Rodolfo 2000; Wiener 1948). Schweppe's group continued the cybernetic tradition of borrowing homeostasis from biology to explain nonbiological phenomena. Applied to the utility industry, homeostasis was to be "an overall concept which tries to maintain an internal equilibrium between supply and demand" (Schweppe et al. 1980, 1151).

More specifically, homeostasis for utilities would mean the "continual updating of electrical rates, based on supply and demand, and continual communication of those rates to customers by the electric utility" (Schweppe, Tabors, and Kirtley 1982, 44). Once again primarily concerned with the consumer-utility relationship, the authors framed "homeostatic utility control" as a way to transcend the "supply follows demand" or "demand follows supply" paradigms—as an effort in the interest of a more equal terrain for the meeting of electricity supply and demand (Schweppe et al. 1980, 1152). At this stage, homeostasis was already an economic formulation to them—a state described as the equilibrium concerning not, say, heat exchange but "supply and demand" between the different parts of a system. While conceptually economic, it was untethered to concrete ideas around markets or deregulation. The article made a very brief and vague attempt at political contextualization, and that, in the company of resolutely nonpolitical developments, mentioning that thanks to the homeostatic method, "vulnerability to equipment failures, oil embargoes, coal strikes, and weather could be reduced to a minimum" (Schweppe et al. 1980, 1151).

Tabors thinks that the group members' different interests "morph[ed] relatively efficiently into concepts of spot pricing." In Tabors's photovoltaics project, the agenda had been how to compensate a producer of solar electricity in a grid that hypothetically incorporated solar power. This question had become relevant after the passage of the Public Utility Regulatory Policies Act (PURPA)—a 1978 act that made an exception to the vertically integrated electricity industry by allowing producers of renewable energy to serve as independent generators of electricity. While specific to the then-nascent and near-negligible industry of renewable energy, PURPA had inspired economists like Tabors to think that competition was possible for other kinds of electricity generators as well. Tabors ceded that solar electricity producers would have different costs—often, very large startup costs, which then might be compensated for partly by government subsidies.

But crucially, Tabors thought, for them to participate in the industry, every unit of the electricity they offered would have to be considered equal in value to the unit of the electricity offered by the incumbent electricity providers.

He told me, "Well, *obviously*, I would value [their compensation] based on the marginal value of what I bumped offline." In other words, solar electricity's price should be that of what it replaces, given that electricity from any source is functionally homogeneous. In this reasoning, Tabors seemed to echo the principles of modern economics. As sociologist Richard Swedberg argues, the abstract idea of markets (i.e., markets that are not necessarily geographic designations of exchange, such as farmers' markets or trade routes) emerged at the end of the nineteenth century with the rise of neoclassical economics: the professionalized, mathematized version of economics, pioneered by the likes of Alfred Marshall (Swedberg 1994). A conceptual innovation of neoclassical economics was to designate markets as hypothetical territories where the price for the same good, or what was assumed to be the same good, was the same. Tabors was poised to foreground this neoclassical dictate in the group's "homeostatic utility control" work.

For his part, Schweppe seems to have been influenced by the conceptual instruments used by the economists with whom he was in touch. As many others, his then-doctoral student Ignacio Pérez-Arriaga remembers Schweppe as a constant inventor who enjoyed talking to nonengineers across campus in the hopes of finding nonengineering, yet still mathematical, answers to his engineering questions. Tabors's and Schweppe's interests merged in a common goal: spot prices as vehicles of information—information to convey the availability of supply in Tabors's case and information to ensure synchronicity and stability in Schweppe's case.

In his Boston office, Tabors showed me the original mockup for the 1980 article called "Homeostatic Utility Control" hanging on the wall prominently, printed out and patched together on big sheets of paper. According to the authors, spot prices were an extension of existing control mechanisms, like the state estimator, only scaled up. While the automatic control devices in a system, the aptly named governors and regulators, could make small adjustments to the balance of electricity flows on the basis of seconds or minutes, larger changes in supply and demand in, say, hourly intervals could be accommodated in an "energy marketplace." The technological interface that they described was akin to today's smart meters—devices of constant communication exchange between utilities and customers. With this interface, the dual goals of the engineers and economists would be achieved. The prices charged to consumers would approach the costs of utilities, satisfying the marginal cost theory that foresees the market price equaling the production cost of every additional unit of an item. The balance of supply and demand would also secure the physical stability of the grid. Anticipating Tabors's glue metaphor, the article described this ideal condition in the following way: "A set of interrelated physical and economic forces maintains the balance between electric supply and customer load" (Schweppe et al. 1980, 1151).

Tabors reminisced to me: "[We thought] we may never be able to do [the "energy marketplace"] and this may be the stupidest idea on the face of the earth. However, [we said] the logic is this, the math is this, the electrical engineering is this. We kind of just kept pounding on it." Over time, the group had a variety of interlocutors, collaborators, temporary and long-term contributors,[6] supporters, and opponents. A year before the "Homeostatic Utility Control" article came out, MIT's Center for Energy Policy Research in the Energy Lab, funded by the Department of Energy as part of its scientific response to the 1973 oil crisis, encouraged the group to share its research with a larger community. The directors, also friends of Tabors's from previous projects, raised funds for what came to be known as the Boxborough Conference, formally titled "New Electric Utility Management and Control Systems," held in 1979 in Boxborough, Massachusetts. An impressive array of people responded to the call issued by MIT's Energy Laboratory: from executives of energy companies like Exxon and Gulf Oil, to utility managers, to regulators. The conference served as a sounding board for Schweppe and Tabors's group—then called the Homeostatic Control Study Group. A draft of the 1980 article was shared with the attendees.

The conference and the four homeostatic researchers' thoughts proved to be polarizing. For instance, William Vickrey, an economics professor from Columbia University who went on to win the Nobel Prize in 1996 for his research on pricing under asymmetrical information, was almost too enthusiastic a participant; his participation had to be limited by the session moderator. On the other hand, also in attendance was the vice president of the Electric Power Research Institute (EPRI), a nonprofit organization founded in 1972 and funded by US electric utilities; he thought the group was out of its mind. After the conference, he wrote the group a letter noting that, as far as he was concerned, its "concept had the same amount of good sense as if every passenger on a 747 had their own joystick and on average they were going to land the plane." A future when prices would be algorithmically decided seemed unsound to both researchers like EPRI's vice president and many utility managers with whom the group had personal connections. Schweppe had enjoyed excellent connections with the American Electric Power (AEP, a major American utility), having developed the state estimator while on a sabbatical at AEP. After the Boxborough Conference, Schweppe received a letter from AEP's CEO, noting how disappointed he was with where Schweppe's career was going.

According to Tabors, the utilities resisted the homeostatic project, because it sounded tantamount to relinquishing control over their own physical operations—it seemed as if their physical operations would be trusted to the whims of an untrustworthy pricing algorithm. In those days, before "the gluing of economics and engineering" in Tabors's words, the "economics" part remained static and predictable over long periods of time, while the utilities were in charge of making sure the "engineering" part functioned stably on a daily basis. From this standpoint, the gluing seemed suspect. According to how Tabors interprets it, his group challenged the pushback by "getting the math right." In a way, the math, the matter of the glue, was to ensure that the new arrangement, "this engineering economic channel" as Tabors put it, was not fickle and untrustworthy just by virtue of being governed by algorithms instead of in meeting rooms by regulators.

Throughout, the group made allies as well. According to Tabors, "the front edge of the business, the front edge of the industry could see the correctness of the math, see the correctness of the logic." Schweppe had a colleague who was on the California Energy Commission (i.e., California's state regulatory agency) and who arranged a meeting for Tabors and Schweppe with the chief commissioner. To their surprise, the chief turned out to be Rusty Schweickart, whom they recognized both from his public appearances as a former astronaut who had served on the Apollo 9 mission and his attendance of faculty meetings as a visiting professor at MIT's Aeronautics and Astronautics Department. This made him a sympathetic acquaintance. Finding their idea "cool" but lacking the financial resources himself as a regulator, Schweickart helped facilitate connections for two major utilities in his area, Southern California Edison and Pacific Gas and Electric, to fund the group's project and provide it with access to their data. The group could now conduct econometric analyses—test their spot-pricing formulae using historical data on supply and demand. Tabors and Schweppe were reputed MIT professors who enjoyed connections with the electricity industry and used those connections toward promoting their project, which was lent credibility by mathematics and appeal by the rhetoric of free markets in the pro-market 1980s.

In the mid-1980s, Schweppe decided that it was time to write a book. By that point, Tabors recalls, they had "all the pieces." The pricing issue was attacked from a variety of ways in papers, reports, and dissertations, though the terminology had not been consistent throughout, in a way that "has evolved in parallel with our growing experience," as they later remarked in the book's preface (Schweppe et al. 1988, xvii). The book was to be "a single, integrated sourcebook" for engineers, economists, regulators, and policymakers willing to see the benefits of a spot price-based energy marketplace for utilities and customers" (xvii–xviii). The process until the book's 1988 publication coincided with a number of personal and political developments. The photovoltaic project that had sustained Tabors was winding down and the two other members of the group, Caramanis and Bohn, were transitioning to permanent academic posts elsewhere. While "Fred [Schweppe] would grind away at stuff" mathematically and theoretically, Tabors, assuming an administrative role as always, would make sure that the chapters fit together, that the writing was readable. It took them two years to get the manuscript to a publisher.

In the book, the authors dropped the concept of homeostasis altogether, not because they did not believe in it anymore but because they had found a framework with more purchase to convey their ideas. They formulated their project exclusively as one of creating a new market. The book opens with the following assertion: "There is need for fundamental changes in the ways society views electric energy. Electric energy must be treated as a commodity which can be bought, sold, and traded, taking into account its time- and space-varying values and costs" (xvii). The spot-price-based energy marketplace is a "win-win situation for both the regulated utility and its customers," the book suggests, because the consumers could get more service for every dollar if they chose to follow the prices falling and rising in real time and adjusted consumption accordingly, and because prices would decrease across the board when utilities operated in a "less uncertain" world where they could reflect their costs in prices (xv). Spot pricing was a logical extension of the trends in the electricity industry and a mandate of the readily available computational technologies. It was necessitated, in a sense, by the scientific and technological achievement already accomplished.

In stark contrast with only a decade before when they started their work, deregulation had become a distinct possibility in 1988, as had already been argued by Schmalensee and Joskow, who had written *Markets for Power* next door on the MIT campus. While originally uninterested in the idea of deregulation, by the end of the process, "we were in it. . . . No question about that," Tabors commented to me. The book marked a transition to their explicit but very cautious involvement with the ongoing debates around electricity markets. His group took up deregulation in a mere eighteen-page chapter of the book, titled "A Possible Future." Although spot pricing was invented for the regulated industry, they noted, "Its implementation opens a door to deregulation of some or all generation." Tabors remarked to me that they wrote "very gently" that the "mentality" of spot pricing, which anticipated a multiplication of prices based on costs, could be the basis of competition and thus deregulation. The last chapter of the book has an unassuming figure: a four-step recipe for a deregulation scenario (124). After the initial step of establishing spot prices between consumers and utilities, the authors foresee further algorithms to organize the relationships between utilities, and then a legal change for utilities to be detached from the geographic utilities that they were obliged to serve. The final step is tongue in cheek: "wait and see what happens." The authors advise against rushing to adopt these steps, as they had never been tested before (111).

In July 1988, Tabors and Schweppe were slated to have a Saturday morning meeting with a small delegation from the Central Electric Generating Board (CEGB), the publicly owned utility that generated, transmitted, and distributed all electricity in the United Kingdom. Tabors and Schweppe had been in touch with officials in the UK including the regulators who were drafting the original wording of a deregulation proposal. In this meeting in Cambridge, Massachusetts, Tabors and Schweppe were to relay their ideas about deregulation to the UK group; they were to "educate them." Toward 10 a.m., Tabors had been waiting with the committee for Schweppe for an hour and he began to "hit the panic button" at Schweppe's no-show. Going through all the connection points, Tabors received the news that Schweppe had died the previous afternoon from a long-standing heart condition. The book came out only months later in December 1988. In 1991, the UK broke up CEGB into four units and privatized them. The UK thus preceded the US in the deregulation process. Tabors recalls that the committee, who were not able to meet with Schweppe that Saturday morning, took the four-step figure from chapter five and "ran with it." Their new structure was largely based on the "yellow book," *The Spot Pricing of Electricity*.

After Schweppe died and Caramanis and Bohn moved away from MIT, the group ceased to be at the forefront of the pricing research. Today, all seven ISOs in the US use a pricing mechanism called Locational Marginal Prices (LMPs)—a mechanism of pricing used exclusively in the US and credited to a Harvard professor, Bill Hogan, who developed the concept of locational prices in electricity over the mid-1990s (1995). PJM, the ISO that runs the electricity market with the most participants and liquidity in the US, introduced LMPs in 2000 and other ISOs followed suit. Schweppe's group had always been in touch with Bill Hogan, a professor of public policy at Harvard's Kennedy School of Government since 1978. Hogan, who was previously a researcher of global energy policy and oil prices, is "a great mathematician," Tabors concedes, even though they have acted as friendly foils to each other over the years. LMPs are prices assigned to every designated "node" in the system: nodes are substations where electricity is injected and withdrawn and its voltage readjusted. Tabors and Schweppe had promoted a zonal system of prices—a system that the UK adopted and is today prevalent in Europe, where designated zones are assigned prices. "I was a zonal guy, he was a nodal guy; nodal won [in the US] but, essentially the implementer of what we had developed was Bill Hogan." Hogan, as Tabors puts it, makes clear his reliance on Schweppe and Tabors's math: "Footnote one, see xyz, Schweppe et al."

LMPs have another major difference from spot prices as imagined by Schweppe and Tabors. Schweppe and Tabors's main objective was to let the consumers see prices, respond to them, and achieve equilibrium between consumers and utilities' supply and demand preferences as a result of such interaction. Hogan's approach, while also fusing marginal cost theory and the physics of electricity transmission, was oriented toward governing the relationships between a multiplicity of generation and distribution companies—or the wholesale level. With the mixed blessing of hindsight, Hogan, like everybody else in the business, observed deregulation as it was happening in the UK and prepared for an impending future in the US. Along with the UK, the US skipped the first step of Schweppe's deregulation recipe and jumped straight into the second: the algorithmic organization of relationships between buyers and sellers of wholesale electricity. The consumer-utility relationship fell out of sight. "[In the US] we've done everything we possibly could do to fix it so the demand side could never see the price still," Tabors remarked to me.

Schweppe's group was chasing after a homeostatic system—a grid that, in its entirety, would serve as a marketplace, where human and nonhuman components would communicate continuously. It was a quite early precursor of the smart-grid vision that has recently become prominent in electric systems engineering and the electricity industry. Today, engineers are hoping to extend electricity markets onto individual homes by developing smart technologies and algorithms to go with them. (In 1986, Schweppe invited an early-career researcher to MIT for her first sabbatical so they could pursue such interests:

Marija Ilić, whose contemporary smart-grid laboratory at Carnegie Mellon University is described in chapter 3.) Reflecting on the contemporary rise of interest in smart grids, Tabors commented, "We're coming back to the simplicity of the original equations; we're coming back to the simplicity of [our] thought process." After many colleagues at MIT, who made the campus a good place to "glue" economics and engineering, left in the 1980s, Tabors moved most of his research to privately run consulting companies—regretfully so, since he found academic venues to be the "logical" places for the gluing he was after.

Scholars in STS and history of science have theorized what it means to do work in the interstices of different kinds of expertise. For instance, John Law has articulated his notion of "heterogenous engineers" who build systems that incorporate social and technical elements simultaneously to address complex sociotechnical challenges like, in his case study, fifteenth-century Portuguese sailors who set sail across the Atlantic (Law 1987). Similarly, Peter Galison wrote of "trading zones"—spaces of collaboration and mutual learning where experts with different specializations experiment with each other's languages, and create new theories and technologies (Galison 1997, 783). Both Law and Galison argue that expert practice and knowledge often emerge through cross-field conversations between experts with different priorities; in Galison's case, such conversations are facilitated by liminal institutional spaces, and in Law's case, by messy engineering projects that know no division between social and technical expertise. The work of Schweppe's group could be explained by existing theorizations of heterogenous engineering or trading zones, as it could be painted as a filtering of electrical engineering concepts (megawatt/hours, transmission capacities, ramp up/down times) through the language of economics (marginal costs, markets, and prices).

I do suggest, however, that the case of the gluing of economics and engineering narrated here is poised to offer more than a validation of these theories that have a certain self-evidence to them. While Law writes against "social constructivist" sociologists who might prioritize the social aspect of sociotechnical assemblages as definitive (Law 1987, 111–13), he would perhaps admit that engineers seldom deny the interconnected and malleable nature of the social and the technical in their work. At stake in the gluing of economics and engineering is more than the mere fact of their interconnectedness; it is the weight and momentum some technological pursuits have over others—what direction is deemed "cool" and worthy of pursing, as well as the interlocutors one is able to enroll in that pursuit. At stake is also what could happen if the gluing came undone (as we see in more detail in the California electricity crisis case)—if the commodities, their buyers and sellers, the designers of their markets no longer acted in predictable ways that could also be widely considered fair and competitive. In the case of electricity, regulation emerged in applications of long-standing scientific interests like homeostasis, which were then rendered legible to wider audiences, including policymakers and industry managers, through the language of microeconomics. The peculiarities of electricity did not find easy or direct translations in economics; existing price algorithms could not inform the pricing of one megawatt/hour in a way that made electricity's trade remain within the capacity of its infrastructure. The gluing ensued with the creation of prices specific for electricity. Regulation is to be found in that gluing.

## The World Deregulates

In 1981, Ignacio Pérez-Arriaga received an electrical engineering doctorate from MIT with a dissertation on the mathematical modeling of the electric grid, especially the effects of small frequency disturbances, written under Fred Schweppe's supervision. Later he returned to his native Spain and started his tenure at the Universidad Pontificia Comillas in Madrid—a position he holds to this day. Yet he continued visiting MIT and stayed in touch with Schweppe's group. Around the same time, the Spanish government, just like the US government, was exploring the possibility of deregulation in electricity.

Schmalensee and Joskow briefly advised the Spanish government during their research for *Markets for Power*. On a Friday night in 1983, the year when the book came out, Pérez-Arriaga received a call from the Spanish Ministry of Energy; the officials on the phone asked him to report on Monday on Schmalensee and Joskow's book. Pérez-Arriaga canceled his plans for the weekend and spent his time taking notes on a photocopy of the book that he had brought back from the US on his last visit. Spain passed its first deregulation law in 1993 and Pérez-Arriaga served for five years on the Spanish National Electric Regulatory Commission beginning in 1995. He has since continued to travel back and forth across the Atlantic, advising regulatory commissions in Europe and Latin America, as well as ISOs in North America. He became skilled in deregulation experiences across the Atlantic. To his knowledge, he is the only person to have ever sat on the electric regulatory commissions of two different countries: Spain and Ireland.[7] "You can probably tell my Irish accent," he likes to joke in the graduate course on electricity regulation that he teaches at MIT—teasing himself on his own unmistakable Spanish accent.

In 1988, Pérez-Arriaga went to Chile as an invitee of the Chilean government. He was selected by the Chilean officials both for his experience in following deregulation debates in multiple contexts and his Spanish fluency. On that trip, he discovered something neither Schweppe's group nor Schmalensee and Joskow knew about at the time—that Chile had already undertaken deregulation several years earlier. In my interview with him, Schmalensee reiterated, "Nobody knew it, but Chile did it." In 1982, under the military dictatorship of Augusto Pinochet, Chile had passed the "Electric Law," making the country the first one in the world to undertake deregulation. The law enforced the separation of generation and transmission companies and introduced a marginal cost-based pricing system. Many regulatory aspects of this process were up in the air, and Pérez-Arriaga was invited to share his opinions.

The Chileans' basic question was how to charge utilities for their use of the shared grid—a question that had become relevant when transmission was opened up to the use of new competitors. Pérez-Arriaga's first instinct was to resort to the dictates of his home discipline of electrical engineering and follow the flows to calculate how much exactly everyone was using the grid. In our 2013 interview, he laughed at the naiveté of his original approach: "I started out like that," he said, "and then I ended up being a regulator!" The challenge was to find a mathematically repeatable algorithm that would allocate the cost proportionately and then formulate that in legal terms into a regulation. While he could not invent the solution the Chileans were looking for on that trip, Pérez-Arriaga was inspired to follow the lead of his doctoral advisor, "whose engineering [had] led him to economics." He remembered buying microeconomics textbooks to teach himself enough microeconomics to "translate into power systems."

As is well known to students of Latin America and neoliberalism, when Pinochet came to power in a US-backed coup in 1973, Chilean and US economists trained in Chicago were appointed to key positions to open Chilean industries to foreign investment and privatize government-owned infrastructures. While the writers of the 1982 Electric Law are not directly associated with the University of Chicago, at least one of them, Renato Agurto, was a graduate of the Catholic University of Chile, which had become dominated by Chicago-trained economists even before Pinochet's overthrow of Salvador Allende, through a Cold War program of the US that trained Chilean students at the University of Chicago's Economics Department (Biglaiser 2002). On his visit, Pérez-Arriaga met the two pioneers of the Electric Law, Agurto and Sebastian Bernstein, whom he remembers as part of the intellectual legacy of the "Chicago Boys." The Pinochet government downsized the regulatory staff and brought in foreign investment in a scale unprecedented in Latin America (for instance, when compared to the deregulatory processes in Argentina and the Dominican Republic, where regulatory authorities, in fact, were bestowed more power than before) (Martinez-Gallardo and Murillo 2011).

It turned out that Chilean "wide-eyed sort of ideologues" had enacted deregulation before anybody else. But the 1982 Electric Law remained unknown to the English-speaking world until Agurto and Bernstein started publishing in English in the 1990s (see Bernstein and Agurto 1992). By that time, Schmalensee, Joskow, and others were already preoccupied with the UK's deregulation project. Schmalensee remarked, "I remember Paul [Joskow] and I saying, my God, [the UK] actually did it. So now let's see if it works; they're running the experiment!"

Electricity deregulation, then, seems to have followed a nonlinear, circuitous trajectory across the globe. The neoliberal Chicago Boys provided the ideological push for electricity deregulation in Chile, but the push does not seem to have taken the form of a force of destruction that spread linearly from imperialist centers to the periphery. While Chile's US-trained economists inspired interest in deregulation and the creation of markets in a number of sectors, at least in electricity's case, deregulation did not serve as a ground of experimentation for US experts as it remained unknown to them. The Chilean electricity industry remained unknown to the US electricity industry as well—thus, no free entry for foreign investors was secured in this particular experiment in deregulation. On the other hand, as we have seen, the creators of the UK deregulation drew on US experts whose work had not yet translated into a deregulation experience in the US. A yet-unfulfilled promise of deregulation, in other words, informed an experience that came to fruition first. The experts thus circulated ideas and techniques of regulation in a way that was informed less by programmatic government agendas than the mandates of professional and disciplinary circuits to which they belonged.

Right after his Chile trip in 1988, Pérez-Arriaga returned to MIT to spend a sabbatical year with his old advisor Fred Schweppe and communicate his experience in Chile. But his plane arrived in Boston exactly three days after that Friday afternoon on which Schweppe had died. He inherited Schweppe's office, a box of his unpublished papers, and the course Schweppe was set to teach in the fall along with two others: Richard Tabors and Marija Ilić, who was visiting MIT at the time. Over the years, he traveled back to Chile and elsewhere in Latin America—Argentina, Colombia, the Dominican Republic—as a consultant to governments carrying out or exploring deregulation. He has recently advised the EU in its explorations to integrate separate national markets of electricity into one single EU electricity market. His experiences have become teaching material for a graduate course at MIT—his own version of Schweppe's course from the 1980s. He had been teaching what proved a popular regulation course since "regulation has [had] more content" since deregulation; for that same reason, he commented to me, the course is heavier on regulation, as opposed to physics, than Schweppe's course had been.

Pérez-Arriaga's style of teaching illustrates two aspects of engineering-economics in transit. First, an understated version of economics, or even political economy, that is generally positive toward competition and markets serves as a uniting language for experts. Pérez-Arriaga opens his course with a quote from Alfred Kahn, whose *Economics of Regulation* he considers the bible of regulation, projected on the screen: "All competition is imperfect; the preferred remedy is to try to diminish the imperfection. Even when highly imperfect, it can often be a valuable supplement to regulation. But to the extent that it is intolerably imperfect, the only acceptable alternative is regulation. And for the inescapable imperfections of regulation, the only available remedy is to try to make it work better" (1998 [1988]: 329). Oftentimes, when the subject concerns the desirability of competition, he throws his hands in the air and says, "It's Adam Smith." The implication of calling a point "Adam Smith" is that it should be considered a basic and universally agreed-on fact much like Smith's oeuvre is believed to be the universally agreed-upon foundation of mainstream economics. For Pérez-Arriaga, a self-taught user of economics, these references go a long way to create a common rhetorical ground between him and his interlocutors. When "it's Adam Smith," the graduate students from electrical engineering, systems research, the business school, and other departments do not disagree with him.

Second, being a regulator involves keeping a constant eye on whether humans and nonhumans are complying with the intended goals of the regulation in place. In a favorite story he tells often in class, Pérez-Arriaga relays how alert an expert needs to be to evaluate the success of market regulations and government policies alike. The Dominican Republic's regulatory board (which corresponds to FERC in the US), he tells his students, had introduced free electricity in poorer neighborhoods with the interests of underprivileged people in mind. On a visit to the country, Pérez-Arriaga realized that, at his hotel, his orders of cold beverages took a while to arrive. It turned out that the hotel, located in a wealthy neighborhood, had relocated its refrigeration units to a poorer neighborhood to take advantage of the new regulation. Experts who devise regulations, Pérez-Arriaga concluded, need to not only to create economically and physically feasible and desirable solutions, but also continuously check whether anyone is putting the measures to unintended uses. The watchful eye helps the circulation of competitive ideas; that is how electricity becomes "Adam Smith."

And what happens when regulation fails—and fails badly? What happens when electricity cannot be distributed on what experts consider competitive or fair grounds—or when it cannot be distributed at all?

## Scandal and Reassessment

In 1998, the first electricity market came online in the US, operated by CAISO, an ISO whose territory covers most of California. Soon, the "world stopped," as Schmalensee likes to put it. Or perhaps, the gluing came undone. The daily price of electricity skyrocketed from the initial average of $45 megawatt-hour to $1400 within a year. Utilities had to buy electricity from the market at enormous prices yet sell it to consumers at rates capped by California's state regulatory agency. Two utilities went bankrupt and blackouts followed. In January 2001, Governor Gray Davis declared a state of emergency. The state of California bought electricity at terribly steep rates on behalf of the now-bankrupt utilities, creating massive debt obligations for the state's budget and resulting in what was only the second gubernatorial recall in US history; Governor Davis was replaced in the 2003 recall elections with an unlikely candidate, the actor Arnold Schwarzenegger. At the heart of the controversy was one market actor, a Texas-based trading firm named Enron—a firm that had actively lobbied the California government to enact deregulation (McLean and Elkind 2003). Enron had entered the market without any assets in California; as a speculator, it bought and sold electricity without producing any of it. When Enron executives were brought to court for accounting fraud in 2001 (unrelated to California's electricity crisis), the company officials were also accused of allowing "market manipulation" and "gaming" during the California crisis.

The "world stopped" because a number of state governments backed out of deregulation after what happened in California. Many, including California, suspended deregulation, meaning they backed out of extending deregulation from wholesale to retail electricity (i.e., the distribution level) and giving consumers the option of selecting from a number of competing utilities. (California's retail deregulation is still suspended.) The US public's introduction to the subject of electricity markets was thus far from positive. Journalists documented the tactics that Enron traders used to drive prices up; one commonly deployed by Enron was encouraging power plant owners to shut down plants with false maintenance excuses at times of peak demand to create artificial shortage of capacity. Traders were caught on tape callously celebrating trading tactics that caused statewide loss of electricity and debt on behalf of Californians.[8] Enron became the face of corporate greed—a subject that, especially after the 2008 financial crisis, became a topic of interest to anthropologists as well (see Oka and Kujit 2014). Like the journalists who scrutinized Enron, the case of Enron served as an opportunity to ask existential questions about electricity markets. Should a service as vital to social life as electricity be traded in markets—venues that may encourage acts of greed like Enron's? To rephrase the question George Stigler once asked of regulation, do market experts think *deregulation* is doing any good?

Experts' explanations tend to fall somewhere under the "structure versus individual" spectrum—it is either the market that was badly designed or a few bad apples, but most often a combination of the two. Along with countless researchers who studied the Enron case, Schmalensee believes that California's market was terribly designed. (Remember the proviso in his suggestion that, "if you design good markets, well, it turns out it *can* work.") He reacts strongly to the suggestion that the case of Enron (or the fact that Enron was a speculator without assets) may invalidate markets as appropriate forms of exchange for electricity:

> I don't think speculation per se [was the problem], it's the fact that Enron supposedly got people to turn off generators, did things like that. Well, . . . that's illegal. If you decide to kill all the cows in Texas, they raise the price of beef; well, that's illegal. The fact that somebody does that doesn't mean that markets can't supply beef.

Just like the fact that there are laws in place that would penalize killing all the cows in Texas, there should have been rules that kept Enron traders from doing and repeating what they did. According to Schmalensee, CAISO rushed to introduce its market ("because California always jumps on bandwagons") and ignored the economists who pointed at the market's flawed design; for instance, it was a fundamental flaw that California had a rule that enforced capped retail rates, which kept utilities from passing some of their skyrocketed costs onto consumers, precipitating eventual bankruptcy. Schmalensee argued that electricity was a commodity; however special a commodity it might be, it could still be governed by the general principles put forward three centuries previously by Adam Smith. While arguing that electricity should be a market commodity, he invoked Adam Smith's famous quote from *The Wealth of Nations*: "It is not from the benevolence of the butcher, the brewer, or the baker that we expect our dinner, but from their regard to their own interest" (2003 [1776]: 22).

When Enron entered the California market, it hired Tabors's firm for consulting services. Tabors and his colleagues trained Enron's lawyers in market rules; it meant a steep learning curve for everyone involved. In the meantime, Tabors had a chance to observe Enron's trading floor. He now remembers Enron's traders as "bright" but "obnoxious," and their trading strategies (famous ones revealed to the press include "Get Shorty" and "Death Star") as "hubris at its finest." These strategies, while a function of the "trader mentality" of making a quick buck without much consideration for the trouble it may cause down the road, did not wind up making Enron much money anyway. Tabors's two years of advising the UK's transmission authority immediately after the country started deregulation strengthened his impression that research focus would now regrettably shift to legal matters. When he and Schweppe were imagining a hypothetical market, they had not quite factored in the participants' efforts to circumvent the rules: "We kind of assumed that people would act economically rationally but hadn't thought our way through all of the things that might mean or might not mean." After the Enron scandal, his firm became more involved with issues of law, liability, and defense, and less with engineering and economics research. While Tabors's explanation points more toward the vices of a few bad apples, "corporate greed" does not feature in it as the main explanatory device since he thinks Enron's bankruptcy was eventual with that sort of behavior, and it was preventable with more of the kind of legal attention that he, alongside others, specialized in later.

I join Schmalensee and Tabors (and Pérez-Arriaga, who also believes that CAISO's original market design was flawed) in their judgment that "corporate greed" is a weak frame of reference. It is weak for them because their frame of reference, or their "economic imagination" (Appel 2014), is one that has markets at its heart as the fairest organizers of exchange. It is a weak frame for me because, as anthropologists have shown, traders and other market experts may inhabit structures with an ethos (Ho 2012; Zaloom 2012), however fragile and open to reinterpretation that ethos may be (Appel 2014). That ethos is lodged in the techniques and principles with which experts approach the organization of electricity exchange—in their dedication to align prices with marginal costs, optimize the balance of electricity's supply and demand, and promote competition as the safeguard of welfare maximization across society. It is in what they consider—and do not consider—fair and competitive.

The Californian electricity crisis concluded with crippling and lasting debt for the state. However, while Enron became the name of corporate excess in public consciousness, the concept of electricity markets emerged on the other side with modest damage. When a major failure in electricity delivery happens, as the California crisis has taught us, experts now tend to agree emphatically that what is to blame is bad regulation—regulation that was not thought through, like Pérez-Arriaga's imaginary basketball regulators who thought the right course of action for competitive play was decreasing play time. Replacing bad regulation with the good kind is a goal that keeps the experts at work. Ideas to amend existing markets with new features and create new ones in goods and services that are peripheral to electricity exchange abound. Deregulation and markets, it appears, are unfinished projects.

Schmalensee shared with me an idea he had been entertaining, which, although just a thought exercise, demonstrates the endlessness of the universe of marketable commodities. One of the issues that power plants that use renewable sources of fuel experience is the inability of the generators to ramp up and down as fast as wind and solar rays become available and unavailable. Some valuable fuel is lost as the power plants are in the process of coming online and offline. Schmalensee offered, rhetorically, what if a market could be designed in which the commodity was not electricity or electricity from renewable resources but the "ability to come up and down rapidly?" He asked: "What would that market look like for ramping? How would you design it?" He did not have an answer, but that did not mean this would not become an answerable question one day for someone else.

A less hypothetical question about the relative merits of starting markets in a service or leaving the decision of its price to a decision-making body concerns the controversial subject of capacity markets. These are markets currently run by four of the seven ISOs. The problem these markets are supposed to fix is that generation owners can only recover their current costs through LMPs and thus have no incentive to invest in building further capacity (i.e., building more power plants or expanding the capacity of their current plants) for the future. This, some ISO boards found, constitutes a risk for the future reliability of the grid.

In the 2000s, Tabors's coworkers helped design a capacity market for PJM Interconnection (the largest ISO in the US, headquartered in Pennsylvania). Pérez-Arriaga invented a capacity market for Colombia, after which ISO-New England then modeled its capacity market. Even though he once created a capacity market, Pérez-Arriaga was (when I interviewed him in 2013) in the midst of preparing a presentation for a European regulation conference in which he was going to propose a mechanism outside of markets to replace capacity markets—an impermanent, contract-based mechanism to be used only when ISOs identify the need to build more capacity in their territory. Tabors thought capacity markets were a "disaster"—a band-aid to the problems that LMPs (which, ultimately, were not his but Bill Hogan's creations) had caused; by providing an after-the-fact calculation of production costs, they had eliminated incentives for producers to build more power plants in the future, the costs of which they would not recover. More cautiously, Pérez-Arriaga commented that in ten years, we might eventually come to the conclusion that capacity markets were the best or the worst idea. At the time of writing, a consensus on the subject—like the consensus there had once been on the unmarketability of electricity—is not on the horizon.

While experts may believe in markets as superior forms of exchange, they do not believe that every market necessarily achieves the results it was intended to achieve. The question of whether deregulation has done any good is not straightforward either. There have been studies in economics to undertake George Stigler's original question about regulation—whether it lowers costs—this time applied to post-deregulation era: compare the rates between states that enacted deregulation and that did not to discern whether deregulation achieved its purported purpose of decreasing the rates for consumers. But Schmalensee believes that these are suspect studies that compare states that are different from each other in too many ways other than the differences that deregulation introduces. In other words, he admits readily that it is hard to isolate the effects of deregulation for a scientific study. One area in which the success of deregulation can be measured more cleanly, he thinks, is the performance of power plants; according to recent studies, coal and nuclear power plants in deregulated states use less fuel to produce the same amount of electricity than the same kinds of plants elsewhere, "because there's stronger incentives for efficiency, which is what the [economic] theory would tell you." Referring to this rare (and again, not definitive) case of relatively good evidence for economic theory to predict well, Schmalensee remarks, "It's nice to get some confirmation of [economic theory]."

Confirmation of economic theory, it appears, is not in plentiful supply. That is all right since the daily functioning of electricity markets is not predicated on whether economic predictions come true but on whether a critical mass of market actors take electricity's trade as generally competitive and on whether electricity is serviced without disruption. Economic theory does play the role of facilitating communication between different kinds of experts—and often glues their causes to one another's—but not necessarily a role of bringing to life a world in its image, as the "performativity of economics" paradigm would hold. In the present century, electricity markets have settled into a routine pace—largely sheltered from public attention. Enron's bankruptcy has been supplanted by that of Lehman Brothers as the largest in history, which occurred during the 2008 financial crisis; in the process, Enron also lost its dubious distinction as the public face of corporate greed—a distinction it had inherited from Samuel Insull's Commonwealth Edison. Electricity markets now operate, one can say, predictably and routinely. Regulation in the interstices of engineering and economics has been the first building block in creating a market commodity from the last century's arguably most market-resistant commodity.

## Extraordinary Commodity, Ordinary Markets

In April 2012, I stood behind a glass divider in a loft overlooking the control room for New England's electric grid. I was on a tour of the ISO-New England along with Pérez-Arriaga's graduate students from MIT—a *public* tour that, nevertheless, required a background check a month ahead of time. We were in an unmarked building in a thinly populated corner of Holyoke, Massachusetts. The diagrammatic sketch of the New England electric grid dominated the control room. Tour participants, including me, instinctively scanned the diagram to find the good-sized rectangle shape representing Cambridge, Massachusetts, where we were coming from. We pointed out to each other when a line connecting the rectangles turned red, which signified, as we correctly guessed, the volume of electricity nearing the carrying limits of transmission lines at the corresponding location. Six men populated seven desks, one left spare with evacuation packs to grab and go, if needed, to the standby control room based out of a van in an undisclosed location. We studied how the operators reacted to the lines turning red, thrilled to witness such a routine yet critical operation. "We're an under-the-radar organization," our tour guide said. "The public doesn't see what we do or challenge," he added. "Governors don't know we exist," he, I hope, exaggerated.

Today, this building's servers receive thousands of bids and offers every day from utilities, producers, retailers—the buyers and sellers of electricity in New England. So do the other ISOs across the country that run electricity markets. The bids and offers are received in the morning; prices binding for all participants are announced in the afternoon. The next day, the process will be repeated, perpetrating a routine largely uninteresting to the general public. People do get captivated when they take a moment to think how electricity reaches them, like I did along with others during my visit to ISO-NE; it is just that most people do not take a moment. Even those who are involved in the daily operations—like traders and market analysts—see their heart pumping in predictable intervals determined by the markets' schedule; in mornings, before the bids and offers are due, they grow focused and solemn, and in the afternoons, they find a moment to crack a joke or two by the water cooler. The next chapter reports on those ordinary operations that see the market process quietly maintained and reproduced on a daily basis. This chapter reports on how markets got to that stage of ordinariness when the commodity in question was considered all but ordinary less than two decades ago.

It is regulation—rulemaking and price-making activity that is legally enforceable—that achieves this kind of ordinariness. Deregulation (or the better-termed restructuring) often has the effect of redistributing responsibility for that activity; private entities often emerge as its major seat. In other words, with deregulation, the actors and the format of regulation may change, which by no means translates into the elimination of regulation—a fact that critics sometimes disregard. ISOs are private nonprofit entities; they have units responsible for the creation, assessment, and upkeep of market design—how different kinds of prices will be calculated, what new services may need to be priced, if the pricing systems prove over time to be competitive and hence fair. These are units that also look to outside consultants, like the engineers and economists discussed in this chapter. This is where the bulk of regulation in electricity takes place today; it is because regulation has shifted away from state regulatory agencies that experts routinely dismiss the significance of the job of "regulator," referring specifically to commissioners on those agencies. Regulators' job—overseeing rates and quality of service at the distribution level—might be too slow-paced compared to the daily operations of electricity markets, but regulation itself is alive and well on ISOs' boards, advised by the likes of experts discussed in this chapter. As we will see in chapter 4, ISOs' oversize decision-making capability despite their private nature, compounded by the fact that their boards are populated by representatives from industry giants, is a subject of critique by a growing public.

Regulation is what invents markets. In electricity, that work was specific to the affordances of electricity, facilitated by its experts, and communicated thanks to language provided by economics. But regulation in itself was not enough for electricity markets to continue operating or to grow. Electricity needed to be turned into mobile prices, communicable and actionable across long distances, through an information infrastructure and thanks to the work of people who can be characterized primarily as information workers—traders, data analysts, database workers. The next chapter turns to a day in the life of electricity markets.

$$\textbf{2}$$

## REPRESENTING

In an upper-floor office of a Boston skyscraper, I sat at my desk with Google Earth open on my computer screen.[1] As I moved the mouse on the mousepad and dragged the cursor across the screen, my eyes followed a high-voltage transmission line in an unpopulated part of Ohio. At times, the line became indistinguishable from its crowded surroundings; at other times, a path that had been cleared of trees to make way for the line helped me spot it again. My eyes hurt from squinting and my wrists ached from repetitive motion. I followed the line into an electrical substation: one of the thousands of nodes in the US where electricity's voltage is adjusted as it joins in and breaks out of transmission lines. It is also one of the thousands of nodes where electricity can be withdrawn and injected, and hence, bought and sold, at different prices. This one must have been Cedar Grove, a substation that I had seen featured in market reports; high electricity traffic and, thus, high prices in that location, the reports had warned.

With relief after an hour of searching, I right-clicked on Cedar Grove to see its geographical coordinates, copied them, and minimized Google Earth on my screen. I returned to my spreadsheet that had been open all day and entered Cedar Grove's coordinates. Later, the software developers in the office would grab these coordinates to add Cedar Grove to a map that they had been developing for months—a price visualization software that showed substations and regularly updated the prices associated with them. Hundreds of more rows on my spreadsheet were waiting to be populated, but taking a peek out of the office window, I saw that the sun was already setting over the Charles River. Most software developers and analysts had already left the office. When the developers incorporated my spreadsheet into the new map, my tiny datum could influence an electricity trader's buying and selling decisions, along with the direction and price of electricity somewhere, sometime. But for now, I savored tracking down the elusive line that had cost me an hour, saved my spreadsheet to return to it the next morning, and stretched my wrists.

Electricity markets may have started as a fanciful thought exercise—an algorithmic challenge, for the few inspired engineers and economists, to marketize a commodity whose physics presented an obstacle to business-as-usual political economy. Despite the not-so-humble beginnings, things on an electricity trading floor, on a given day, can seem rather dull to an observer. After all, in this day and age, a trading floor simply consists of a number of people watching their computer monitors and moving their hands to operate a keyboard, a mouse, or a coffee mug. Sure, an observer might notice some movement around the room. For instance, in the mornings, when traders need to meet markets' morning deadlines to submit their bids and offers, a few of those people might get up and huddle around one monitor, point at certain things on it, and talk with each other with some gravity while their eyes are still glued to said monitor. They might shout short questions at each other across the aisle with no trace of a smile. Or in the afternoon, after the morning stress, one might observe quite a bit of chatter in the kitchen and during visits to each other's desks. But most of the time, a trading floor might look like any other office where things are mostly done with computers; there is a lot of looking at one's monitor. An electricity trading floor, like other trading floors with the Bloomberg channel constantly on for all to occasionally look at, might not look like much to observe.

Still, there is benefit to follow Susan Leigh Star's much-repeated (Larkin 2013) advice to "study boring things" (1999, 377), so we notice a quiet transformation, reminiscent of the quietness with which traders, data analysts, and others with a varying level of intimacy with data have been watching their monitors. In the last decade, electricity trading has been transforming into a science of data analysis and practice. Increasing numbers of computer programmers, data scientists, and data analysts have been becoming traders, market analysts, or developers of trading or price prediction software. These include those developers at the firm I call EnTech who would later put Cedar Grove in the map. Then there are people like me, with limited data management experience but a spare weekend to teach themselves how to use spreadsheet software like Microsoft Excel; these people acquire jobs helping maintain the databases that support traders, analysts, and developers, acting as what I call "database workers." Familiarity with or interest in the physical specificities of electricity, or even energy broadly, is becoming a secondary or tertiary requirement for hiring purposes. With the "glue" between electricity and its price formula now in place, these actors work on representing electricity in the form of standardized data, which is what allows electricity to be acted on—that is, traded—remotely across large swaths of territory and by an increasing number of parties.

In this chapter, I describe electricity trade and its market analysis as practices of data—practices steeped in a work culture centered on collecting, organizing, maintaining, and analyzing data. I argue that electricity trade's becoming a practice of data creation and management has allowed the steady expansion of electricity markets in terms of the people employed, the electricity traded, and the footprint covered. If electricity markets are growing in trade volume and footprint, that is due in no small part to the datafication of electricity trade, which has allowed into the field the influx of nonspecialists of electricity who are specialists of data. In that way, this chapter's argument is key to this book's overall argument—the argument that specific scientific and technological work cultures spur the invention of new patterns of economic relationships proliferating around us. The unpronounced premise of electricity trade's work culture is that electricity be rendered neatly in spreadsheets in the form of representable information, ready for the eyes of machines bent on seeing everything in 1s and 0s—that it become no different for the profit-seeking human eyes from any other commodity, be it petroleum, cotton, or gold. But, as this book maintains, electricity always kicks back. That a data-savvy trader of, say, gold, can be an equally successful trader of electricity overnight remains rarely heard of. The work of equating electricity with spreadsheet-friendly information is always incomplete and often goes well into the evening after the sun has set over the Charles River.

This chapter's larger theoretical ambition is to theorize "information"—that which circulates in representation—in the context of economic anthropology. The story of techno-economics here concerns how data experts reorganize our markets and economies in the form of information bits; in that vein, it is a story that bridges the questions of political economy and the findings of the social studies of information. The work of data standardization and the phenomenon of data proliferation described here will certainly not be unfamiliar to students of STS. Anthropologists and STS scholars have theorized how scientists and engineers, as well as less prestigious workers like "data janitors" (Irani 2015), work to represent reality in shared data formalizations. They have demonstrated in various settings, from climate change science (Walford 2017) to geological exploration (Almklov 2008), that this work is no neutral representation—that it is selective, imperfect, and always incomplete. In that regard, this chapter's ethnography is an empirical continuation of this growing body of theory; I describe the daily work of electricity trade and analysis as a constant effort to tame electricity and its massive infrastructure into bits of moving information, or what Bruno Latour calls "immutable mobiles" (1990), to its own practitioners' varying levels of satisfaction. But we need not stop at an illustration of already existing theory. This chapter's ambition, then, is to take a further theoretical step and explore the effect of electricity's data-forward representations in electricity's economy. In other words, I ask: What is gained and what is lost by creating "immutable mobiles" from electricity flows? What is gained and what is lost by trusting electricity's exchange to those more familiar with data practice than the physics of electricity or the economics of power plant operations?

When it comes to electricity, data practitioners who produce, organize, and maintain an abundance of data on a daily basis for purposes of profit and/or employment keep electricity markets viable and poised for growth. Importantly, they are engaged in this practice as a mandate of their training, professional habit, and work culture. As this book has posited before, the 1992 legal action to deregulate the electricity industry did not blueprint or foresee the current state of electricity markets. It is because electricity trade was increasingly populated by information workers, who built their "immutable mobiles" for profit's sake, that electricity markets have now grown much larger than a niche platform for a limited number of electricity suppliers and load servers who simply wanted to pool their resources for efficiency purposes. One of the major examples of this growth has been the exponential (and somewhat controversial) rise of "virtual trading" in electricity—that is, trading by entities who do not produce or physically acquire electricity; entities who only buy and sell electricity on paper for arbitrage purposes.

Representing electricity in the form of mobile prices, then, is the second building block of the current economy that this book explores. In this new moment of economic exchange, the focus of market actors seeking profit and competitive edge has shifted away from observing each other for each other's next move, to capturing the commodities and their surrounding infrastructures in electronic representation. From this perspective, a key implication for contemporary techno-economics is that, in several markets, we now have to contend with the gradual replacement of commodity-specific expertise with the expertise of data, which often tends to spur new layers of standardization and unleashes a spiral of marketization.

Anchoring my descriptions on the floor of EnTech is particularly useful for this purpose. EnTech is not a trading company, and its floor is not a trading floor, although it closely resembles one. Instead, EnTech is a market intelligence firm that sells trading advice to anyone interested—anyone who trades in one of the seven electricity markets in the US, from energy production giants (who sell electricity) to utility companies (who buy electricity on behalf of consumers) to virtual traders (who buy and sell on paper to make money). EnTech's very existence, in other words, encapsulates the growth effect that the proliferation of data culture has had in the electricity industry—many auxiliary companies like EnTech have emerged since the early 2000s to serve the needs of electricity traders who (or rather whose companies) can spare the budget for subscription to these companies' various information-related services, if convinced that the added value justifies the subscription fees. EnTech's promise is simple; it can predict, better than anyone, how the prices in specific locations will act the next day, so a trader buys and sells accordingly. Pulling up the location of the Cedar Grove substation is among the tens of thousands of things that may allow EnTech to produce a more precise prediction for prices at that location. Data about generators' fuel type, generation capacity, age, and location gives clues into supply; data about weather gives clues into demand. This is in addition to endless other predictors, like data on historical supply and demand, that a time-pressed trader might overlook.

In terms of spatial structure and demographics, EnTech's floor looks like a contemporary trading floor; most of the office consists of long shared desks, each dedicated to one of the US electricity markets operated by ISOs across the country. These desks are populated by "analysts." A market intelligence firm's equivalent of traders, analysts do everything related to electricity trading except carrying out the actual trade. They communicate their trading advice to their clients on the phone and in emailed reports. These decisions go into the trades made by clients; depending on the client, these trades could be in thousands of megawatt/hours per day and consequently, involve tens of thousands of dollars per bid or offer.[2] Their work being closely tied to that of their clients', the schedule of their workday is similar to that of a trader, except more flexible given that they do not execute the trades. They command salaries a few notches above the US median income—not comparable to the remunerative glory of Wall Street financiers with their bonuses for trades well done, but also pleasantly comfortable for young people not so many years away from their college graduation. Analysts certainly bear a resemblance to traders by virtue of their focus on identifying good trades, but they are first and foremost part of an information provision mission as encapsulated by EnTech. Most of the analysts at EnTech were either former traders or gearing up for a career in trading in pursuit of higher salaries; however, those who grew attached to building out EnTech's underlying information infrastructure could transition to developer roles (reverse transitions were also seen for those who missed the day-to-day thrill of market operations).

The rest of the floor consists of cubicles that house the developers, usually commanding a degree beyond bachelor's and relatively higher salaries. The rest of the staff—like "database workers"—that support the analysts were also in or near these cubicles, out of the analysts' way so that their time-sensitive work was not disturbed, especially in the mornings before the market deadlines to submit bids and offers. At the time of my fieldwork, the Boston floor (the company had branches elsewhere in the US focusing on other energy commodities) employed around twenty-five analysts, ten developers, and two meteorologists,[3] in addition to administrative and marketing staff. A few of these employees had studied electrical engineering prior to coming to EnTech; others had learned the first thing about electricity on the job. The floor was equally populated by women and men, both in supervisory roles and otherwise—a relative novelty for market analysts, as well as traders, of the present century.

Below, I first elaborate on how techno-economics as seen from the EnTech floor may bridge political economy and the recent scholarly insights into big data. Then we follow the rhythm of a workday at EnTech, which itself follows the rhythm of a day in electricity markets. We follow different kinds of information workers—first, analysts as they analyze data under "real-time" pressures, and second, developers and database workers, as they collect, organize, and maintain the data that supports analysts.

## Of Representing Electricity

The EnTech floor is replete with monitors. A testament to my temporary position, I worked with only two monitors, unlike developers who had three or analysts who had three or four depending on preference. The number of monitors depended on one's position in the office; it also served as a statement on work style. Analysts liked having more monitors since it signaled their ability to process more information simultaneously. Some developers scoffed at that statement; looking at more information at the same time did not necessarily mean processing it well. A developer once reminisced to me about a day in the office when one analyst quit her job and her monitors became up for grabs. The other analysts turned into "vultures" at the sight of the monitors, the developer joked. But what is the information that seems to radiate from all these monitors—the information that presumably asks to be processed? How might our attachment to this kind of information be transforming our economic worlds?

The connections between information and economies, of course, have been explored for a long time. According to Friedrich Hayek, for instance, information came lodged in prices and revealed on an as-needed basis to economic actors, so they could adjust their supply of goods to the available demand, and their demand to the available supply (1945). Hayek's definition is not conclusive (although it does have an emic value, in that it resonates with the views of many actors in contemporary electricity markets), but a conclusive definition of information is not desirable for a techno-economics of information cultures anyway. What is necessary is to take information as an anthropological object—to take it as an object that acquires meanings in only the worlds we study. That way, information is "neither true nor false"—it is "information as reality" as opposed to information about or for reality (Floridi 2004, 560). Hayek's contemporary Gregory Bateson, who sought to apply the epistemology of the then-emergent information theory onto anthropology, thought of an information bit, in more than one occasion, as a "difference which makes a difference" (1971, 5; 2000, 462)—as the fundamental unit of that which leaves a trace in neural pathways and, thus, the mind. For our purposes, this definition holds water, again, not necessarily as ontological reality, but as an ethnographic finding—as an insight into how the actors we study conceptualize and work with information. At EnTech, information is anything that offers the potential of a difference in profit, if worked into price predictions.

Taking information as an anthropological object takes us where Hayek did not have a chance to observe—to computing cultures that have cultivated a specific kind of information: data. An "artifact of the 20th century," data is[4] a form of information "specific to electronic computing" (Rosenberg 2013, 15). It exists as distinct from "information" in its discreetness and divisibility into bits of *datum* (Gitelman and Jackson 2013, 5) as instantiated in the cells of the spreadsheet I used at EnTech to collect the location of electrical substations. Data is information that "has no truth" (Rosenberg 2013, 37) as opposed to, say, a fact. "When a fact is proven false, it ceases to be a fact. False data is data nonetheless" (Rosenberg 2013, 18). If I have grabbed the wrong coordinates for Cedar Grove, for instance, I have produced erroneous data that is data nonetheless; erroneous data's intrusions into databases are more or less expected by all data practitioners (Walford 2017).

"Data" may not be so neatly distinguished from "information" in market participants' spoken language. For instance, at the time of my fieldwork, EnTech's public relations department tried to reach the customer base with the tagline "Information is power"—a pun on power's secondary meaning as electricity. But it is clearly not generic information that has been proliferating in markets—it is spreadsheet-friendly bits that have the potential to make a difference in prices and profit, collected, organized, maintained, and analyzed both by market operators and market participants, in a process that no one (not even the market operators) claims can ever be completed or perfected. While data is EnTech's trade, information is the product sold, drawn on heaps of data.

And as we all know by now, the size of those heaps matters. Anthropologists have been concerned with theorizing the phenomenon of *big data*—the practice of tying science, technology, and policy decisions to the collection and analysis of large amounts of information, measured in increasingly larger multiples of bytes (Gitelman and Jackson 2013; Mayer-Schönberger and Cukier 2013). In the practice of sciences, scholars have shown, *big data* has often been coupled with the conviction that, if data itself has no truth, the gathering of large amounts of data is the necessary path to the discovery of the truth (Bell 2015). We know, however, much less about the daily experience and the long-term consequences of big data's entry into market operations. How is the exchange of goods and services being transformed in an age where more and more bits of information about those goods and services are being accumulated by the parties that supply and demand them? How do the prerogatives of big data management transform the demographics of the workforce, as well as the experience of those who are subjected to those markets? How does, in sum, the entry of big data into markets, of electricity and otherwise, change our economic lives?

Caitlin Zaloom has provided valuable clues into the initial moments of financial markets' turn towards electronic computing—data's home environment—at the turn of the present century (2006). Before the switch to electronic computing at the Chicago Board of Trade, Zaloom shows, the market used to be instantiated by traders' aggressive and manifestly masculine bodily performances; after the switch, traders began to submit their bids and offers electronically in the form of sheer numbers, with no body language to serve as a vehicle. While the switch had the very real effect of large numbers of people losing their jobs to a computer-savvy new generation of traders, it did not have the effect intended by market designers—the effect of eliminating the "social" from the markets, conceived as traders' biases and irrationalities. Traders learned to see the numbers, not as "objective descriptions of supply and demand," but as clues into the actions of "competitors around whom they generate specific strategies" (2006, 159). In electronic markets, Zaloom argues, numbers have emerged as the fabric of the social—as that which informs how actors relate to each other. Zaloom's argument holds water for competitive electricity exchange, which has been an electronic environment from the beginning; the actors of electricity markets have always depended on electronic communication across the humans and machines of the electric grid.

Nevertheless, the way data informs the social goes beyond the electronic submission of bids and offers today. Since the early 2000s, market participants' accumulation of data about relevant commodities prior to forming those electronic bids and offers has grown exponentially. The datum I created about Cedar Grove's location was a drop in EnTech's sea of databases, some larger in size, some smaller—it was perhaps the multiplicity of databases, the kind of information that was seen as potentially relevant to prices, that was more significant than individual databases' sizes. Every morning, traders' proprietary software pulled these databases to predict how prices would move given how they did on similar days in past years—the record of similar days being kept in databases and the terms of similarity being decided by the algorithms in proprietary software. Electronic computing has enabled this environment of intense focus on increasing one's competitive edge with creative uses of data and databases. Traders of yesteryear read each other's bodies to glean information—more information than simply their bids and offers—about the current and future movements of supply and demand. They assessed if their competitors were bluffing, if they had more or less in store to buy or sell, as Zaloom has argued (2006). In electronic markets, of electricity or otherwise, not only traders themselves have become data-processing actors, but also firms like EnTech have emerged, dedicating resources completely to the creation and management of information.

In many ways, then, Zaloom's early insights into electronic markets at the turn of the present century still hold, although the intervening two decades have seen significant changes, too. First, the trading workforce in a variety of markets has changed since the turn toward electronic computing (in the case of financial markets) and the introduction of deregulation and competition (in the case of electricity). Today, it is safe to say that there are virtually no traders left without computing skills. While individual trading talent is still a recognized feat, it is no longer necessarily a function of traders' bodily performances (in the case of financial markets) or their intimacy with power plant management (in the case of electricity). It is, instead, a function of their creativeness with data—their ability to tell which kinds of data are relevant to prices and worth keeping databases of; their ability to recognize erroneous data and improvise with substitute data; their ability to detect opportunities of arbitrage and profit using data analysis before others can. At EnTech and on electricity trading floors, women have emerged as leading analysts and traders—a far cry from the overtly masculine environment Zaloom observed in financial markets before the electronic revolution (though manipulating the floor's gender dynamics was not the market designers' intention). In sum, the work culture of trading has fundamentally turned many markets into a culture of collecting, organizing, maintaining, and analyzing data.

Second, as Zaloom also held, the "social" was not eliminated as a result of the change in work culture. Neither bids and offers nor the data that precede them are seen as final truths by market participants in electricity—they are instruments or "prostheses" (Çalışkan 2010) in their quest to profit, not just today, but in the near future, that allow market participants to read others' near-term movements. However, we must not lose sight of the fact that data is a *different* instrument than, say, a trader's body parts that communicate market conditions. In other words, for a study of contemporary techno-economics, we must ask: If not eliminated, how is the social being transformed in this moment of data proliferation? In the case of electricity, data proliferation has centered the market participants' focus on building electronic representations of the electric infrastructure—representing it in the digital environment as extensively as possible. In building its digital representations, market participants exhibit no ambition to reach a certain truth about the electric grid, unlike what scientists in data-forward sciences might hope to do with their use of big data (Bell 2015). Their hope, instead, is to increase their price prediction potential. We can deduce, then, that in this new moment of data proliferation, market participants' focus has shifted from each other's bodies and minds, readily observable in-person encounters (Çalışkan 2010) or in trading pits, to the commodities and infrastructures out there in the world—like electric substations, transformers, and power plants, waiting to be transplanted into digital work environments.

Once again, the location of the Cedar Grove substation is an infinitesimal part of this ambitious effort to represent the electric grid in the electronic computing environment. But how can we understand this transplantation— the process through which an electrical substation becomes the functional equivalent of a spreadsheet cell? How does a satellite image sourced by Google Earth become a datum that may ultimately be an ingredient, albeit tremendously small, in the buying and selling decisions of a market actor? In what state does a practitioner find a datum, and to what transformations does she subject it? Data practitioners often speak of "raw data"—especially in reference to data collected by instruments and sensors before it goes through "cleaning" and sorting (Walford 2017). To anthropologists and STS scholars, there has been ample issue to take with the implications of the term "raw"—the implications that data might simply be found in nature in pristine state, that it might exist prior to humans' interpretation and interference. Invoking Claude Lévi-Strauss's canonical work in which the binary of "the raw vs. the cooked" maps on the binary of "nature vs. culture" (1969), Geoffrey Bowker has categorically rejected the notion that data can ever be raw; "on the contrary, data should be cooked with care" (2005, 184). Tom Boellstroff (2013) has introduced further nuance into this debate by invoking Lévi-Strauss's "culinary triangle" (1997), in which the raw appears no longer as the opposite of the cooked; instead, it is the origin point for cultural transformation (i.e., the cooked) and natural transformation (i.e., the rotten). Rotten data comes to being when collected data, over time, loses its association to its underlying object, as the underlying object itself changes, the digital environment gets corrupted, and electronic connections (like hyperlinks) disappear (Eriksson 2013).

In electricity markets, as well as in other data-forward work cultures, raw, cooked, and rotten data coexist in a fluid state; data transforms from one state to another, and reversibly so. In other words, we need not dismiss raw data as an "oxymoron" (Bowker 2005, 184) as long as we take care not to associate rawness with an immutable origin point—that is, as long as we recognize the complex infrastructures it takes to *produce* raw data (Walford 2017). After all, to introduce a further analogy into the debate, we get our undeniably raw fruit from undeniably complex and human-made systems of agriculture. All seven of electricity market operators in the US dump spreadsheets of information on their official websites periodically. EnTech's software developers write algorithms that automatically "scrape" these spreadsheets to update their existing databases.[5] In this case, the dumped spreadsheet can appear as "raw" for EnTech's purposes, while it certainly does not appear so from the perspective of the workers at the market operators who put them together. One's raw data, then, is another's final product. Furthermore, automatic scraping is enabled by servers of great computing capacity and developers with advanced coding skills. In other words, it is a complex infrastructure that wills rawness into being. Electricity markets abound with "cooked" data—that is, cleaned or accepted as cleaned by a group of relevant people—and "rotten" data, as well as, and not instead of, raw data, which are nonetheless produced to be accepted as raw.

At EnTech, I witnessed constant conversations on the question of which data was worth the teams' efforts to chase after to include in existing databases (or build entirely new databases for). One example concerned weather. While all electricity market actors (including market operators) looked to weather as an indicator of demand, they frequently limited their study of weather to temperature averages. But at the time of my fieldwork, at EnTech as elsewhere, many were starting to look into cloud cover as a factor that further complicated demand—a factor that could play a role in making consumers turn their heating up or down. However minimal a factor it might be, the reasoning went, it could be worth representing via heaps of data and integrating into the price models. While pursuing new kinds of relevant data that other market actors might be neglecting, they also entertained doubts about the usefulness of certain ongoing data collection endeavors. For instance, some analysts I spoke with were not convinced that knowing the exact geographical coordinates of electrical substations—the bulk of what I did at EnTech as part of my participation—would make much difference in the trading software's price predictions. They entertained a healthy dose of skepticism, which was presented more as a hunch than an evidence-backed assessment.

Those constant conversations about data—its kind, quality, value—are part and parcel of the work culture I describe here. It is a culture that asks for an ever-better representation of the commodity and the infrastructure in question—in our case electricity and the electric grid. It encourages an endless quest to flatten the three-dimensional electric grid into spreadsheet-ready bits. A familiar subject to students of STS, of course, is the work of standardization in sciences and technology—the creation of decontextualized artifacts of representation that travel far, only to be decoded and operationalized again by members of the same work culture—Latours's "immutable mobiles" (1990; Bowker and Star 2000). From environmental accountants who turn carbon dioxide in the air to emission numbers in corporate offices (Lippert 2015) to scientists who model unpredictable rivers in ways that align with national political goals (Barnes 2016), we know that data practitioners engage in an endeavor of creating stable, transferable, mobile representations out of messy realities. But why and to what effect? Are there grand motives and overarching consequences to the well-illustrated phenomenon of increased data standardization, classification, and circulation?

The answer, once again, is not to be searched far away from the work culture. In a brilliant case study of how data tools facilitate petroleum geologists' understanding of an oil reservoir, Petter Almklov shows that the tools available to scientists and engineers overdetermine what they see (2008). The log of a well—the memory of a drill's encounters in the reservoir—stands as a "decontextualized abstraction of the actual well" (2008, 884) for the geologists working on shore; it is also a function of the rules with which those abstractions must be made as per the information infrastructure shared with other geologists. Sure, there are advantages to following those shared rules, like "facilitating communication over long ranges in time and space, and enabling comparisons and combinations to be made of objectified entities and their measured and ascribed properties" (2008, 883). This kind of facilitation is, indeed, essential for a Boston-based firm like EnTech to serve clients operating in California, Texas, and elsewhere in the country alike, and without a hitch. But Almklov observes that his interlocutors, in their everyday practice, did not work with the motivation to enable far-flung communication: "Instead, standardization was as much the result of professional habit and embodied practice than of any need to communicate with external agents. It seemed they were most comfortable when working and thinking with such objects" (2008, 881).

And here lies a fundamental insight for the techno-economics of electricity's representation. Data practitioners are most at home creating electronic representations of particular kinds. At EnTech, more employees are recruited because of their familiarity with data standardization than the ones recruited for their familiarity with electricity. It is not their belief in the superiority of markets as an organizing feature of society that compels these information workers to create and circulate electronic representations; it is their "professional habit and embodied practice" (2008, 881) as data practitioners. If that is the "why" of standardization, the consequence of it is that, as these actors' standardizations proliferate, the electric grid becomes increasingly more actionable to people whose trade is data, not electricity. During my fieldwork at EnTech, I once ran into a new employee in the kitchen, who was in charge of auditing and improving the company-wide information infrastructure. He cited a journalism firm as a previous employer. When I asked if this was his first experience in the energy sector, he looked at me as if I had asked the most irrelevant question possible and laughed; did the creators of Microsoft Excel have to know what kind of calculations its users were going to carry out with it? Did it matter if users kept a grocery list or calculate market prices with it? The platform agnosticism promoted by the data culture in markets, then, has the consequence of expanding the market participant pool to include people who know more about data representations than the underlying commodity.

Proliferating data standardizations also expand markets in different ways; as more of the electric grid becomes subject to a variety of actors' electronic representation and remote action, it becomes possible for distant actors to trade—and even desirable for those interested in increasing their market shares and possibilities of profit. But it is important to remember that a motive for expansion is not to be found on an electricity trading floor or the floor of EnTech. What one finds there is a work culture reproducing itself, day in, day out. What one observes is information workers creating immutable mobiles from electricity's flows with a certain tenacity and no long-term agenda. We now turn to the information workers at EnTech and the daily practice of working with electricity's representations. During my time there, every day I emerged out of a long elevator ride, greeted the receptionist, and walked through the analysts' floor before getting to my desk in the developers' cubicles. I observed different kinds of information workers—analysts, developers, and database workers—as they worked on a continuum of raw, cooked, and rotten data on the EnTech floor. In the next section of this chapter, we dwell on the analysts' floor with the analysts, before we walk together to my desk in the section after.

## Analysis in Real Time

As an electronically mediated endeavor, electricity markets happen at many places at once. An ISO is one of them; it is usually hosted in an unmarked building somewhere in its service territory far from urban centers. Since the very beginnings of electricity markets at the turn of the present century, thousands of bids and offers, for every hour and location, have been meeting each other in ISOs' software. An ISO's out-of-the-way location is a security measure; it is also immaterial to market operations since buyers and sellers connect to its control rooms thanks to the Open Access Same-Time Information System. OASIS is an Internet-based network where all registered requesters can see and reserve transmission lines.[6] Now, thousands of firms can communicate with ISOs through OASIS. Where a market actor is located does not matter for market observation or participation purposes as long as they have a reliable connection to the internet. But EnTech happens to be in one of the upper floors of a skyscraper in Boston overlooking the Charles River.

Analysts at EnTech were young people with informal or formal backgrounds in data practice; most of them had taught themselves data management and coding skills. Some of them were former traders who wanted to escape the extensive work hours of trading. Others were gearing up for future jobs as traders—more stressful, but higher paying. Most of them had come to EnTech with no prior knowledge about electricity or electricity markets; during their short training periods, they had learned how to represent electricity in data form by observing experienced analysts. Some of them were either former or aspiring future traders of other energy commodities. The familiarity gained with, say, natural gas prices while studying how they affect electricity prices could be leveraged later for a career in natural gas trading.

At EnTech, analysts' main job was to work with a pricing software designed by the firm's developers to mimic the pricing models of the ISOs. In the form of spreadsheets, the model offered price predictions for the different price locations of the grid, like Cedar Grove. While ISOs' pricing algorithm stacks actual bids and offers to produce prices for every location, EnTech's software needed to take guesses for tomorrow's bids and offers to predict tomorrow's prices. Its pricing model was attached to databases that kept data about any factor that might help the model predict tomorrow's bids and offers, and hence tomorrow's actual prices—from fuel type, to generation capacity, to age, to location.

Those databases were put together in the cubicles next to the analysts' floor by developers and database workers like me.

The analysts' floor consisted of long shared desks. Each desk was populated by two rows of analysts facing each other, or rather facing their monitors. Those who worked on the same electricity market (i.e., the same ISO) sat in close proximity to each other either on the same or neighboring desks. Each analyst had headphones on and at least three monitors facing him or her, often supplemented with tablets and laptops and cluttered with sticky notes. In the mornings, the floor was eerily quiet, especially in comparison with the chatter of the afternoons. Fingers worked busily on keyboards. The analysts did not take their eyes off of their many screens. When those who worked on the same electricity market huddled to puzzle over an image or a spreadsheet on one of their screens, no eye contact was made between the analysts. Their screen showed either the pricing model or a map at all times.

The reason why mornings were quiet at EnTech has to do with the timeline of electricity markets, as well as the reason why afternoons saw more chatter. All seven of US electricity markets have two major types of settlement, referred to as different "markets." Every morning, by a set deadline, the ISOs accept bids and offers from market participants that convey at what price they are willing to buy or sell one megawatt/hour of electricity at each hour *tomorrow* at different locations. For instance, a buyer within the PJM Interconnection territory might be willing to pay $25 for one megawatt/hour electricity tomorrow at 1 p.m. at the Cedar Grove location; $26 at 4 p.m. at the Orchard Road location—all of which she needs to communicate to PJM by 10 a.m. today. PJM publishes the results—that is, the prices at every hour at each location for tomorrow—at 1:30 p.m. *today.* This process of determining tomorrow's prices is called the "day-ahead market."

Some rebidding and readjustment periods later (depending on the individual ISO), the day-ahead market closes; every participant takes the resulting prices. Tomorrow comes. Necessarily, some unforeseen deviations from what was agreed-upon in the day-ahead market occur. (Let us say, a utility underestimated how much electricity its consumers needed and had to buy more during the day. Or a power plant had an unplanned service interruption.) The control room of the operator makes sure every participant is serviced during the day and no one went without electricity. Its market unit, on the other hand, calculates new prices for very short intervals (e.g., every fifteen minutes) for those buyers and sellers who have deviated from their day-ahead commitments. This process of calculating prices for actual consumption is called the "real-time market." The majority of the trade volume clears in the day ahead, which is why traders (and by extension, analysts) are busiest in the morning. Analysts email their morning reports to their clients approximately an hour before the deadline of their ISO. Then they stay on call to examine real-time market implications with them for the rest of the day (hence the headphones).

If physical location has seen a diminished role in electricity exchange since deregulation, time has seen an intensified one. The concept of real time is key to how actors in electricity markets perceive their role in the operations of markets. In electricity, real time is not simply a figure of speech or the social scientist's category; it refers to a specific market operation as one of the markets' settlement types. In financial markets, as anthropologists have explored in other contexts, market actors might feel a certain anxiety around the temporality of the market—a sense of being constantly behind and a need to catch up to markets' present moment (Miyazaki 2003). In the case of the central bank of Japan, as Annelise Riles has documented, the technocrats generated a real-time settlement scheme between the different banks to replace the daily settlement; the real-time machine, then, was hoped to eliminate the problems associated with too much reliance on planning (2004). "Real time" has a certain irony to it; despite being a creation of the technocrats' knowledge, it is supposed to liberate markets from it, in what Riles calls the "unwinding of technocratic knowledge" (2004, 398).

Time, then, is a marker of who is inside and who is outside the market; people, like electricity traders and EnTech's analysts, who participate in markets by buying, selling, or affecting buying and selling decisions, rhetorically externalize themselves to the operations of markets by resorting to the concept of real time as a market device. Perhaps for the pragmatic reason that the majority of trade volume clears in the day ahead, traders and analysts focus most of their attention on the day-ahead settlement, and not the real-time settlement. In more than one occasion, the real-time markets were described to me as "what actually happens" with a shrug—as in the market simply taking its course when the time comes, with all market participants being reduced to observers at that moment. The most a trader or an analyst could do, it was implied, was to be prepared to "real-time" in the day ahead. What is more, many market actors, like traders at utilities and generators, experience the real time (i.e., the real-time market) only in hindsight; they get the most precise account of their profits when they receive a bill from the ISO that has accounted for their deviations from their day-ahead commitments. Real time, in other words, is an act of account balancing. Electricity traders and analysts mostly live in the day ahead in an effort to be prepared for real time. When time turns to real time, they are still too busy with the day ahead to pay attention to the present moment.

In the mornings, the analysis happens under a deadline—under the pressure to create a stable enough fact, or a report to be shared with their clients, by a certain time. Analysts arrived in the office around 6 a.m. or earlier and first *recalibrated* their models. Recalibrating meant updating the model with the real-time results of the day before, published by ISOs' websites. From that time onward, until the submission of their reports at 9 a.m., the analysts looked at their monitors with an expression of tunnel vision. The nonanalyst staff would joke to me that they would take utmost care to get out of the analysts' way in the morning. John, the lead EnTech analyst for ERCOT (the ISO of Texas), once invited me to observe the ERCOT desk closely, so one morning, I obliged. I had known beforehand that two rows of ERCOT analysts occupied two different desks, sitting back to back. That morning I realized that this was a design feature meant to enable analysts to see each other's monitors easily by simply turning back on their rolling chairs. It turns out that if EnTech's physical location was immaterial to the markets, its spatial organization was not; the close proximity of relevant people had to be enabled by furniture arrangement for timely collaboration (Beunza and Stark 2004). Around 8 a.m., I pulled a rolling chair myself, perched in the in-between space, ready to get out of the way.

Around 8:30 a.m., the lead analyst John checked in with the other two analysts to see whether their forecasted prices for different nodes correlated. Another team member asked whether everybody else was seeing a particular line congest. "Seeing a line congest" meant that the projected load of a line came close to its electricity-carrying limit. Dan, an analyst in training, mentioned remembering that he had come across a "constraint" that might result in congestion on the same line. "Constraint" is the generic name for any ISO announcement signaling that a line may underperform—due to peak in demand, scheduled maintenance, weather events that might physically hurt the lines, and a variety of other reasons, all of which are often presented without detail on ISOs' websites and daily reports. John opened a map of ERCOT's transmission system on one of his monitors, and all four of them huddled around it.

John had intuited where that line might be located, and collectively they found the line on the map. Not quite knowing the exact effect of the underperformance on the grid surrounding it—and not trusting their ability to find it out before 9 a.m.—the analysts returned to their chairs and decided to make this observation into a note about "slight risk" in the report. The analyst sitting next to John was the one who suggested "slight" as a qualifier. Based on his earlier conversations with the in-house meteorologist, he anticipated that congestion would be limited because the electricity in question was coming from a wind power plant and the wind would probably die down in the afternoon. Slight risk was entered into the report as a textual note.

This textual note was not as desirable as a quantified observation would have been. Like John and the others, Dan reminded me that the report had to be concise and give traders exactly what they needed to know; otherwise traders would not bother to read it. For Dan, conciseness usually meant a numerical prediction of prices rising or falling in a particular location, as opposed to a textual note that they might rise or fall—communication through numbers, however imprecise, like that undertaken by Caitlin Zaloom's interlocutors. Yet, in the mornings, when analysts had limited time to quantify intuitions, some of EnTech's suggestions and observations came in the form of text. Textual interpretation relayed the collective process of intuition behind the report to the client in honest terms of probability.

Text is not the only part where inexact inputs could find a place for themselves in the report; the process of intuition extended to the mathematics of the analysis. As the analysts were seeking each other's opinions on the generation levels of a particular wind farm and its effects on the prices in nearby nodes, Dan told me that this was a new wind farm that did not exist in EnTech's model of ERCOT yet. Therefore, the model (which usually updated itself on a daily basis by scraping data from online sources coded into it) could not automatically scrape published price data about this plant. While the analysts waited for the developers to update the model with the specifics of this new unit, the ERCOT analysts decided to create a duplicate entry for another wind farm in the model—a wind farm that they thought had "similar economics" to the missing plant (e.g., same energy source, location with similar weather conditions). This existing plant would, however imperfectly, make up for the missing plant. The analysts made sure to remind each other of the dissimilarities between the two during the remainder of their discussions. This would allow them to introduce further, yet still intuitive, adjustments to the prices around the missing unit. It was not exact information, but it would do for a while.

This was, in a nutshell, the everyday of the data analysis process in electricity at EnTech. Analysts made stable *enough* reports out of unstable, uncertain facts in the early hours of the day. They utilized numbers not as final descriptions of demand and supply levels but as heuristics for the movements of demand and supply (Zaloom 2006). Numbers and text complemented each other as heuristic instruments. Analysts' work wound down toward the afternoon, after the ISOs' rebidding and readjustment periods ended. Most of them would leave the office around 3 p.m. in the afternoon, when I, as a database worker, still had a few more hours of spreadsheet maintenance work ahead of me. I would be brewing yet another pot of coffee in the kitchen to get me through the work, when the analysts would be wishing me a "good night" already, even though it was only afternoon. There were always some other analysts lingering on the floor well past the closure of the day-ahead market, studying their data quietly on their own. They wanted to be prepared for a real time that would only ever be experienced as the future or the past.

This preparation work is central to EnTech's promise, yet it could be easily lost on an observer. Economic anthropology has had a tendency to focus exclusively on the analysis and execution of trades, as well as a habit to study embodied behavior as the locus of trading. For instance, Daniel Beunza and David Stark explicitly argue against the study of the "economies of information" on the grounds that "information is [now] almost instantaneously available to nearly every market actor" and that arbitrage is only enabled by traders' "socio-cognitive processes of interpretation" (2004, 372). I believe, however, that economic anthropology needs no pitting of "information" and "interpretation" against each other; that would be an unwitting affirmation of information's ontology as outside the social. While traders and analysts are charismatic actors whose time-constrained activities have recently constituted an anthropological curiosity, I believe that they need to be studied as information workers who are effective only to the extent that they work well with other information workers. We need to attend to not only what happens under morning deadlines but also the process of preparation for that deadline—how action under a deadline is supported by other temporalities that sometimes see the sun set over the Charles River.

I came to this argument gradually over the course of my participation in EnTech's work as a database worker. But I admit that I did not come to it fast; I spent months ready to come to conclusions on the preeminence of analyst- and trader-embodied interpretation. If part of the reason why I was conditioned to come to that conclusion was economic anthropology's near-exclusive focus on traders, a larger part was how my interlocutors at EnTech viewed their own work; in conversations they seemed to share the majority of economic anthropologists' view that the locus of action in markets was individual traders' bodies.

"I would cost a lot of people a lot of money if I were doing your job," I once joked to an analyst, "because I'm just not a morning person."

"Well," he said, "you'd have to drink a lot of coffee in the morning."

On another occasion, a developer who used to be an analyst told me that new analysts arrived early and stayed late to study the market manual with the help, of course, of a lot of coffee. Several others highlighted that an analyst (or a trader, for that matter) needed to develop alertness and the ability to recall and mobilize several sources of information quickly, just like John, who remembered the location of a congested line from memory under the pressure of the 9 a.m. deadline. Like economic anthropologists, they seemed to be locating the necessary skills for the job in the person of the analyst. "If all the analysts got hit by a bus one day, we would be done for. We would have to start from scratch," the same developer said. The comment was meant to explain the dependency of developers and the company in general on analysts' accumulated experience or tacit knowledge (Polanyi 1966), while hinting at the pedagogical processes through which this knowledge passes on to new analysts (Collins 1985). At EnTech, it was commonly accepted that expertise was embodied by analysts and sustained by the commercial-sized coffee machine in the kitchen.

I learned not to trust the accuracy of this joking commentary while observing what happened after the exciting early hours passed—wondering why the analysts were trickling into developers' cubicles every afternoon to collectively examine the predictions they had made in the morning. I found that traders did not subscribe to EnTech's services only because of the analysts' interpretative skills. EnTech's promise to traders was that these interpretative skills were supported by a team of software developers, whose work was less constrained by market timelines. The same former analyst and current developer told me, "When a trader is screaming at you on the phone, the last thing you want to do is go back and organize your data." Developers provided the extra time to calculate and refine—the kind of time that analysts and traders did not have. In other words, developers, assisted by database workers, brought to electricity markets another layer of time, a more stretched, longer-term layer, that is neither day ahead nor real time.

At EnTech, afternoons saw analysts relaxed and cracking jokes across desks while they enjoyed a moment or two to "go back to the data," as several of them put it. For instance, going back to the data would help John (or rather, having developers going back to the data for him) to process and quantify the meanings of the congestion of that line in ERCOT if it congested again another morning (which it most certainly would). Developers adding the missing wind farm to the ERCOT model would save John and his teammates the guesswork involved in working with substitute data under a deadline. Whereas the interpretative work of traders and analysts, or their embodied knowledge, has received a good amount of attention in economic anthropology and sociology, the infra-structural activity associated with interpretation, that is, *data* management and processing, is less well understood. The "economies of information" that Beunza and Stark have construed as passé constitute a techno-economic field that is only beginning to be explored.

It is true that traders and analysts might experience an embarrassment of riches these days when it comes to information. ISOs publish electricity prices and information about their transmission equipment on their websites on a daily basis. They also publish their own estimations of demand. Many ISOs, through their public relations departments, boast about the amount of infor-mation they share with the public as an evidence of the transparency of their operations. But this must not lead us to believe that the available information is automatically received and processed by all actors to only make a difference depending on how it is interpreted. The bits found on ISO websites, as well as through other public and proprietary channels require significant work to *become* information—work conducted by a variety of people ranging from electrical engineering PhDs to programmers, to even mathematically under-qualified people like me. What constitutes data itself is under constant debate in this process, as we will see next. As Lisa Gitelman and Virginia Jackson put it, "the imagination of data entails an interpretive base" (2013, 3); inventing data is interpretive work par excellence. Analysts' and traders' interpretative and associative skills do not follow, but also encompass, their imagination of data.

"Information is there," a developer once told me, "you just want to automate it." But as my daily practice taught me, information was never readily found as information; it took collaborative work to produce and accept a bit as information. And as that developer himself conceded, the work to automate is exacting—it takes endless design, quality checks, and maintenance. While one might think of information and automation's many imperfections as an obstacle to overcome, for analysts and traders, it is what they take to be the reality of working with data—an extension of their work culture. It is also the stuff of opportunity and space of possibility. Producing better, more complete representations of electricity, which rest on partial and exclusive information, presents the possibility of competitive advantage over other market actors. In crafting better representations of electricity and the electric grid, analysts have to collaborate with other information workers like developers and database workers. If analysts and traders had a guiding ideal, it would not be perfect information; it would be the perfect database. Alas, the perfect database also remains elusive.

## Database Work and Granularity

In the afternoon, I often bypassed the analysts' floor to head straight for my desk in the developers' cubicles. My ritual was to turn on my computer, log into the shared computing environment of the firm, and log into Skype. In the quiet quarters of the developers, I would sometimes sit for the entire afternoon without saying anything out loud, occasionally lifting my head over my two monitors to take a peek at the Boston view. If you watched me work, you could think my "screenwork" (Boyer 2013, 13) was unsupervised. If you watched anyone in our quarters work, you could think the work here was solitary. But within the computing environment, we were all connected. Tasks were assigned, findings were entered as comments, and the feed showed who was working on what. We discussed the tasks over Skype's instant messaging interface. Occasionally, I did delve into solitary work, cleaning data on spreadsheets for hours on end. Along with some developers, I often stayed later than the analysts, some of whom teased me for "burning the 5 p.m. candle." But even then, I knew that my supervisor would vet my spreadsheet the next morning. Until approved, my work was simply a comment entry. Once approved, it was data.

Fantasy writer Jorge Luis Borges has a short story called "On Exactitude in Science" (1999 [1946]). It is a tale of an empire, where the ambitious imperial cartographers make a map so detailed that it grows to be the same size as the territory to be charted, eventually becoming the empire itself. The tale features prominently in Jean Baudrillard's theorization of simulacra as an allegory for the "hyperreal" representations surrounding us, which have become realities of their own (1988). Database work and software developing—two processes that support analysis—can be described as a kind of hyperreal cartography. Database work consists of mundane acts of determining what is useful data— what needs to be extracted from the world to be put in a spreadsheet cell and what serves as proper representation in electronic format. As such, it adds up to a continuous process of imaginative investigation.

In other words, database work is an effort to capture a territory, in this case the electric infrastructure, in electronic databases in as much detail as possible. Software developing, on the other hand, is designing digital instruments with which to effectively navigate those databases—in this case to ask how the prices will act tomorrow. Like the Borgesian imperial map, electronic databases and models are "information as reality" as much as they are "information about reality" (Floridi 2004, 560); they are selective, imperfect, and always incomplete snapshots of the represented territory that acquire lives of their own. Like the Borgesian imperial cartographers, database workers and developers perpetually seek a greater overlap between the infrastructure and its representation. A satisfying level of overlap, however satisfaction is defined, they call "granularity." The perpetual chase for granularity is a mandate of information workers' work culture. Finally, like the Borgesian imperial map, database work is no neutral representation; it stretches the expanse of electricity markets, that is the empire itself, by allowing the influx of data-conversant practitioners into it. It is also what makes electricity tradable farther and wider than before.

My participation in EnTech was itself wrapped up in a mapping endeavor. By the time I arrived there, the software developers had been working for a few months on creating a new original product: a real-time, interactive map of the US transmission infrastructure. The map visualized transmission lines in the form of lines and electric substations (i.e., the transmission lines' departure and arrival points) in the form of dots. When the user hovered on the lines with the mouse cursor, a dialog box would pop open to show the amount of electricity flowing through it at the moment, along with an arrow showing in what direction electricity was flowing. Transmission lines close to their carrying limits were visualized with red lines, others with green lines. The map, EnTech managers believed, would help the traders subscribed to EnTech's services and their analysts see easily and quickly where too much load—congestion—might drive prices up. (ISOs' formula calculates Locational Marginal Prices based on three kinds of data; supply, demand, and congestion.) For instance, it would help analysts like John locate a congested line easily in the morning rush; when they saw a congested line reported on ISO reports only by name, they could look up its location on the map and determine what else might be affected by that congestion.

All this could very be useful to improve "our granularity," people at EnTech often said, but there was one problem. The map showed only a few lines and substations on it, and not thousands as the managers wished. Databases had to be built with the information of many more transmission lines and substations for the software to translate them into visuals and "scrape" real-time information about them. To better spend the time of the developers with coding skills, interns with a passing knowledge of Excel, like me, were hired temporarily to collect bits of information and build out those databases. We were a team of five—me, another intern in the Boston office, another intern and an employee based in EnTech's Midwest office, and a supervisor also based in the Midwest office. On my first day, my supervisor, who was visiting the Boston office, gave me a quick overview of the work. She would identify the equipment she wanted in the database and the rest of us would locate it and enter its information on spreadsheets shared in a digital work environment. If it was a transmission line, we would enter its location and carrying limit. If it was a power plant, we would enter its location, age, and fuel type—or however many of these data points we could find. With these databases attached to it, the software could scrape real-time information about the equipment from public and proprietary sources. In other words, when an ISO announced that, say, 500MW of electricity was flowing into Cedar Grove at a particular moment, the map could translate that into a red dot since it now knew that the transmission lines going into and out of Cedar Grove could not carry much more than that. On that first day, my supervisor remarked to me with some pride how pretty and sleek the interface of the software looked—how fun it would be for traders and analysts to work with it. Like that, we all set out to map the electric infrastructure onto spreadsheets.

One might wonder why all this information should be considered new—if the allegorical empire had not been charted before. It is true that no one has ever put together a complete database of the US electric infrastructure, including the ISOs. All actors have partial knowledge of the steel and copper of the infrastructure, which they represent differently. Take PJM Interconnection: the largest ISO in North America, PJM is headquartered in Pennsylvania and covers all or parts of thirteen states. The spreadsheets published on the PJM website include the names, code names, and voltages of various equipment, such as transmission lines, substations, and transformers. These spreadsheets exclude any information about the line limits or locations of this equipment, partly because PJM has no perfect knowledge about the properties of the equipment either. Equipment gets old, its properties change, it gets replaced or removed, all of which make it hard to capture it in a database. Transmission is supervised by PJM but divided into territories, each operated by a transmission owner. Each one of PJM's spreadsheets is devoted to one transmission owner and has stylistic differences, if not an altogether different convention. Whereas lines are given names closer to plain English in the territory of one owner, another one has chosen to be more cryptic with names. And given that PJM has approximately 10,000 transmission lines and more substations, collecting, standardizing, and squeezing all this data into one database is a lofty goal. So, where does one start?

Where one does not start is the perfectionist attitude of Borges's imperial cartographers. Like the analysts and electricity traders elsewhere, who favor action over inaction at any cost, our supervisor wanted the product to be useful as quickly as possible and not necessarily complete or perfect. The definitions of useful information on the analysts' floor applied to this product, too; it is useful if it assists analysts and traders in predicting prices while being easily cognizable. For that reason, database work was necessarily a selective process. We started by accumulating the higher voltage lines whose code names appeared frequently on ISOs' congestion list. Those were the ones "the customers wanted to see," as my supervisor put it, because the prices around them fluctuated more, opening up possibilities of arbitrage and profit. Selection continued as the database was being expanded as well. We left aside the equipment that did not readily factor into our models—at least for the time being. My supervisor reminded us that we would eventually want to have "everything" in the database. But my coworkers were often quick to remind me that "everything" was a figure of speech—operating on the same receding horizon as that of granularity.

In the absence of a central database for equipment location, I spent hours on end on Google Earth, visually following transmission lines and substations to find their locations, which I then exported to a spreadsheet in the form of GPS coordinates. Short of going to each location and seeing for ourselves, hovering over the digital earth of Google was the next best thing. As a database worker, I connected the dots using Google's different tools. Using the web search tool, for instance, I collected textual information about the equipment we wanted to have in the databases. This information included everything ranging from official announcements by construction companies, to reports of citizens unhappy with infrastructural constructions, to expert reports used in siting permission processes and, where those processes have failed, lawsuits. While looking for the landmarks that the equipment might have been named after, I became familiar with the host communities of the electric equipment in states I had never physically visited. My clues existed to end in GPS coordinates—and to be revived in another search later. My supervisor sent me tasks for equipment in a corner of Ohio, for instance, because I had "been in the area for a while."

As I was virtually transported to Ohio, analysts were tuned into the local time and weather of their ISOs' service territories. Our being in Boston was incidental—we only remembered it when yet another snowstorm was about to strike New England and we showered our in-house meteorologists with questions about the local weather.

Information collection, maintenance, and organization in electricity markets works like a perpetual motion machine, drawing its energy from itself more than anything else. In a competitive trading environment, where EnTech is not the only market intelligence firm aspiring to predict prices, the search for granularity means erring on the side of more information. Especially in the context of a market intelligence firm, granularity becomes its own goal, even when its connection to profitability is not easily verifiable. Would our new map actually help traders and analysts make better trading decisions? Would their marginal profits justify traders' subscription fees or EnTech's labor costs for building the map? I kept on asking these questions to the analysts on the floor. Some of them—typically those who took pride in taking into account the most information sources as possible and had more monitors at their disposal—were already taking occasional looks at our beta version and expressed interest in giving it a try when we fully launched the product. Others—typically those who took pride in trusting their intuition more than anything else—repeated to me that they did not see much use to a geographically exact map of the electric grid; what mattered most to them was the equipment's relative locations to each other. The fact of the matter was, we could not exactly measure how much the map would improve chances at profits, even after the full launch. But as a potential booster of granularity, it was a welcome and logical addition to EnTech's portfolio of instruments, and it had the full support of the management.

The culture of data work, in other words, dictated that, as dutiful cartographers, we keep on expanding the map of the proverbial empire—the electric grid. This is why I dispute Beunza and Stark's claim that we have entered a phase where, information having become plentiful and readily available, the locus of profit making has shifted to creative interpretation of already existing data (2004). I argue, instead, that we have entered a phase where market actors *create* more data about commodities than before, in addition to endlessly maintaining it, even when the potential of data creation at boosting profitability is not easily verifiable. Creating "immutable mobiles" (Latour 1990) about electricity that easily travel electronically and decoded at the destination (like a price prediction by EnTech analysts) has the effect of expanding electricity markets themselves, alongside the databases we keep about them. Let us remember what I mean by expansion. First, the employment pool has expanded from being limited largely to specialists of electricity (like electrical engineers) to encompass information workers—including database workers like me. Second, the very physical footprints of electricity markets continue to expand as previously monopolistic utilities see reason to voluntarily join market territories. Market actors now have the opportunity to encounter each other in a disembodied, data-mediated fashion; they often take advantage of this new "hyperreal" in order to plug into control rooms far away and expand their market shares. For anthropologists, the gradual ascendance of data work in market environments should not signal simply a new moment of interpretation for market actors—we should regard it as a vehicle of market expansion.

ISOs take pride in claiming that information has become public and plentiful in the era of electricity markets; in press communications, they often cite how they share spreadsheets of information on their website every day as an illustration of the transparency of markets relative to the monopoly days. But we have enough reason not to take this claim at face value; data does not precede actors' interpretation—it is created and maintained interpretatively as well. Actors in electricity markets strive for the perfect database, the ever-receding horizon, in the meantime operating with messy but usable data. The challenges facing the perfect database are many and often silly. There is "metadata friction" (Edwards et al. 2011) between the various databases at EnTech and elsewhere due to reasons as mundane as homonymous equipment and misspellings. There are simply too many streets and landmarks in the US named Cedar Grove and almost as many equipment pieces named after them. Looking for a transmission line on a spreadsheet to no avail often resulted in the line being spelled in yet another way by an ISO or a transmission owner employee. While learning to anticipate how certain common words were likely to be misspelled in particular regions, we also had discussions of automating misspelling detection. Here again, however, the automation had to be preceded by defining what misspelling was, which proved close to impossible in the face of the misspelling varieties we encountered.

Contacting an ISO representative for the clarification of public information was always a possibility, though the process yielded varying results. After consulting EnTech's analysts of PJM Interconnection and developers with backgrounds in electrical engineering, our team still struggled to figure out what the code "RAD" in front of some line names meant. I finally clicked the Live

Chat button on PJM's website. After being referred to one representative after another for half an hour, one representative finally got back to me reporting that RAD stood for radial line in PJM parlance. As I ran by him our understanding of what a radial line was, that is, a line that carries electricity in only one direction, he said, "Correct," and added honestly, "as I understand it."

Database work in the midst of all this data friction is a collective process. Circling around equipment for hours on Google Earth, collecting textual and numerical clues—at times, nothing seemed to work to help us find what we were looking for. A line we had been searching for over hours could turn out to be an underground line, impossible to see on Google Earth or on the other satellite maps to which we resorted in regions where Google Earth's aerial photos were not up to date. If we wanted to have the location of that equipment in the database to be able to scrape public data about it, we simply had to compare best guesses and drop the pin on one spot. As my supervisor once said, it was "better to have something if not the exact perfect thing." Once the best guess was agreed on, the bit went into the database, and once the database was refreshed in the server, the bit was set to appear on the map; it had become data. It was made raw; it contained exactly as much as would be usable in analysts' models—no more, no less.

Developers who dealt with much larger databases of thousands of rows (such as historical demand) reminded me playfully that whatever I entered as data would remain as data. Massive databases could not be fully controlled all that often for quality. Yet our team still preserved the hope that in the future, with better clues, we would go back to the database and make data more precise. The database had a temporality—it operated on a more stretched layer of time, that was neither day ahead nor real time. In this layer, information did not steadily move along toward a higher quality form. Once, while importing data from both the textual and geographic annotations of the same subscription-based database, I noticed discrepancies and was slightly panicked to learn from a team member that the geographic annotation on which I was mostly relying was an older version. Upon reassuring her that I would now rely on the newer, textual version, she advised not to assume that older necessarily meant less perfect. She had seen cases of older databases being preferred by developers. In electricity markets, constant database maintenance is not a guarantee of quality improvement—it simply is a precondition of keeping data usable and its messiness under control.

Representing electricity in electronic bits changes how we *know* electricity.

To tell a story of techno-economics, we should attend to the epistemology of acting in markets saturated with the culture of data work. We should ask: Now that market actors create and keep more information about commodities and their underlying infrastructures than before, do we know more or less about these commodities? Does a trader, analyst, or developer have to know anything about the physics of electricity to operate in its markets? How, in other words, is expertise in markets changing in a data-driven economic world?

Anthropologists once held that market actors were keen on cultivating familiarity with the commodities and financial instruments they traded. A successful fish merchant needed to master the conditions of perishability and exchangeability of each fish (Bestor 2004); a dealer in the booming business of Islamic mortgages needed to be conversant with Islamic jurisprudence (Maurer 2006b). More recently, especially since the 2008 global financial crisis, traders' expertise in the tools they wielded began to be the subject of doubt; scholars have problematized the proliferation of quantitative analysts specializing in physics and mathematics in financial markets (cf. Patterson 2012). Anthropologists, in addition, have found that the world's major cotton traders have no interest in cotton as an organism or crop (Çalışkan 2010) and that the creators of financial instruments in investment banks pass their new creations imperfectly onto back-office employees charged with keeping these instruments alive (Lépinay 2011). Scholars, then, are concerned that market actors are jettisoning an intimate knowledge of commodities while embracing those commodities' electronic representations. Is it true that we are forgetting that the world has more physicality to it than its electronic representations might be able to capture? And if so, what are the consequences?

The nature of economic expertise has surely changed in the electricity industry in the market era. The increasing focus on creating and standardizing information about electricity spurred the influx of people into the industry who know more about that particular skill—information creation and standardization—than the object of the information. But this does not mean that it was forgotten on the EnTech floor, or elsewhere in electricity markets, that electricity kicks back. Forgetting that would not create a dramatic system failure like a blackout—that kind of consequence would result from failures at sites like ISOs' control rooms—but it would, over the long run, decrease EnTech's ability to predict prices. Remember, for instance, my effort to decode PJM's "RAD" code in front of some line names. When the online assistance representative decoded RAD as "radial line" for me, my supervisor and I knew who exactly to ask what that meant: Alicia, a PJM analyst who had an electrical engineering background and who was known to have better familiarity with electricity-specific terminology and physics. What is more, she was an experienced analyst of PJM. I sent Alicia an instant message to ask what a "radial line" was and received her explanation right away—a line that carries electricity in only one direction. It was true that at EnTech, programming, developing, and general data management got one hired, while a background in electricity was considered simply a "plus." But, either prior to one's time at EnTech or during it, one was expected to learn how electricity moves (or learn how to find that out), along with how that information can be translated into bits in ways that would allow successful price prediction.

We need to be alert to the ways in which the proliferation of information work in markets can take precious attention away from the specificities of the traded commodities and services—sometimes with catastrophic results. For instance, financial traders who created "credit-derivative obligations" viewed subprime mortgages as yet another kind of debt that could be bundled neatly into a new financial instrument; ignoring the specifics of housing debt—when and under what conditions people tend to default—famously spurred the global 2008 crisis (Tett 2009). But this should not lead anthropologists to assume that representing a commodity in the form of data precludes knowing that commodity. To disentangle a commodity from its representation, information workers have to look for what exactly needs to be extricated from that commodity in the form of information—what about it, they have to ask, is enough for market actors to know and utilize for profit-making purposes. Information creation, then, requires an imaginative investigation of the underlying commodity and its infrastructures. Information workers participate actively in the imagination of what kinds of information may provide competitive advantage in markets, as we have seen in the example of the debate at EnTech around whether exact geographical coordinates offered any value as information.

The process of information proliferation is political, both in instances of crises and during the everyday operations of markets, but not because electronic representation is necessarily unfair to what is represented; it is political because it works selectively to serve the agenda of a particular group of people—in this case, traders (and their allies in market intelligence firms) who seek a competitive edge in electricity markets. What information workers leave out of their representations can kick back, either in the form of system failures or in the form of discontent. As the reader might recall, in my quests for transmission equipment location at EnTech, I resorted to, among other things, reports of citizens unhappy with infrastructural constructions—siting permission reports and records of lawsuits. As an information worker, I extricated location information from those documents and safely discarded the reported controversy since neither was it relevant for EnTech's agenda, nor was it representable in any way I knew. I am certain that if citizen discontent had a more significant history of disrupting electricity prices, EnTech would have found a way to represent it in spreadsheet cells and calculate its effect on prices via models. (As an anthropologist, however, I did pursue those controversies and citizen discontent, which turned into the ethnography in chapter 4.)

The reader might wonder what happened to our ambitious map-making project. Did we succeed to map the electric grid in detail on par with Borges's imperial map? At the end of my time at EnTech, my supervisor was pleased with the progress our team had made; thousands of spreadsheet rows were filled and, as a result, hundreds of new equipment populated the interactive map with all their color-coded glory. But ultimately the product suffered the fate of many other experimental software; after my time there, it got integrated into a different EnTech product that also came in the form of a map—one showing real-time data of generation. It was not discontinued, but it went from being its own product to being a feature of another. While products come and go, data may live on, being transferred from context to context. But what makes data durable also makes it hard to isolate its effect. Now it is even harder to discern the impact of our mapping journey—whether the feature of transmission information, as separate from generation information, has increased EnTech's promise to predict prices better than any other market actor. I hear anecdotally from EnTech's analysts that how they feel about our map has not changed since I left; those who enjoy working with as many information sources as possible tell me they like it, while those who take pride in trusting their intuitions more than anything else answer with a shrug.

## Those Left Behind

The terms of electronic calculation in ISOs' control rooms—the LMPs and how they are calculated—have remained largely the same since their inception, but the world of electricity trading outside—the world of those who sent in the bids and offers—has changed substantially. In the early days of electricity trading, power plant engineers and utility planners provisionally filled in their new roles as traders, scrambling to produce "bids and offers" from what they had previously considered as the "costs" of electricity production and provision. Virtual trading—trading by actors who cannot physically acquire or provide electricity, but who can buy and sell on paper to make profit—was unheard of. Today, it is more likely that a bid or offer is sent into an ISO by a coding whiz than an electricity specialist (even if the coding whiz is working for a power producer or a utility). Droves of computer programmers, data scientists, and data analysts have become traders, markets analysts, or database workers supporting traders and analysts. A quick online job search for an electricity trading position would go to show that strong Microsoft Excel skills are considered a "must" for hiring, whereas prior experience in the energy sector is "preferred" at most.

At a place like EnTech, the work culture of data is taken for granted, since the datafication of electricity markets is the very reason of EnTech's existence. But how does a data-forward trading culture sit in places where electricity is produced or provisioned to consumers? It appears that those scrambling engineers and planners still exist, and they have conflicted feelings about the trading of electricity, precisely because of its data-saturated work culture. Meet Ted, a power plant engineer specializing in construction and safety at a major utility and generation company in New England. During my week at ISO-NE's market participant training in 2013, Ted sat to my left, generously sharing his real-time running commentary on the course material with me. As I had learned on my first day at the market training, Ted had become responsible for his company's trading division when the head trader abruptly left a few months prior. His traders, he said, had already been "doing the bids" for the last ten years; he was at the training to learn the process in order to supervise them better. A self-identified learner-by-doing, as well as a holder of an undergraduate engineering degree, Ted was confident he would grasp trading's basics quickly. He resented, however, that the ISOs' market operatives, some of whom served as instructors at the training, often lacked a reciprocal interest in power plant engineering, which had a direct effect on how they designed the markets.

Throughout the week, Ted interjected electricity- and engineering-specific nuances and correctives to the instructors' hypothetical scenarios—either by whispering them to me or heckling the instructor. If the instructor gave an example of a transaction in the real-time market, Ted would say, "Not everyone can ramp up a plant that fast"—at his work he managed coal-based power plants with slow ramp-up times. Once, the instructor found himself at pains to explain the concepts of "eco min" and "eco max." An example of the "gluing of economics and engineering" we saw in the previous chapter of this book, economic minimum and economic maximum signify the window of a power producer's offer to sell electricity, based on its generators' physical capacity. When the trader sitting to my right, an electricity novice but a coding whiz, could not get a satisfying answer from the instructor to his question, "Who decides the eco min and eco max?" Ted turned to him to simply say, "Heat rate." When the trader looked confused, the usually chatty Ted repeated the same two words as if that was a perfectly self-explanatory answer, immediately intelligible to all. Finally, a participant sitting in the row in front of us turned to the confused trader to relieve him of his misery: "[The instructor] doesn't know because he's not an engineer, but there's an efficient point where a plant can run, economizing on fuel the most. That's what the economic max is." This explanation was surely an exaggeration; the instructor did know what the concepts meant, but he did not explain them to the satisfaction of the engineers in the crowd. Nevertheless, Ted nodded aggressively at his fellow engineer's explanation.

Ted's continued frustration did not concern only some ISO representatives' tabling of engineering matters for the purposes of the training. He negatively reacted to a number of market design developments that resulted from the influx of data practitioners into electricity trading—these developments, he thought, catered mostly to market actors who had no interest in producing or providing electricity, while making life more complicated for engineers like himself. He despised (and admitted to not fully understanding) virtual trading, which he characterized as "legalized gambling." He also dreaded ISO-NE's plan to shrink the real-time market transaction intervals to every five minutes—again, a measure that services the likes of EnTech, which find a reason for business in such challenges of information gathering and bid/offer formation under tight deadlines. I suspect that Ted could have chosen to acculturate himself to trading. Work cultures are not impermeable—like in any other culture, there is room to grow, stand out, move on, within certain boundaries. But he seems to have chosen not to, as only two years later, he returned to full-time engineering as a hydroelectric dam safety engineer.

Ted's frustration with the proliferation of data practices in the electricity industry is understandable for professional reasons. He used to believe that the raison d'être of his employment in a utility company was keeping the lights on for customers. The location of the faraway Cedar Grove substation—the stuff of information workers' trade—was several layers separated from what he considered work and what his everyday toolkit was able to address. For Ted, data practices constituted distractions from the "actual" work; for the growing body of information workers in electricity trading, to the contrary, the same data practices are the raison d'être of their employment. As anthropologists of the techno-economic field, we should take notice of how data practitioners find and create for themselves opportunities for profit and/or employment in economic arrangements where they have limited familiarity with the traded commodity. While increased profit appears as many market actors' motive to turn to data, data's work culture perpetuates itself even when enhanced data management's causal relationship with increased profit does not lend itself to granular verification—at least not on markets' own timelines, whether day ahead or real time.

While the information workers tracked in this chapter steadily expand the footprint of already existing electricity markets, there is also a different process of expansion at work—a process that transforms the footprint of everyday life itself into an electricity market. The professionals in charge of that process aim to draw everyday users of electricity into a market-like form of economic life, if not into organized exchanges like those held by ISOs. The next chapter turns to the engineers of smart grids.

( 3 )

# OPTIMIZING

There are no oscilloscopes, multimeters, circuits, power supplies or other instruments typically found in electrical engineering laboratories here. There are about twenty cubicles, instead, equipped with laptop computers. On the shelves are found textbooks; nearly each one has the word "optimization" in the title—"Optimization of Power Systems Operations," "The Principles of Power Flow Optimization," among others. The whiteboard is awash with Greek letters signifying the constraints in an optimization problem. The pin board sports science fiction and Japanese anime-themed drawings. If the lab members are not in their cubicles gazing at MATLAB (a computing software) on their computer screens, they can be found either in the conference room next door for lab meetings or in the adjacent kitchen, where the recreational reading material includes copies of *Physics Today* and *Power and Energy*, in addition to a lone copy of *Socio-Economic Review*, presumably left there by the occasional grid engineer reading up on economic sociology.

This basement lab was the work environment of a group based in the Electrical and Computer Engineering Department of Carnegie Mellon University, Pittsburgh, comprised of graduate students and postdocs, and led by a professor, Marija Ilić. I had arrived there in the fall of 2013 for a semester's stay in the wake of an illustrious occasion—the publication of a book by lab members, current and alumni, many years in the making. The book put forward ways to build an electric grid equipped with information technologies (Ilić et al. 2013). As a shorthand for their agenda, the authors used the term "smart grid," like a good many other engineering research groups in the country and the world. This new grid, the lab members claimed, would allow for cleaner sources of fuel than allowed by current grids. And it would do so by expertly forecasting and coordinating, thanks to superior computing software, every single input of supply and demand out there. For illustration's sake, imagine harvesting the littlest gust of wind to power a wind turbine just enough to electrify your toaster, just in time for breakfast. The book shared the results of grid simulations conducted on MATLAB with historical electricity consumption data from a place far away from Pittsburgh—the Azorean archipelago in the middle of the Atlantic. The islands, the book held, were a testbed for results replicable elsewhere.

When I had first arrived in Pittsburgh, I was excited to get my hands on a copy of the book; it had, I found out, gone to print with a generous acknowledgment for me. The acknowledgment was for my summer stint in the Azores two years prior as a research assistant to the lab leader, Ilić, who had tasked me with gathering insights into the social aspects of electricity consumption on the islands. The book's content was as I anticipated—abundant discussion about matching generation to consumption under different circumstances, presented in the optimization language. One thing, however, still stood out to me: the frequent use of the phrase "just-in." The book's editors reassured the readers that, with the proposed software changes in place, electricity would be produced and delivered to consumers just-in-time, just-in-place, just-in-context. This phrasing—denoting things being delivered just when and where needed—seemed to characterize many other economic forms that are proliferating in everyday life, from ride-sharing apps to internet-based crowd-working arrangements. Many critics also think that "just-in-time" encapsulates the changes to production and consumption under neoliberal arrangements—to stand in for the increasingly decentralized and modular processes through which our goods are assembled and brought to us through global supply chains (cf. Harvey 2005). How did the phrase belong in a book about engineering electric grids?

In this chapter, I describe the work culture of optimization in Ilić's lab, where a precise balance of supply and demand of electricity is sought above all. As one of the lab members once told me, "'The point of all we do is to better match supply and demand'" (Özden-Schilling 2015, 578). I argue that optimizing engineers are techno-economic practitioners who, in electricity and elsewhere, create market-like lived realities here and now, without waiting for legal change and without necessarily a base in personal ideological conviction; they do so as a function of the optimization toolkit and its attending conjectures about the world. This culture of optimization explains the proliferation of decentralized, modular, and everyday forms of economic life surrounding us. When we anchor our study of these new economic forms within settings like Ilić's lab, we can craft a nuanced story that captures the specificities of the optimizers' imagination, informed and enriched by specific mathematical toolkits.

Optimization is a set of mathematical techniques to select the best outcome, depending on a criterion, out of a set of possible outcomes. There are different traditions of optimization across computer science, engineering, economics, and systems sciences. In Ilić's lab, "optimal" means when fewest possible resources go to waste because consumers' electricity needs are matched to resources as closely as possible. In her spartan laboratory, you might think you have arrived in an economics department, as you overhear people talking endlessly about the "balance of supply and demand." Ilić and her students see the smart grid as a continuation of the age-old problem in electrical engineering of keeping the grid balanced and stable—now aided by advanced communication technologies and heaps of data available.

Often, she receives new students coming to her flagship graduate-level course because of the hype surrounding smart grids; she needs to set the record straight as to what the term means. Smart grid is not a complete replacement for the electric grid according to her. It can best be described as an agenda of improvements—an agenda to upgrade the electric grid with digital communication technologies, selectively and judiciously, across both the transmission and the distribution levels of the grid. The improvements involve anything from smart transmission lines that can reroute electricity in the event of bottlenecks to networked consumer devices like dishwashers and air conditioners that coordinate consumption within and across consumers' homes. Indeed, the point of the agenda, as smart-grid engineers see it, is precisely not to differentiate between different parts of the grid as the current structure does—not to differentiate between wholesale exchanges at ISOs' markets and retail consumption at home. For that reason, smart-grid engineers' research often also extends to the psychology of electricity consumption—the consumer's mind appearing as yet another determinant of grid operations to be understood and modeled into optimizing algorithms.

The optimizers strive to create the formalisms and algorithms for a smart grid set to function like a pervasive, everyday market, constantly calculating electricity prices based on consumers' real-time use and the changing cost of electricity production. In that endeavor aided by digital communication technologies, they observe no distinction between the grid's different voltage levels. The smart grid is set to be a market humming in the background of our lives and we, everyday consumers, are to be conscripted to it simply by virtue of using electricity.

Ilić's team picks up where her one-time collaborator Fred Schweppe's team had left off—laying down the mathematical terms for an electric grid that weaves consumers, producers, and machines alike in a web of constant communication. Like Schweppe's team, Ilić and her lab members have roots in systems sciences— a field that ponders the complex dynamics of multicomponent assemblages like the electric grid, which is also home to several brands of optimization. Due to historically intersecting intellectual lineages between their field and certain neoliberal thought traditions, there are, sometimes, family resemblances in thinking and articulation between the optimizers and neoliberal economists. An explicit concern with factoring time's work into calculations and engineering just-in-time solutions is an example of these intersections. But upon a closer look, they diverge on several fronts as well—for instance, on the role of competition. While competition is key to unlock information and a good in itself according to many neoliberal thought traditions, it is one route among others to refine the balance of supply and demand according to the optimizers. Indeed, Ilić is dissatisfied with contemporary markets, first envisaged by what Richard Schmalensee had called the "wide-eyed" neoliberal ideologues, precisely because she thinks that competition for competition's sake can produce suboptimal results.

Ilić and her students, then, conceive of this everyday market in contrast with ISOs' existing markets—let's call those "actually existing markets," the likes of which we saw being assembled in chapter 1 and operating routinely in chapter 2, since those are already in operation, while the smart grid remains an orientation for the future, being implemented gradually. Much of solar and wind power, the smart-grid engineers point out, currently cannot be harvested due to sensing imperfections and suboptimal calculations abundant across the ISOs and the electric grid. Imagine an "intermittent" resource, like the sun or the wind, becoming available for half an hour today, without having been predicted by traders in yesterday's day-ahead timeline. The sun may stop shining or the wind may die down before the relevant power plants ramp up and the real-time market recalculates. Suboptimality abounds on the consumption side as well, the optimizing engineers tell us. We, everyday electricity consumers, tend to use electricity all at the same time, overloading the grid in the evenings (and typically, ISOs schedule the dirtiest resources for this time to meet the peak in demand) and leaving it underused past midnight. But what if, optimizing grid engineers ask, our dishwashers could sense resources lying around and come online at times of underuse, even if it was three in the morning? As a response, they strive to turn the fabric of everyday life, featuring such near-subconscious acts as turning the lights on at one's home, into a form of market itself—one I call an "everyday optimizing market."

This chapter builds on the argument of this book by continuing to depict the current economy as a field of techno-economics where original economic reasonings come to being in the thick of science and engineering endeavors. Ilić and her group are experts who have no claim to economic expertise or are not primarily guided by an interest in contributing to economic theory yet create the economic forms of life with which we live. As we will see, they at times conceive of their expertise in contrast with that of economists. The choice to envision the electric grid in the image of a pervasive market is surely technical and po-litical at the same time. But it is not political in the sense of overt association with a belief system concerning how society should be governed. In the many months I spent working alongside them, some members of the lab showed no interest in such conversations; others expressed left-leaning views commonly associated with hesitation toward markets. Instead, it was optimization that was overtly articulated—that appeared as a common language and a mutually agreed-upon necessity for the betterment of social organization. It animated a culture naturalizing the balance of supply and demand as the main way to secure social welfare—a culture allowing one to be a market builder who does not necessarily articulate a belief in markets as solutions to social ills.

Scholars have explored what it means to make political choices through technical work—a field of activities that has been called "techno-politics" (Mitchell 2002). They have investigated how governments introduce technolo-gies to institute forms of citizenship on the ground, be it by meters that regulate access to household water (von Schnitzler 2008) or media forms like radio and cinema that are supposed to create modern political subjectivities (Larkin 2008). Langdon Winner's classic piece on how artifacts can acquire their politics points at two specific ways this can occur (1980). Either, Winner finds, there is an intentionality built into the artifact in question, like a bridge that is too low for public transport buses (and their low-income users) to go under, or the artifact's continued maintenance is most compatible with a certain political arrangement, like a nuclear power plant whose safe operation demands a hierarchically and often undemocratically organized human force (Winner 1980). Here I follow the second route identified by Winner and start my inquiry from within an electrical engineering lab to tease out its economic vision. However, I do so not to find out what set of political beliefs matches this lab's activities best but to capture the nuances of original economic and political reasonings that emerge in this setting, which does not lend itself to easy categorization or complete overlap with given ideological agendas. In his discussion of techno-politics, Brian Larkin highlights the field of possibility that specific technologies and infrastructures open up, unintended by the political forces that put them in place (2008). There is a similar field of possibility instantiated in the work culture of optimization—visions for the present and the future of the electric grid that come to being during sessions of brainstorming for new optimizing algorithms. These visions constitute the third building block in the making of the current economy that this book explores.

Exploring the work culture of optimization can help usher in a new critique of contemporary political economy. All around us a new economic form of life, like the smart grid, has been proliferating. It is a form that concerns matching; matching supply to demand, just-in-time, just-in-place, in the background of everyday life. It is, for instance, in the digital ride-sharing apps that match people who need a ride with people who are willing to give a ride, exactly when and where the ride is needed.

This new form can be detected by its three attributes. It is decentralized; it does not go through a central authority for approval or calculation. It is modular; the parties to the transaction are free from long-term commitment, as in the contractor style of work. Finally, it is ordinary; it targets ordinary people in the thick of their everyday lives—while they are commuting to work, socializing with family, or using electricity. This is as opposed to organized exchanges where buyers and sellers are preregistered, intentional economic actors. To target ordinary people, this form of economic life leverages their connectivity to what has been called "ubiquitous computing" (Weiser 1993) or the "Internet of Things." Economists sometimes call this form "matching markets" (cf. Roth 1986), and other social scientists, "Überization" (cf. Fleming 2017) or the "sharing economy," which also concerns the marketization of the ordinary aspects of life predicated on networked communication technologies. I call it everyday optimizing markets. These markets are created in laboratories such as Ilić's, and we need to enter those laboratories to make sense of why and how market-like forms of social life have been proliferating around us.

Moving forward, an economic anthropology focusing on optimization needs to develop two things. First, an "otherwise," a counterfactual. Aren't we all optimizing, the reader may ask; isn't optimization all there is in one form or another? The answer is no. Optimization is only one logic of economic organization among others—has been so in the electricity industry where industrialists historically raked in large profits by, for instance, leveraging economies of scale, which is a logic focused on expanding the supply side, not matching supply to demand in ever-finer scales. The other thing we need to develop is a critique. Can there be any issues with efficiency, the reader may ask; aren't matching resources to needs and avoiding waste always good things? True; matching is no social ill, neither is efficiency. That is why, when we explore the larger terrain of optimization, we must look at the particulars—at how the exact variables to optimize are selected in each case and whose continued interests that selective optimization serves. A ride-sharing app might expertly match people who need a ride with people who are willing to give a ride—a perfect balance of supply and demand between those handpicked variables might be within reach. In the meantime, the app's management might be actively preventing workers from being matched to stable employment. Indeed, modular operations accompanying the optimization agenda has ushered in an environment of rampant unstable contract work in several industries (Appel 2012; Hall and Krueger 2018). However, similarities notwithstanding, the social goods or ills that may accompany optimization are not identical across domains; neither should its critique be. In the case of the electric grid, experts' leveraging of the optimization agenda to offer solutions for climate change mitigation should be welcome, while their exclusive commitment to a market form, which may sidestep issues of equal access or fair pricing, can give us a reason for pause.

In what follows, I first specify the analytical intervention of focusing on optimization to investigate everyday optimizing markets; to do so, I attempt a modern-day kinship chart of expertise that involves both the optimizers and neoliberal thinkers. Next, I move on to how the optimization agenda allows smart-grid engineers to conceptualize the grid as a market. Then, I dwell on the new role assigned to humans in the technologically saturated economies of optimization and the new meanings of the social. I conclude with reflections on what a fine-grained critique might look like for optimization's proliferation in daily life.

## Of Electric Optimization

Optimization is about finding the best outcome in a window of feasible outcomes. I would like to run one mile as fast as possible, subject to the constraint of my energy level. I would like to run as many errands as possible, subject to the constraint of my budget for transportation. The reader might notice that these questions are concerned with some form of resource management; I would like to conserve my money, my energy, or my well-being, to the extent possible while still achieving a satisfying outcome. Indeed, research in mathematical optimization historically peaked during times of concerted effort around resource management. While its theoretical roots can be traced back to modern mathematicians like Fermat or Lagrange, optimization received a definitive boost during the two world wars, when governments funded logistics efforts to plan for a steady supply of fuel for their troops (Cowen 2014, 25–30).

World War II coupled the concern for logistics with an obsession with improved ballistics. The US government recruited civil scientists and engineers in droves to improve the accuracy of military pursuits, like predictions of enemy aircraft location (Galison 1994). What flourished was an agenda of matching under uncertain circumstances—from matching fired ammunition with moving targets to matching raw materials with production goals—in the meantime spooling out the institutions and disciplines in which optimization was to live and prosper, like the RAND Corporation or the discipline of operations research. A mainstay of this time, the RAND Corporation, was particularly instrumental in spinning wartime systems thinking into managerial techniques for organizations and businesses (Knafo et al. 2019). Optimization thus had a solid foray into problems that can be easily recognized as economic, like optimal budgeting across the divisions of a firm.

These military roots are well documented by historians of science (Bowker 1993; Galison 1994), but optimization also has a less often-told electric history that illuminates its forays into the everyday, outside of government purview. Some of the famed polymaths who would later pioneer cybernetics and operations research started out as electrical engineers in the early twentieth century, working on the practical problems of an increasingly interconnected North American electric grid. They were commissioned projects by industrialists, like General Electric, which wanted them to assess the feasibility of their long-distance high-voltage transmission line projects—whether a particular new line would end up destabilizing the entire system (Mindell 2004). The practical question facing these industrialists and their academic engineer allies was how to keep a growing system stable and functional as they experimented with adding and subtracting parts (Mindell 2004).

This question had become pressing in the early twentieth century—after the end of the "Battle of Currents" between Thomas Edison's direct current (DC) and George Westinghouse's alternating current (AC), when AC emerged victorious and gradually completely replaced DC (T. Hughes 1993). AC was replete with transient phenomena—short-lived changes in a circuit, like bursts or withdrawals of electricity—that demanded treatment by differential equations, which was "a bewildering topic" (Puchta 1996, 50) to an earlier generation of electrical engineers who knew only simple algebra (McMahon 1984). For a while, stopgap measures were invented, like the Steinmetz method, which generated steady-state versions of transient phenomena, rendering the complexity of AC grids imperfectly solvable with the tools of algebra. But long-distance, high-voltage AC systems were outrunning their makers' abilities. Unprecedented amounts of current and levels of voltage could cause damage to manufacturers' expensive equipment if not coordinated well across large distances. In the first half of the twentieth century, then, manufacturers sought a different, higher level of mathematical sophistication. By the same coin, well-educated mathematicians were now attracted to the problems posed by grid physics.

The emergent mutual attraction between mathematicians and engineers found itself a fertile breeding ground at the Massachusetts Institute of Technology (MIT) during the interwar period. Critical to its growth was Vannevar Bush, now widely known for brokering a groundbreaking relationship of scientific collaboration between the US military and universities (Shurkin 1996, 101). Bush was originally an electrical engineer; having written a doctoral dissertation at MIT on the behavior of electrical circuits, he returned to MIT in 1919 as a professor of electricity transmission after stints in academia and the electricity industry. Bush's laboratory received generous funds from the industry, including his former employer General Electric, to estimate the feasibility of long-distance transmission construction projects to prevent the construction of costly but ultimately unfeasible transmission lines (Mindell 2004). In 1925, he supervised a graduate student's work on a machine to mechanically solve

Carson's equations, a theory of conductors used to calculate transmission line impedance. The result was the product intergraph; a contraption of integrators made of wheels and discs—the first analog computer that came out of Bush's laboratory. By 1928, Bush had acquired access to MIT funds to build a larger model to solve differential equations of a higher order (Barnet 2013, 14–15). The differential analyzer, the pioneering general-purpose computer, was born in this environment.

A very specific engineering concern—how to continue to build electric grids while keeping them stable and reliable—was, then, at the heart of the twin growth of computing and optimization. Optimization's early pioneers learned from their experience with the electric grid when they developed the *nonlinear* and *dynamic* versions of its *linear* variants to make room for random, previously unknown situations, like unforeseen additions to and subtractions from electric flows. As a new generation of mathematically sophisticated electrical engineers tinkered with analog grid models in their laboratories, they questioned how complexity and uncertainty in a growing system could be addressed with the least cost to the system's manufacturers. Their concerns were economic in a commonsensical way; their clients wanted to maintain their costly infrastructure and make sure to profit. But their concerns were also economic in a specific way—economic as in having achieved a good match between the input and output flowing through an uncertain system. Not so coincidentally, Bush theorized that the computer helped the grid engineer do his work "economically" and referred to the mental load of calculation without a computer as an "economic waste" (quoted in Puchta 1996, 57).

Ilić and her students descend from that line of polymaths, like control theory expert Schweppe, not because of shared roots in electric grid studies but because they inherited variants of their tools. The cyborgs, those human-nonhuman processors of information, were born in electrical engineering departments, but they soon left to congregate in the newly formed discipline of computer science (Ceruzzi 1996).[1] In the postwar period, the study of electric grids themselves fell out of fashion in academic electrical engineering, and grid optimization practice moved to the industry. It would take other theoretically interesting problems for mathematically sophisticated engineers, like Ilić, to become interested in grids again. In the late 1970s when Ilić entered the field, the problem consisted of the recent US blackouts of 1965 and 1977 that had encouraged systems thinkers to pour over grids again. The smart-grid agenda is the result of the latest, twenty-first century interest in applying improved optimization to electric grids—this time as a response to the northeastern US blackout of 2001 and climate change concerns around resource management. Ilić's internationally diverse researchers came to grid optimization not necessarily via their interests in electricity, then, but via their training in applied mathematics and systems engineering. Many readily admitted to not having visited a power plant before, neither did they necessarily have a relationship with the grid unmediated by optimization software. First and foremost, they identified with their toolkit—optimization; to what the toolkit was "applied" came after, just like data workers at EnTech who found in electricity yet another object in the world to transform into spreadsheet-friendly bits.

Today, experts in a dizzying array of fields choose to nestle optimization tools in ubiquitous computing devices to create transactional spaces in everyday life. It may be hard to trace this moment back to a singular influence because optimization tools are so widely traveled. This is the same kind of difficulty anthropologists have experienced in tracing the trajectories of neoliberalism. For anthropologists, our close involvement with the "social lives and concerns of [our] interlocutors," which is surely an ethnographic asset, is also a reason why our "scal[ing] up from the particular to the general" may result in the overuse of broad explanations, like neoliberalism referred to as an all-encompassing context (Ganti 2014, 93). As anthropologists themselves bemoaned, the overuse of the term has, by now, diminished the concept's analytical value to near-nonexistent (Eriksen et al. 2015). What I suggest is not to dismiss neoliberalism as an explanatory term categorically; I suggest that its history should be told as one of a "thought collective," like the historically specific assembling of neoliberal thought collectives to respond to issues like the postwar rise of the social state (Plehwe 2009)—in other words, a phenomenon instead of a context. We can analyze its family resemblances with the optimizers to explain their mutual techniques and beliefs; we can acknowledge the overlaps between the two phenomena while making sure that we do not see "neoliberalism" everywhere there is "optimization."

Let me clarify what I take neoliberalism to be and how I view its relationship to optimizers past and present. In his study of post-Soviet neoliberal reformers, Stephen Collier takes neoliberalism not as a hegemony or ideology but a Foucauldian, biopolitical project—a form of "critical reflection on governmental practice" (quoted in Collier 2011, 18), concerned with giving new life to the principles of classical liberalism, like individual freedom, in the context of the rise of the social state. Collier traces a tradition within neoliberal thought focused on infrastructures and their regulation, especially George Stigler's meditations on the regulation of the electricity industry—on whether existing regulations had kept costs for producers and prices down for consumers (Stigler and Friedland 1962). Assuming that any economic domain can be analyzed as consisting of individual calculative agents, thinkers associated with Stigler's line of thought (and, through complex genealogical links, their post-Soviet intellectual kin) aim to recode domains of economic life to resemble markets, even in "areas where competitive markets could not function" (Collier 2011, 224). Their policymaking counterparts develop "microeconomic devices" facilitating "calculative choice, competition, and price based on supply and demand"—things as simple as electricity meters and thermostats (Collier 2011, 227).

With their penchant for decentralization, ubiquitous calculation, and competition in public life, Collier's neoliberal reformers clearly show family resemblances with the experts I follow—the thinkers and tinkerers of electricity meters. These family resemblances are best explained, once again, with the overlap of the tools that they wield. Collier, for instance, asserts that post-Soviet neoliberal reformers were supported in their reform endeavor by a "toolkit of techniques and mechanisms of programming that have been assembled over many decades" (2011, 216), but does not elaborate on the toolkit or identify the brand of its mathematics. A comprehensive account of optimization's uses by neoliberal founders is not within the scope of this book, but, to bring the argument full circle, I will look for clues in historian Philip Mirowski's work on the mid-twentieth-century transformations of the discipline of economics, which features foundational neoliberal thinkers (2002).

The answers might be in the toolkits that the cyborgization of economics gifted to the discipline. As Mirowski explored (1989), modern economics emerged in the late nineteenth century as the science we know, in its contemporary mathematical form. It is called *neoclassical economics* to differentiate it from the classical political economy of the likes of Adam Smith and David Ricardo. Founded on the image of individual actors maximizing their utility, this tradition still constitutes the mainstream in economics. But that mainstream was challenged in many sciences, from biology to chemistry, in the middle of the twentieth century. Like other historians who have studied "cyborg sciences"—twentieth-century disciplines that recast themselves as sciences of information processing (Pickering 1995)—Mirowski traces the origins of the cyborg offshoot of economics to the military uses of science and technology in World War II in the US, especially wartime mathematics that undergirded the concurrent development of the computer and the field of operations research.

Polymaths who deployed the same mathematical techniques across disciplines, like John von Neumann, introduced cyborg theory to different groups of economists, although to variable extents, in the form of the "novel mathematical techniques of optimization with inequality constraints, measure-theoretic approaches to probability, fixed-point theorems, and limit sets" (Mirowski 2002, 282). Cyborg economists, some of whom are neoliberal founders like Friedrich Hayek, put a premium on information processing under uncertainty, regardless of whether the processing was done by humans, nonhumans, or a little bit of both. They were dissatisfied with neoclassical rationality, the rationality of the integral human agent with defined preferences. While certain techniques of optimization "such as linear programming or maximum likelihood algorithms" (Mirowski 2002, 285) were used by economists of both neoclassical and cyborg lineage, others, like dynamic programming, came to signify the groups that open-heartedly embraced cyborgs and their obsession with uncertainty (Mirowski 2002, 260).

What makes my interlocutors have overlaps with neoliberal articulations at times is that they, too, wield these exact techniques of programming; they, too, come from a cyborg science lineage. Their reach is not coterminous with that of neoliberals—it is sometimes longer, sometimes shorter than them, depending on the reach of the infrastructures with which they tinker. As Ilić and her students engineer the electric grid as a decentralized, modular, everyday market, they also engineer it to bring more aspects of social life—and more people overall—into the fold of market relationships. The optimizers have their own agenda, complete with a toolkit, to recode public infrastructures in a way that decentralizes decision making and relegates it onto human and nonhuman assemblages, now augmented with continuous calculative capacities. Think of electric grids where your refrigerator constantly trades electricity with your neighbor's electric car. To continue, like Collier, within the Foucauldian biopolitical paradigm, we could say that optimization-minded experts have shifted the locus of governance away from the well-being of human populations and toward cyborgs—those continuously optimizing human-nonhuman machines.

To be sure, looking to mathematical methods (e.g., optimization) instead of ideologies (e.g., neoliberalism) to understand economic approaches to social life would be a futile exercise if the method and the ideology were necessarily coterminous (i.e., if using optimization necessarily landed a practitioner in neoliberalism). That would amount, in effect, to reaffirming a story of widespread neoliberalization, only in a roundabout way. In fact, optimization experts, even the wielders of optimization variants most favored by neoliberal thinkers, can arrive at economic approaches expressly denounced by those neoliberal thinkers—like those lacking competition among different entities. A case in point is given by Eden Medina's analysis of socialist cybernetics in Chile—specifically, Project *Cybersyn*, an industrial production model commissioned by Salvador Allende and developed by cyberneticist Stafford Beer (Medina 2011). Encapsulating the Allende regime's interest in decentralized governance and worker participation in management, Cybersyn modeled the Chilean industry as autonomous components, which only alerted higher management if production problems could not be solved within each component's feedback loop within a given time period.

We need not go far from the US electric grid to find non-neoliberal, noncompetitive uses of optimization. Up until the mid-1990s, the US electric grid was home to natural monopolies functioning without competition in their demarcated territories. The electric history of optimization I have sketched above took place in an environment dominated by private initiative, which was, still, uncompetitive. Optimization became a common managerial practice (Knafo et al. 2019) after that initial moment of discovery, at which point electricity monopolists, just like other industries, used optimization tools to optimize their operations—to make decisions about what power plant in their fleet was more economical to run at what time to meet the demand in their territory. (Optimization, here, was not as pervasive as imagined by Ilić's team for the grid's futures, but it was optimization nonetheless.) The introduction of competition into the operations of the US electric grid was undertaken by ideologues who can be classified as neoliberals, as their reasoning primarily revolved around the replication of successful deregulation stories. But as we will see, Ilić considers the initial introduction of competition into electricity as ineffective and suboptimal—she is an optimizer whose work rebuts or pays no heed to the work of electricity's neoliberal ideologues from the 1990s.

More generally, these examples go to show that "neoliberalism" or "socialism" as analytical categories cannot rise to the explanatory tasks that we expect from them. They do not alone account for the differences between Chilean socialism and Soviet socialism (Medina 2011), the similarities between the economics of US neoclassical economists and Yugoslav democratic socialists (Bockman 2011) or, for my purposes, why smart-grid engineers are compelled to conceive of our electric grid in the image of a market. The task is to trace everyday optimizing markets back to histories of science and engineering and to their origins in laboratory spaces.

## Enter the Lab: A Market-Like Grid

Like the laboratory where the group was based, the classroom where Ilić taught her graduate seminar was spartan, equipped with not much except chairs, a blackboard, a projector, and a screen. There were upwards of ten graduate students in the seminar, coming from engineering departments, computer science, mathematics, and elsewhere. They were vaguely interested in energy—they had heard of smart grids, they liked mathematics—so here they were, hoping to see it for themselves. The seminar, "Smart Grids and Future Electric Energy Systems," encompassed all that Ilić's smart-grid vision had to offer. It was where new members were recruited, recent ones were trained if recruited elsewhere, and senior members served as teaching assistants. In the first few weeks, Ilić needed to win over students on the fence about staying in the class before they were lost to either the complexity of the mathematics or the vision that the course advanced. On the first point, Ilić could compromise and even plead. If they suffered the first few manual examples, she reassured the students, a lot of their mathematical work later would simply consist of learning which buttons to press on MATLAB's interface. Tony,[2] the teaching assistant, could teach them that in recitation sessions. She wondered aloud to herself how they used to do calculations by hand before MATLAB's rise in the 2000s—she strained to remember; were they modeling unrealistically simple systems with just two substations?

On the second point, the vision of the seminar, Ilić was unbending. The grid was not a collection of technologies—it was not this substation, that inverter, or this transformer. It was the totality of the relationships between them—it was a system. And despite what novice students surrounded by Pittsburgh's startup culture might believe, it could not be fixed with the insertion of a magical new technology—like superior "facts" (flexible AC transmission systems) or even a mighty powerful battery that would go on to solve the storage problem inherent in electric grids. Ilić's teaching environment did not have analog models of the grid, like the one in Vannevar Bush's laboratory; the digital computing software, MATLAB, was usually worked on by one person at a time. So, she used her body language to model to her students a way to think about the grid.

When a novice student started singing the praises of a great new inverter or a game-changer technology of storage, Ilić would reflexively put her hands out as if she was holding a basketball and enunciate every syllable: "The system, tell me how it affects the system."

The system, it turns out, was economic, but in an inherent way, not because humans had decided it should be so. When asked about the desirability of this or that technology, Ilić often merely uttered one word and smiled, "Cost." Cost here was a near-natural process. Systems simply incurred costs as they functioned, sometimes in the form of wear and tear, sometimes in the form of resources wasted, like the unharvested wind and sun. Electric systems incurred even more costs than most systems because of the absence of grid-level storage; what was not used was simply wasted, if it did not destabilize the system. Ilić often grounded her explanations in realism rooted in her experience with the industry; she depicted an imaginary version of herself talking to ISOs, utilities, and transmission owners, telling them in vain they should undertake costly infrastructure investment when the efficiency (read: cost-cutting) benefits were not sufficiently clear. I often thought she channeled Vannevar Bush, who wanted to please General Electric both by keeping the lights on and saving the company money, when she would say, "Cost. You need to justify what you're putting in the grid before you put it in!"

It was a long time before Ilić mentioned anything to me about her life story, but snippets started coming up eventually. She was born in socialist Yugoslavia in 1951. Influenced by her mother, her first role model who taught her the value of hard work, she was a motivated student, with an early love for books and science classes. Playing competitive basketball was her first love; that is, by her own account, how she learned teamwork. Good students were encouraged to study engineering in college at the time in Yugoslavia; she enrolled in electrical engineering at the University of Belgrade in 1969. From the 300 entering students, only ten were women, and only five of them would go on to graduate in an environment not so friendly to women students. She found inspiration in one of her female recitation leaders and soldiered on—a foretelling moment for her career as a woman in a field dominated by men. She got through all the essentials of electrical engineering with flying colors in the four years of her five-year program: electronics, automation, control.

Then in the fifth year, she got interested in "systems thinking" and "optimization"; she told me, "That's when they sent me to America." The early 1970s was a time of turmoil in Yugoslavia—where the country's brand of socialism stood relative to Soviet socialism and US capitalism was questioned by activists, but Ilić was steeped in her craft. She arrived in a "Systems Science and Mathematics" department in the US for graduate work right after the 1977 New York City blackout. Her advisor thought this was a good time to study electric systems as a systems scientist; the US electric grid had failed yet again after the last large blackout in 1965. Her professors assumed she would have to take a year to come up to speed in this specific field, but Ilić dove into electric systems, fell in love with them, excelled. After becoming an illustrious electric grid researcher herself, she would remember the statue of Nikola Tesla, the Serbian developer of AC electric grids, outside her alma mater in Belgrade—a statue to which she had not paid attention during her time there. She eventually got in the habit of getting her picture taken with it on visits back.

Ilić thought of her research circle the way she thought of the electric grid; her collaborators, students, and I were the sum of our relationships and her job, that of a facilitator, managing relationships as she went. Tony would tell me repeatedly what I already knew: "She is interested in the scope." Each member of the group worked on a different problem of control and dynamics—Tony on controllers, one graduate student on electric vehicles, another one on flexible transmission, another one on demand management—but Ilić constantly reminded them to think together just like the parts of the electric grid they were studying.

Tony, who had loved mathematics for as long as he could remember, had chanced upon grid studies while in college in his native Greece. After having taken several applied math and electric grid courses in Greece and the US, he had stumbled on Ilić's work and realized, by his own account, how cutting-edge it was. Just like the engineers of the early twentieth century, who became attracted to the grid's physics as the grid became more complicated, Tony thought grid dynamics were now more complicated and exciting than ever for applied mathematicians like himself. The 2003 North American blackout had made it apparent that the electric grid had grown complicated while academia overlooked it. Then, of course, there was the continuing challenge of intermittent resources that left us bewildered. Tony told me that we still had limited knowledge about how the grid's stability would be affected if the contribution of solar and wind power rose dramatically—what kind of faster controllers we would have to place, how resources like wind could be kept from being wasted (or "spilled" as they say in the field). Just like Ilić, Tony thought he had come to grid optimization when he did because his skills applied to electric systems—and it was urgent at this particular time to apply them.

Ilić, Tony, and others in the lab thought of the electric grid as an inherently economic entity. But was the grid also a market? It was, at best, a mismanaged market—one that Ilić intended to turn into what I call an everyday optimizing market. In the 1990s, Ilić had been engaged in the activity of "gluing economics and engineering" that helped bring electricity markets as we know them alive. She contributed to the theorization of markets by, just like Schweppe and others, assessing how ISOs could put a price tag on usage, transmission loss, and voltage constraints, among other electric grid phenomena (Ilić et al. 1993). But over time, as her smart-grid work took off, she also came to disagree with certain aspects of ISOs' existing markets on mathematical terms and, by extension, those markets' neoclassical brand of economics.

At the root of that disagreement was, then, a mathematical conviction. The actually existing markets used a static version of optimization, solving the optimization problem only once for a future time. Buyers and sellers did their best today to predict what their needs and capabilities would be tomorrow—but what if those changed between today and tomorrow? What if the weather forecast was wrong and everyone cranked up their air conditioners unexpectedly? Those in the trading world might dream of the perfect database that reflected all the information out there—a receding horizon they nevertheless strove to attain every day. To Ilić and her group, that effort was a mere band-aid for the simple reality that the electric grid's parts—things and humans alike—changed constantly. "You are assuming perfect information," Ilić acted out speaking with her economist friends and the original designers of actually existing markets. "Perfect information," the original sin of neoclassical economics, was "where economics ends," she often said.

For the same reason, the arrival of restructuring in the 1990s and the subsequent arrival of markets did not constitute a true milestone to Ilić. In her class, she once put up a formula of "optimal power flow" on the screen—the static optimization formula that monopolistic utilities used to use to make decisions about their own operations. She circled with her finger the letter C standing for cost. Then, she said, when markets began, the bid makers at utilities replaced this C with a B, standing for bids. "We used to say 'cost and benefit,' now we say 'bids and offers.' That's all that changed when restructuring began," she said throwing her hands in the air. Her indictment offered a striking dismissal of markets as we know them. The arrival of markets consisted of a mere change of words, she implied—a competitive appearance, a rhetorical change brought about by the wide-eyed ideologues and the free market apologists of the 1990s.

The declaration of markets by law meant nothing if the underlying mathematics was not changed to improve the balance of supply and demand. The question was whether we could match *today's* demand to *today's* supply as *today* took its course—as every actor's needs and capabilities changed, unforeseen and unbeknownst to a central authority. Ilić and her team used *dynamic optimization* to write algorithmic rules for our fridges, electric cars, and the utilities that sell us electricity to interact near constantly. That was the decentralized, modular, ordinary market—the everyday optimizing market Ilić thought the grid would eventually become, if only optimizing engineers attended to its inherent complexity.

When she talked about the grid, Ilić put her hands out as if she was holding a basketball. When she talked about actually existing markets, her hand went up an inch, as if she was talking about something superimposed, arbitrary. If only we could attend to "this"—the basketball, the grid—in all its inherent economic ontology, then there would not be any need for arbitrary markets or its attending science, economics (or neoclassical economics). The grid itself would be a well-managed market. When Ilić and her students used these hand gestures, I was often reminded of the way orthodox Marxists might speak of a base and a superstructure in any mode of production. For Ilić, the grid was the base—it was where economic relations happened and what was to be revolutionized, so to speak—into a new mode of everyday life where the given supply and demand of anything automatically balanced each other. Acknowledging and addressing the uncertainty inherent to the grid was an economic act per se that negated the need for neoclassical economics and its arbitrary assumptions about information.

She found inspiration in thinkers of other systems. Once we attended an evening chat with the women's electrical engineering club on campus where she presented on her career. There, she bemoaned how she did not have a role model for years as a woman in the field, until she came across only a few years back Elinor Ostrom, the 2009 Nobel laureate for her work in the management of the "commons." Anything from fisheries to forests, according to Ostrom, could be theorized as "social-ecological systems" consisting of endless subsystems. In the span of a few pages that Ilić shared with me later, Ostrom proposed a new science to unite all sciences underneath, from political science to biology (2009, 419). (Around the same time as that evening chat, the word "ecosystem" started popping up more and more in Ilić's lectures.) I couldn't help but think of Ostrom and Ilić in the same breath. Ostrom received her Nobel Prize in economic sciences, which confused and surprised many economists; she was virtually unknown in the field in which she was awarded her prize (Rampell 2012). It was reported that many economists had to look her up after receiving the news (Rampell 2012). Like Ilić, Ostrom had focused her attention on systems and managing them more efficiently; if her work was recognizable as economic to some, it was not so to most economists.

I suggest here that Ilić's intended grid is market-like—although a market not in the neoclassical sense instantiated in the actually existing electricity markets but in the "cyborg" sense where the discovery of information is actively enabled through novel communication channels. Let me be clear that Ilić and her lab members did not necessarily phrase where they stood in relation to market building in those terms. They were not interested in theorizing what a market must mean or using the concept in semantically precise ways. I myself was often confused before I could tell the difference between what I have come to term actually existing markets and the everyday optimizing markets. When I first arrived in the lab, for instance, I was still unclear on the premise of the group's recent book—on how the Azores' monopolistic, publicly owned grid with no competition could serve as a model to extrapolate conclusions for deregulated industries like those in the US.

When I sat down with two graduate students, they did not seem to pick up on any contradiction; once again, whether the market was declared by legal authorities or not was a moot point. In their calculations for the book, they had used the "cost" signal instead of the "bid" signal—the signals that Ilić had said were mathematically the same. They had shown, via simulations, that the Azorean system would have balanced itself better while utilizing the islands' ample green resources if only they used the algorithms that the group had developed, regardless of whether there was a market in the Azores in the style of ISOs. One of them struggled for a minute to put this even more simply. "I guess in some sense it [the system] can still act as a *market* even though there is no actual *market*," he said. By "a market," as a manner in which a system could act, he referred to something more abstract than actually existing markets—an image that systems could be fashioned after. It was an everyday optimizing market.

I suggest here that Ilić's intended grid is market-like—but let us get back to the question of whether it is a neoliberal market. To be sure, phrasings uncannily close to those of cyborg economists and foundational neoliberal thinkers were ample in the lab. Once during her seminar, Ilić paused to sigh after an hourlong mathematical lecture on grid control and automation, tapped the blackboard full of her scribblings from earlier in the hour, and, without breaking eye contact with students, said: "There's no human who has all this information. It's all happening very fast." It was impossible not be reminded of one of the twentieth century's most-cited economics articles, Friedrich Hayek's "The Use of Knowledge in Society" (1945), which discusses how no central authority can process all "circumstances of time and place"—that planning is best decentralized and left to the "man on the spot." Again echoing Hayek's writings, Ilić's graduate student Jhi-Young Joo noted in an elaboration of her home optimization systems (more on these systems in the next section) that it would require "the least amount of information from the local entities" (2013, 45). Like cyborg economists, Ilić and Joo conceptualized information's travels as ideally decentralized, to be managed by decentralized, modular methods in the everyday instead of centralized markets.

There are further overlaps, but also very significant differences between Ilić and Hayek's visions—this time concerning competition. Just like Ilić, who is skeptical of neoclassical economists' idea of competition, Hayek disparages the "conception of competition currently employed by economists" (1948, 360), which assumes that the "data for the different individuals are fully adjusted to each other" (1948, 362). Competition, in this view, begins after participants have already acquired information about each other, just like in existing electricity markets. In other words, a firm like EnTech exists because, in the current state of affairs, it is accepted that an individual buyer and seller must rely on accumulated information about the entire system to form individual bids and offers competitively. But to Hayek (1948), competition is the very process of information discovery—it is how participants discover facts about each other, as well as facts about how to make their own operations smoother.

Ilić also often said, "There is a huge cost to information discovery [in centralized markets]." Just think of firms like EnTech—the resources devoted to knowing the electric grid in its entirety. But to her, competition between individual private entities was not necessarily the key to information discovery—optimization through communication was. If her distributed system actualized—if the individual participants were empowered to optimize—EnTech's ability to collect information and the need for EnTech's services would both diminish dramatically. Hayek could not conceptualize information discovery under the monopolistic, publicly owned grid of the Azores the way Ilić could.

During my fieldwork, I usually wrestled alone with the questions of where my interlocutors found a place for themselves in the history of economic ideas. A true exception to this routine came during my conversations with one member of Ilić's group named Lin. She had some formal background in the discipline of economics (i.e., she had been a double major as an undergraduate in economics and engineering at a US liberal arts college), and unlike other group members, she enjoyed musing over the economic theory work in the lab. Economics, she said, "is basically optimization. Firms want to maximize profit; customers want to maximize utility. That's basically what the supply and demand curve is." Unlike Ilić, she did name the foil to her agenda specifically as "neoclassical" economics and its specific "limitations," like the assumption of perfect information. Her project was born precisely out of her desire to address those limitations with the tools of dynamic optimization—the opportunity accorded by these tools to create markets where there might not have been any. It was the creation of a market in electricity's transmission; what if buyers and sellers also competed for bandwidth space in the wires of the electric grid, just like they compete to buy or sell their electricity?

Here is why Lin's vision was provocative. Even the seasoned advocates of competition in wholesale and retail electricity regard competition in transmission as a theoretical impossibility. In the electricity regulation classes I attended and the market training I received by ISO-NE, I had been drilled that it was impossible to track how much each participant was *actually* using the grid. In other words, while they had gone after the natural monopoly assumption in wholesale and retail electricity, those advocates had reaffirmed transmission as the *true* natural monopoly because we did not have the technology to apportion or accurately track transmission; once electricity was injected into the grid, it was a drop in the ocean, impossible to differentiate from the next drop. Lin maintained, on the other hand, that those economists and engineers' despair was mathematical, more so than technological—the relevant sensing technologies already exist, she would say, but the fact that they could not see the possibility of market where it could have been was a function of the mathematical tools they wielded. She said as much: "[Only] those who look *solely* from the [neoclassical] economist's perspective and think of the system in static equilibrium in deterministic terms think it's a natural monopoly."

A market in transmission had to take place in the thick of the grid—within the automatic optimization conversations between users of the grids (buyers and sellers of electricity) and transmission owners, as they submitted endless bids and offers to each other, and the grid automatically made way for the winning bidders. "In the static sense, [neoclassical economics] *is* true. How you extend it to a dynamic realm, *that's* the issue and I think we can do this mathematically," Lin said. Competitive prices would help put in place a better match between supply and demand—this time the supply and demand of transmission use. Individual users' wishes would be honored; if a hospital valued booking transmission bandwidth for reliability purposes, it would be allowed to do so.

Economic sociologists Wendy Espeland and Mitchell Stevens once argued that "[w]here markets do not exist, they are often created" (1998, 323). I believe that smart-grid engineers rise to the occasion of this passive-voice argument. In their personal lives, the optimizers may be committed to a variety of causes, ranging from income equality to climate change mitigation. But those were not the causes they translated into their professional work, whereas, with the optimization toolkit at hand, market building could be formulated as professional, apolitical, mathematical work. In the specific case of electricity, the persistent need to balance supply and demand—a goal historically inherent to the management of the electric grid—renders the optimizers even more predisposed to conceive of the grid as an everyday optimizing market, one where the balance of supply and demand is granular and constant. The optimization toolkit, together with the material mandates of electricity, in other words, had informed a culture of building markets where there had been none. Many of my interlocutors were in it for the math.

The young optimizers I met often narrativized their ideas in an arc of personal professional growth. Lin had started her graduate school trajectory somewhere else, where she thought she was not putting her skills to addressing big, *systemic* enough questions. She was thrilled to be in Ilić's group where she could write an innovating dissertation, not something that "a consultancy firm can do for me"—not something about the parts but about the *system*. She followed her skill set to what she considered its logical conclusion—apply them to an issue that mattered. Along the way, she contributed to a mission that promised to integrate more renewable resources into the grid—a progressive cause to which she was happy to contribute. She was acculturated into optimization and found herself a creator of markets where they did not exist.

The logical conclusion of Lin's skill set is the grid market—a distinct entity from existing markets in its arrangement of time and space. In chapter 2, we saw that market participants conceptualized real time, based on how they experienced the "real-time market," as that which took its course, with limited to no participation from humans; most of my interlocutors from that chapter would complete their work up to a day before time became real time. In Ilić's lab of control and dynamics, a few more time scales opened up, too granular for even the analysts and traders obsessed with granularity to cognize. In lectures and group meetings, Ilić walked her students through these time scales as they became shorter and shorter. ISOs' algorithms were making decisions in the scale of hours in the day ahead, which were then adjusted by generators and utilities within the twenty-five- to thirty-minute range, after which humans and their optimization algorithms were replaced by control mechanisms. At the scale of seconds, new machinery came into view—regulators, governors, excitors that kept the electric grid intact during small mismatches of supply and demand. In other words, real time simply taking its course depended on a number of nonhuman, nonoptimizing engineering mechanisms. The question was, according to Ilić's team, how deep into these time scales could we embed optimization methods? Traders and analysts' cognition stopped at the hour scale. Could we continue to optimize past the hour?

We could, by reorganizing space. While in the existing markets, decision making went through a central authority, in Ilić's hoped-for grid, optimization would be distributed across the electric grid. While in the existing markets, bids and offers were made on behalf of individual producers and consumers, assuming information could ever be collected fully about them, in Ilić's grid, optimization would come directly from those very entities—each entity would optimize for itself and update their calculations in interactions with other optimizing entities. An entity could be a wind power plant that needed to ramp up exactly when the wind was blowing. Or it could be an electric vehicle that could be charged anytime between when its owner got home and left in the morning. The grid market could honor all of these entities' preferences—human and machine-generated alike—including flexibility and inflexibility with regard to time. This meant an infinite decentralization of optimization, both into shorter time scales and across the space of social life.[3] It would encompass all of electrified life, reweaving the fabric of the social along the way.

## Into the Wild: The Cyborg Social

Ilić was always passionate in her seminars, ready to point out the differences of her vision from that of the neoclassical economics of actually existing markets. Outside the classroom after a seminar one day, I asked her bluntly—why the rift? If dynamic optimization is intuitively better than static optimization for making room for corrections, why did she think this answer would not be obvious to those adherents of neoclassical economics? She nodded to admit that the rift was not a simple matter of right and wrong, as she might imply in her jokes in the classroom. She said, "[They once didn't have it, but] we now have the data." Smart meters, smart thermostats, smart voltage-meters—what is known as "ubiquitous computing"—that generate and retrieve a stream of data from everyday infrastructures now let the potential of constant calculation shine. Ilić was very compelled by the idea that every person and thing plugged into the grid, previously neglected by actually existing markets, could now be brought into the fold of the grid market—everyday people as they use their air conditioners, charge their electric vehicles, mindlessly turn on and off their lights.

The optimizers are fascinated with the social. As they strive to enact pervasive everyday optimizing markets that will encompass everyday people, they have realized that humans remain a mystery to them. They are impatient to generate or borrow a working theory of how humans behave. By "the social" (or the "social aspects"), they largely refer to consumer behavior as it lends itself to manipulation. What do people do with electricity when it enters their houses? What would motivate them to use less electricity? What would motivate them to use it at a particular time of the day? How could we convince them to channel their demand for electricity to times when it is plentiful—when it is cheap and green? How do we enroll everyday people in the quest to match supply to demand? As we saw earlier, the optimizing engineers are not driven by the goal to contribute to economic theory; they want to theorize the psychology of the electricity consumer just so they can begin to model the consumer as part of the electric grid.

Ilić's interest in the social was the premise of how we started working together. Two years before my fieldwork in Pittsburgh, when we first met, she patiently listened to my self-introduction as a social scientist and my research interests. She then quickly cobbled together a summer research stint for me in the Azores to explore the islands' consumption culture. "What would motivate them to change their behavior?" she asked. "Should we give them rebates, free tickets to the movies, charts comparing them to their neighbors?" I was set to help with the "social parts" of the work of Jhi-Young Joo, her student who worked on leading the "demand-side management" of the Azores project. Demand-side management means the practice of discerning what people do with their electricity once it enters their houses, how to manipulate that usage for a finer balance of supply and demand, how to manipulate users themselves, as the experts in the field often put it. Demand-side management is not simply an academic area of inquiry; it is a thriving business, though many businesses do start as academic inquiries. There are several firms in the field that contract with utilities to help them manage consumers' consumption in a way that, ideally, would save money to both parties by lowering overall costs. An arguable poster-child firm for the industry, named O'Power, made a splash in the early 2010s with its simple premise—comparing consumers to their neighbors and mailing out smiley face stickers to those using less electricity.

If the optimizing engineers create the economic forms of life we live with, as I argue, they do so with a working theory of an economic actor in mind. While they do not explicitly theorize the characteristics of this economic actor, observing their working assumptions and beliefs about the electricity user led me to believe that it is best characterized as a cyborg—an assemblage of human and nonhuman parts that together produce optimal calculations. It would be immaterial to the optimizing engineers if the decisions and acts of the electricity user came from the human or the machine part of this hybrid actor. What is more, this cyborg actor, true to its roots in systems thinking, was not expected to have access to perfect information; it was hoped to optimize while mired in uncertainty.

This cyborg actor, it should come as no surprise, stands in contrast with the economic actor operationalized in neoclassical economics, sometimes pejoratively called by critics *homo economicus* (Persky 1995, 222). It is the latest instantiation of what was envisaged by Herbert Simon, the influential decision-making scientist and one-time Carnegie Mellon faculty member, who developed the notion of "bounded rationality" or "rationality as optimization" directly in opposition to *homo economicus* (2004, 47). At Carnegie Mellon today, Herbert Simon's legacy is alive. There is no traditional neoclassical economics department; there are, instead, the cyborg sciences, like a decision-making science department that doubles as a behavioral economics department. Some of the researchers connected to Ilić's lab, who are focused on the human parts of the grid, are based there; others belong to an "engineering and policy" department. These people are researching the psychology of electricity consumption in the hopes of bringing electricity consumers into the fold of the grid market—by finding ways to turn them into continuously optimizing cyborgs.

We have established by now that electricity poses challenges to conventional political economy as we know it, by virtue of the fact that it effectively does not allow storage. On the consumption front, too, electricity seems to pose a fascinating challenge to political economy as we know it. "Electricity is too cheap," I have seen experts lament in unison over the years in lectures of energy economics, electricity regulation, and electricity market design. They would repeat routinely that the "price signal" was not doing its job to induce behavior change—it did not meaningfully reward frugal consumers and punish big spenders. What is more, it also did not do its job to communicate to consumers the "true cost of producing electricity" because the retail price—the price at which consumers buy electricity from utilities—changes perhaps once or twice a year at most.[4] Energy economists are constantly disappointed in the users' "literacy" in energy use. In countless lectures over the years, I witnessed experts addressing the audience by a version of this rhetorical accusation: "You make sure to know the price of oranges before you buy them; do you know the price of electricity when you consume electricity?" This inscrutability of the electricity consumer, energy economists (like those I discuss in chapter 1) explain as the "inelasticity of demand" in electricity; demand is inelastic when it does not respond to prices and, hence, to changes in supply. But for Ilić and the psychologists of electricity consumption, engineering that elasticity is the new frontier.

As economist Deirdre McCloskey puts it, "The economist has from time to time inquired at the psychology shop for premises of behavior more complex than simple greed" (1998, 31). As critics pointed out, the birth of neoclassical economics was wrapped up in the conceptualization of homo economicus; whereas the earlier political economy of the likes of Adam Smith or David Ricardo was a "science of wealth," late nineteenth-century economists conceived economics as we know it as a "study of *the man* in quest of wealth" (Kirzner 1960, 56, italics added). Later, William Stanley Jevons, the neoclassical pioneer of the late nineteenth century, broadened the desire of homo economicus from wealth to utility in general—the economic man wanted to "maximize happiness by purchasing pleasure, as it were, at the lowest cost of pain" (quoted in Kirzner 1960, 58). The economic man,[5] then, optimized as well—but did so with certainty about his own preferences as well as those of others. When these economic men met at the marketplace, the system overall also optimized itself, according to neoclassical economics.

The optimizing engineers also reckon that the economic actor has preferences—prefers, for instance, the room temperature at home to be between 68 and 74 degrees Fahrenheit. He or she (let's say she) also prefers, most probably, to spend less money for the same comforts. The trouble is, this economic actor does not seem to optimize for herself—in the sense that her actions do not always seem to be in her best interests. She does not study the prices or shop around for electricity (when she has the chance), perhaps because she senses that her minimal savings will not justify the time she invests in that study. She does not optimize for the grid either—she wants to use electricity exactly when everyone else wants to use it, overloading the system and driving up the costs. She is not an optimizer the way Jevons assumed she would be because she is too uncertain to process all the information needed to optimize. But she can be an optimizer if she is given a hand—if the optimizing engineers equip her with the right tools.

That is why I believe that the economic actor the optimizing engineers hope to groom for everyday optimizing markets is a "cyborg"—an assemblage of human and nonhuman parts that together produce optimal calculations. Herbert Simon and other mid- to late twentieth-century polymaths whom I consider to be Ilić's predecessors conceived of communication as categorically the same across humans, animals, and machines—as information processing whether by way of neurons or silicon (Wiener 1948). I once attended a conference in Ponta Delgada, the Azores, a year after my research there, to present my findings from my limited Azorean research experience about how different groups of people across businesses and residences consume electricity. Along with Ilić, I attended a presentation about optimizing home devices, where the presenter, Linda, was asked in the question-and-answer period about what kind of user she targeted. Linda said the user needs to be just the right blend of active and passive: active enough to adopt and install the device, but passive enough not to override the device's decisions. The user, in everyday optimizing markets, is conceived of as that blend—as long as optimal decisions are produced from that blend, the optimizers see no need to ontologically distinguish human from nonhuman agency.

One might think, if Ilić did not concern herself with the specificities of human agency, she would not have sent me to the Azores to explore Azorean consumption culture. "I know enough to know that I don't know enough," she always said to me jokingly in our conversations about what social science could do for her. But it is important to note that, when she asked me to "figure out the social," she and her team were aiming to finally model human agency such that it would be the equivalent of machines that lend themselves to modeling—that humans' "active" quality could be rendered the mathematical equivalent of their "passive" machine companions. When Ilić is done, the humans will optimize in seamless harmony with the inverters, electric substations, your fridge, and electric vehicles. They will have been brought into the fold of the grid market, made equally out of metal and flesh. That is the humming, optimizing cyborg social. Its final difference from the neoclassical economist's social is that it is not readily found in nature—it is to be engineered.

The optimizers who pursue demand-side management (or those who are interested in it but do not pursue it themselves, like Ilić) do not always agree on how to engineer the elasticity of electricity consumers' behavior. On one end of the spectrum, there are those who believe that humans can be worked with—they would willingly engage in optimization as long as we give them the appropriate motivators and signals, in the absence of the price signals. On the other end of the spectrum, there are those whose hope in humans' involvement in optimization is limited to getting them to sign up for a comprehensive home-based optimization system—these researchers want to expand the scale of automation in decision making to the extent possible. Those researchers who come from a psychology or decision-making science angle experiment with cases on the former end of the spectrum. Jay, for instance, was researching how people make decisions about purchasing lightbulbs when I met him.

Like so many others in his field, he hoped to understand how humans made decisions so as to produce the appropriate nudge for them to make more optimal decisions on a routine basis, like purchasing a more efficient lightbulb. To research this, Jay had booked what was called a "data truck"—a 13 by 36 foot vehicle with two rooms and eight laptop computers, made available by Carnegie Mellon University to those who would like to take their research into the wild (if the streets of Pittsburgh count as such). Jay parked the data truck on a street in Pittsburgh, stood outside with flyers advertising the project, and invited the interested passersby into the truck. He showed them pictures of lightbulbs on his laptop, captioned with information about their cost, brightness, lifetime, and asked, "Which one would you choose?" The participants answered and left the truck with a gift card. Others came, and now Jay asked the same question, this time also presenting information about the lightbulbs' annual operating cost. All participants were asked to fill out a survey asking them their gender, age, and occupation.

Those researchers who focus on demand-side management tend to have come to the field with more explicit interests in energy, climate change, and the environment than those in Ilić's group; Jay was one of them. Throughout his earlier experience—education in environmental policy and experience building a startup in energy efficiency in his native South Korea—he came to think that unlocking individuals' decision making was at the heart of solving energy issues, that is, reducing energy consumption overall in an effort of climate change mitigation. After his experiment, he would go on to analyze his data to conclude that his participants' demographics had made an insignificant impact in their decision making; whether they were given the information on annual operating cost had made a significant impact. This finding seemed to suggest that electricity consumers were, in fact, driven by the motivation to save money—what they suffered from was clear signals as to how to achieve that. Despite his efforts to glean predictability into people's decision-making habits in his writing, Jay was cynical in person about whether he had solved the mystery of the electricity consumer. "The truck is unreal," he offered. While his research said one thing, his common sense suggested that consumers would not compare every single choice when they shopped at Home Depot—that they would want to check lightbulbs off their shopping list as quickly as possible. As to what *really* motivated humans in their electricity consumption, Jay remained uncertain, like the consumers he studied.

In the absence of an agreed-upon theory on the economic actor, the optimizers often tap into their common sense and anecdotal evidence to explain why humans behave the way they do. Renan, a finishing graduate student who had already launched his energy efficiency startup, displayed confidence in his commonsensical theory, unlike Jay. He downplayed psychological studies when he advanced his own, primarily psychological premise. Unlike O'Power's assumption that human beings enjoyed competing with their peers for competition's sake, they were only ever motivated by saving money. Renan's strong suit was in machine learning and data management. His startup's premise was to identify and communicate to the consumer exactly how much each behavior would yield for them in savings. Renan, in other words, hoped his technology to overcome the weak price signal problem in electricity that so many experts bemoaned. Renan was used to getting questions about what set his company apart from other companies in the field. In our conversations, he would quickly launch into a rebuke of the other players and their attending working theories of what motivates the economic actor. For instance, Google, at the time, had recently started developing smart-home displays, like screens showing daily energy consumption data across the household—a kind of display that Fred Schweppe had called "family's home computer" and surmised would become commonplace by year 2000 (Schweppe 1978, 43). Their hypothesis about human behavior was blind to human motivation; it did, instead, privilege the vehicle of information.

If the consumers were shown their consumption data numerically on a display, Google's hypothesis went, they would begin to change their behavior, whether they were motivated to help the environment or save money. Renan did not agree. "No one will stare at a monitor all day," he said to me defiantly. Renan, then, still operated under the assumption that humans could be worked with—that they would take an active role in making specific adjustments to their consumption behavior—if only those adjustments were translated into dollar amounts for them by Renan's systems. He coded (first for his dissertation, then for his startup) a machine-learning algorithm that deduced those dollar amounts by processing data about electricity household use and corresponding bills. As I mentioned earlier, what people actually do with electricity once it enters their houses remains a difficult puzzle to solve. Renan is trying to solve it by feeding his machine-learning algorithm as much data from public sources as possible—about, say, house square footage and resident demographics—to discern the relationship between different household characteristics and wattage used. Jay and Renan, while bringing different assumptions about humans to the table, held out hope that humans will, to a certain extent, enroll themselves in optimization, if only they are nudged to that effect. Many others remained more pessimistic. Linda, the demand-side management researcher who had made the comment about the simultaneously active and passive user, bemoaned to me during a chat after her presentation that users, at least in her pilot experiments with her home optimization system, constantly wanted to override her system's decisions.

While Renan and Linda dipped into commonsense assumptions about human motivation, others were keen on conducting "experimental psychology" projects to test hypotheses on real consumers before reaching conclusions. In my conversations with two researchers with the then-nascent Energy Behavior Group at Carnegie Mellon, I often wondered if they were not intimidated by the scale of their question—the question of what drove people to consume the way they did when commonsense answers, like saving money or quality of service, scarcely applied. They would reassure me that, whereas the question was, in fact, a big one, we could begin to answer it by isolating parts of it—asking questions about how humans behaved in specific consumption acts, from purchasing light bulbs to turning off the lights when not needed. Their first big project was meant to test whether the Hawthorne Effect—the theory that subjects react to being observed by changing their behavior (Landsberger 1958)—applied to electricity consumption. For that project, they gained access to the data of the consumer base of PEPCO, a utility that had received subsidies from the federal government as part of the 2009 American Recovery and Reinvestment Act to research energy efficiency and smart-grid measures. For a month, they sent postcards to PEPCO's consumers with a simple note that they might be eligible for a study, although no action was needed yet. Studying the consumption patterns of those consumers who received the note, they found that after this minimalistic note, the observed consumers had cut down their usage by about 5 percent (Schwartz et al. 2013).

This result encouraged them to borrow other theories of human behavior from psychology and test them out on the electricity consumer—for instance, the theory that asking people for a small favor first might increase the chances of having them accept a bigger favor later. The energy and behavior researchers found that, when asked to sign up for more information on an efficiency project, consumers who had already signed up for an initial study responded more positively. Through it all, they were on the most hopeful end of the spectrum about the prospects of collaborating with humans. They thought experts, including themselves, could gradually change consumers' norms; they wanted to instill in consumers a sense to seek out the more energy efficient behavior as opposed to simply a preference for compact fluorescent light bulbs. They knew how tricky the cooperation with humans would be—that unlike homo economicus, the electricity consumer did not have endless patience and processing power for all the information they were "thrown," as they put it. Experts had to carefully nurse their relationship with electricity consumers, ensuring that the favors they asked from consumers corresponded to their different values. One of them once told me, for instance, that consumers sometimes did not want to save money when they did good for the environment, "Because if people are paid to do something, then they'll lose the value that they get from having done good." She had formed this observation by blending conclusions from behavioral research in other fields and their fledgling foray into the electricity consumer's mind. In the group's vision, even human norms become manipulable and programmable parts of the grid market.

The optimizers have, as we have seen, competing visions on how to bring the humans into the fold of the grid market. But regardless of these disagreements, they have a working theory about the economic across that has roots, again, in a work culture of optimization. First, following Herbert Simon, they do not assume the economic actor to be rational the way Stanley Jevons assumed she was. If she were rational in that way, she would not need her information to be carefully curated by experts, as the energy and behavior researchers believed. Second, optimizer psychologists are interested in the consumers only as part of the cyborg whole—the grid. Ilić once said to me, "When people say they care enough about the environment to change their consumption behavior, I need to figure out what exactly 'enough' means mathematically." Finally, optimizer psychologists are guided by the concern to match—match supply to demand—by enrolling the inscrutable electricity consumer into that project. When promoting his startup, Renan often made this motivation explicit, if jokingly. He would say, "We are the *match.com* of energy," referring to the dating website that matches romantic partners.

Decentralized, modular, and ordinary, the grid will encompass everyone and everything plugged into it, the optimizers believe. When we all communicate with each other—people with electric substations, air conditioners with inverters—by way of neurons and silicon, we will live in optimized harmony, match automatically what we have to what we want, here and now as we enroll and are enrolled by electricity. All there is, in the grid, will be the humming cyborg social, quietly balancing supply and demand—the activity of matching our electric needs to one another.

## Conclusion

Several years after I began working with her, Ilić disbanded her group at Carnegie Mellon and started a new one at MIT. Some years after my fieldwork, I visited her in her Cambridge, Massachusetts, office. Her picture with the Tesla statue had migrated to an upper shelf in her new office. As she gave me a tour of the floor, she interrupted herself many times, introducing me to her new collaborators, remembering yet another person she should put me in touch with, but always keeping on top of what we were talking about. I realized, again, she thought of her research circle the way she thought of the electric grid; we were the sum of our relationships and her job, that of a facilitator, managing relationships as she went. We sat down with the graduate student researcher whom she supported most enthusiastically—a young woman from India, who excitedly told me about their joint upcoming pilot project with a utility in Austin, Texas. In their excited conversation about the impending possibilities, once again I saw how a future market is actively imagined in an office space, at the intersection of new algorithms, new data, and new partnerships. Snippets from Ilić's life story came up inevitably—snippets of overcoming the odds as a woman in the field of electric systems. The two women commented on the male-dominated culture of the field, one Ilić has done much to dismantle with her very active support to women researchers.

In this chapter, as in this book, I also rely on the concept of culture, but to identify a culture of optimization, which gives birth to decentralized, modular, and everyday forms of life all around us. This culture is animated by a toolkit that encourages those who wield it to see the world as a sum of inputs and outputs to match—it is further reproduced by a technological problem presented by the electric grid, that privileges the balance of inputs and outputs as the fundamental concern. I develop a narrative of techno-economics against a rival theorization—that of widespread neoliberalization, a theory that assumes that agendas to reprogram government action trickles down to the constitution of everyday life—a theory where neoliberalism appears as something not assembled but prepackaged, and "neoliberal" appears as a label for economic realities that already exist in the world, awaiting the scholar's verdict. An anthropology of optimization opens up to view those places, like Ilić's lab, for the generative places they are, not as passive receivers of top-down ideologies. This focus *may* land us in studies of neoliberalism—it may, by the same coin, land us in studies of socialism (Medina 2011). What it *will* show, for certain, is that broad ideological categories like "neoliberalism" and "socialism" often do not rise to the explanatory task we expect from them—the task being accounting for the political economy of the twenty-first century, marked by decentralization, modularization, and ordinariness. To rise to that latter task, I have proposed to focus on the generative techno-economics of spaces like that of an electrical engineering lab.

And where to go next? What good does it do to point the finger at optimization instead of an overtly political agenda? Well, a little granularity, if I am allowed to learn from my interlocutors, helps us tell what we want to amplify and what we want to critique as scholars—and such work requires a finer brush than imputations of neoliberalism. I believe optimization is good, for instance, for allowing us to eliminate big, costly, polluting power plants and to incorporate small, flexible, green power plants, as Ilić's group was intent on doing. Optimization can also be limiting, for making alternatives to markets harder to conceptualize, like the conception of electricity, say, as a human right—bad for discouraging public ownership, which might be less flexible but more stable.

In the larger optimization terrain, corporations with monopolistic ambitions frequently obscure their not-so-optimal practices even as they present themselves as pioneers of efficiency. Ride-sharing services, for instance, have lost huge sums of investors' money while trying to drive their competitors out of business (Horan 2019). More infamously, these businesses also just cannot seem to match their contractors to stable monthly incomes. Optimization is good when supply and demand are a given, perhaps not so good when we want to change the terms of supply and demand. It is this level of nitty-gritty that attention to techno-economics allows us to discern.

The optimizers of the electric grid, as we have seen, aim to expand the grid market to encompass as much of social life as possible. They hope to turn people—everyday users of electricity—into optimizing components of the cyborg whole, which is the grid. But what do those everyday users have to say to that vision? How to they formulate their own electric counter-politics and counter-economics? The next chapter turns to the citizen activists of the electric grid.

# PROTESTING

When the GPS navigator in my car showed that I was only minutes away from Keryn's house, I had been driving for eight hours from Boston but had only recently crossed the Potomac River into West Virginia. Shepherdstown, a quiet, suburban town in West Virginia's Jefferson County, is located at the very tip of West Virginia's eastern panhandle, and as such, is more integrated into Maryland and Washington D.C. than it is to the rest of the state. As the locals would tell me later, it is a "bedroom community for D.C.," hosting upper-middle-class professionals who tolerate two-hour commutes for the opportunity to live in a quiet and pleasant suburban environment. Driving through narrow, idyllic roads lined with lush poplar trees, I soon found the street leading into the subdivision where Keryn,[1] a homemaker in her fifties, lived with her husband: not gated but marked by a sign that read "Private Community."

Keryn, her friend Patience who lives in the same subdivision, and their husbands emerged as I was pulling into the driveway of Keryn's house. They all laughed seeing that I struggled to keep my car clear from the beautifully maintained lawn: "This is not the city," Patience's husband exclaimed and encouraged me to park without hesitation. Later, in the backyard, I was regaled with stories of Jefferson County's not-so-quiet recent past, joining Keryn and company over delivered pizza and "Raging Bitch," the beer that had become Keryn and Patience's favorite over the past five years. At one point, Patience's husband, an otherwise buoyant man and a former standup comic, assumed a solemn expression and made sure that I understood the stakes of the fight that they had led: "Elderly women still stop me in the street to tell me they are grateful for what my wife and Keryn have done for them."

Keryn and Patience spearheaded a movement between 2008 and 2012 against a proposed 765 kV transmission line that would cut through their neighborhood and likely swallow many of their neighbors' land by eminent domain. 765 kV is the highest standard voltage for a transmission line in the US, which translates into taller structures to uphold the line's multiple wires and significant acreage devoted to these structures' security. The line was meant to bring electricity from a coal-fired power plant in St. Albans, West Virginia, to a substation in Maryland, crossing 275 miles of southwestern West Virginia and Virginia, to eventually feed electricity-hungry centers of the East Coast. Keryn and Patience took on some mighty foes. The line had been proposed by some of the nation's largest private utilities and approved for reliability purposes by PJM Interconnection—the world's second largest electricity market by megawatts traded (next to the EU's recently integrated market). The line never materialized; it was eventually canceled by PJM in 2012. But what Keryn and Patience did was more than getting the line to disappear. They educated themselves on the obscure regulations—physical and economic—of electricity and articulated a sophisticated critique of its markets, which asked how expanding physical infrastructures fit into the markets' raison d'être. Finding a place for themselves in the current economy, they became what I call *citizens electric*.

During my summer 2013 stay, I was hosted in the basement of Keryn's elegantly decorated, spacious house. The duo—Keryn and Patience—often took me on drives around West Virginia's eastern panhandle. We logged miles and miles passing underneath transmission lines, each of which, it turned out, had a history. Over weeks, our conversations settled into a familiar rhythm. Keryn, with her hands on the steering wheel, would jubilantly recall the moments she and her friends had outwitted the private companies' generously paid lawyers, while Patience, a journalist by profession, would make a point from her passenger seat to connect their fight to larger issues like income inequality and climate change. They both would take a moment to point to each other a beautiful house that we were passing and appreciate a well-maintained lawn. Despite their occasional good-natured disagreements on the "big picture" issues (Patience's term), they would mostly agree on what house and what lawn had been well cared for. Once, Patience paused after praising a majestic suburban house sitting on notable acreage, turned to the back seat, and told me,

Figure 4–1. The eastern panhandle of West Virginia is cut across by transmission lines. Often, they parallel each other since transmission builders find it easier to acquire right-of-ways next to existing transmission lines or to use existing right-of-ways.

"Property is how you become invested as a citizen." Keryn nodded, her hands on the steering wheel.

In the last chapter we saw expert visions on humans' role in electricity's economy. Humans, there, were anticipated to become well-oiled components of the grid market, seamlessly optimizing in the human-machine assemblages in which they took part. But what do humans have to say about these visions? Many are oblivious; an average US customer may worry about his or her bill, but scarcely gives a thought to the machinations that bring the bill in the mail. There are groups, however, that have come to a certain consciousness as consumers of electricity and citizens of an electric economy. The gateway to their politicization is usually something big and concrete encroaching in their environments—a transmission line proposed to cut through their backyard. But they soon move past "not-in-my-backyard" politics (and resent dearly how the term belittles their discontent) to explore the strange new territory of the current economy. They ask what purposes electricity markets, past and future, serve and why they have not been consulted in these markets' making. I have followed two of such groups: Keryn and Patience's StopPATH was a pioneering movement that influenced and educated many others around the country, including Block RICL, a grassroots organization linking landowners across northern Illinois. The two groups were at times ideologically and demographically different but were nevertheless united in their infrastructure politics. Together, they have propelled other groups to existence elsewhere in the country. This chapter documents their critique—what I have found to be the most substantial, elaborate critique posed to electricity markets.

Their example goes to show how people formulate political stances through experiences within the infrastructures they inhabit—especially when the infrastructure becomes noticeable to its denizens for a reason of encroachment or failure (Star 1999; also see Larkin 2013, 336, for a counterpoint). As is the case with the experts this book has tracked so far, laypeople's political stances may be produced independently from overtly pronounced ideologies or explicit social values; that is why ideologically diverse groups can form a united front in their infrastructural politics. In articulating their vision, these groups are also informed by the toolkits available to them with which they experience the economic and physical infrastructures of electricity—this time not spreadsheets, databases, or mathematical traditions, but their land, farms, and the metal bulk that crosses those. In other words, citizen critique and discontent over markets also play out in the techno-economic field, where one's economic vision is a function of the technologies at one's disposal.

Their example also goes to show that while techno-economic critique emanates from within work practice, that practice does not always have to be tied to gainful employment or formal studies, as is the case with the work cultures from earlier chapters. Activists in both groups were involved in the taxing work of managing their lands, houses, farms—overall property. Both fights were overwhelmingly led and populated by women; a good many were in charge of managing their households and invested in the work of caring for affected families and communities. And unlike forms of women's activism that might increase their household work and intensify gender roles (Glabau 2019), their activism took them outside the house as they discovered new back roads in their old neighborhoods, organized others across neighboring towns, and took their fight to county seats and state capitals.

My interlocutors believe that electricity markets are machinations (some use the word "cartels") that seek to advance the participant corporations' profit margins at the expense of consumers' welfare. The ISOs, my interlocutors say, wear their "transmission operator" hat when they pronounce new, bulky, land-hungry transmission lines necessary for future physical reliability, when in fact they wear their "market operator" hat in soliciting and approving these lines to enhance long-distance trade within the market footprints. Markets' land demands are in conflict with both groups' property-based economics. In the case of Block RICL, market expansion also runs counter to the demands of land use as seen through the farming lens, such as the need for contiguous land for efficient farm maintenance and harvesting. Because of these specific clashes, the groups' unease is focused mostly on the already existing markets. They are aware of the advancing vision of everyday optimizing markets as utilities around them begin to introduce piecemeal smart-grid technologies. They might welcome technologies in the service of a finer balance of supply and demand to the extent that these prevent unnecessary infrastructure construction, but they remain unpersuaded by any technological assemblage that does not prioritize meaningful citizen involvement and representation.

While formulating these thoughts over time, my interlocutors have generated a politics of negative liberty—a politics of citizenship based on inviolable private property, which should not be encroached upon for private gain. It is a politics strongly reminiscent of strands of classical liberalism (think John Locke), though I argue that their politics was not a ready-made ideological repository for them to draw on. It was instead arrived at through the experience of inhabiting the infrastructure and protesting its operations. Their critique is anti-market because of how they view the specific operations of ISOs, but it is not anti-capitalistic. It is a moderate, law-abiding, anti-radical critique that is concerned with violations of what citizenship should entail. Citizenship, here, is conceived based on a consumerist model; it concerns the freedom to enjoy private property and paid-for services fairly, the violation of which, thus, amounts to disenfranchisement.

I refer to Keryn and Patience, alongside Block RICL's Mary and Susan, as citizens electric—who formulate this kind of citizenship through the particularities of their experience with the electric grids. This citizen electric, I must be clear, is not a universal category through which to understand how people relate to the infrastructures they inhabit. Anthropologists have now widely tracked the political controversies embedded in infrastructures in a variety of contexts. In South Africa, as Antina von Schnitzler documents, the prepaid meter for water was first devised by the government-owned utilities as a measure to fight the anti-apartheid rent boycotts. The prepayment technology acquired a new life in the post-apartheid era as an enforcer of a new kind of fiscal relationship between citizens and their government, which expected citizens-turned-customers to engage in calculative behavior and assume an "entrepreneurial comportment" (2008, 889). Sowetans protest that the expectation of rational budgeting rests on the assumption of the availability of a predictable monthly income, which many customers of the prepaid meter cannot access (2008, 915). In Mumbai, too, we learn from Nikhil Anand, water access is more vexed and less standardized than what the government officials may wish. "Settlers" who have no government-guaranteed access to water have to apply "pressure"—to relevant authorities and to water alike (2011, 543). This incessant process of making claims to the city's infrastructure, Anand calls "hydraulic citizenship" (2011, 545). The infrastructural terrains explored by von Schnitzler and Anand, where users cultivate modes of political consciousness and belonging, parallel the techno-economics of citizen experience I describe here.

The political subjectivities that emerge in each case, however, is unique precisely because those subjectivities emerge as a function of their specific material environments. In Soweto and Mumbai, users (alternatively referred to as citizens, settlers, or residents) exhibit different conceptions of belonging to infrastructures and fair use of services than what the authorities expect from them. They share this particularity with citizen electric, but that is about where their similarities end. Anand's "hydraulic citizenship" emerges where the governments' aspirations to "liberal, modern citizenship" fail; von Schnitzler's interlocutors' discontent similarly emerges when they are unable to meet citizenship criteria that are impossible to meet because of a history of discrimination (the legacy of apartheid in Soweto and poverty and segregation in Mumbai) that the liberal model simply ignores. They do not view illicit connections to the infrastructure as immoral because they call to question the morality of licit connections. Citizen electric, on the other hand, believes firmly in her capacity as a self-sufficient, individual consumer: responsible to pay her bills on time and only ever licitly connected to infrastructures.[2] She is mainly discontented that the authorities are not holding up their end of the bargain—that they are rewarding responsible behavior with encroachments on individual rights. One might say that she accuses the authorities of not being *liberal enough*. In her ease in evoking the rule of law, she is firmly a "citizen"; citizenship is, in fact, central to how she understands where she fits and how she needs to be treated.

I must stress that if citizen electric's politics can be found to align with a certain classically liberal position, it is not because of her a priori values; her infrastructural politics is assembled throughout the process of her engagements. From a techno-economic standpoint, where specific material affordances matter to one's political and economic consciousness, it is no coincidence that von Schnitzler and Anand's embattled residents have come to a certain consciousness as infrastructural citizens at the level of distribution where they are end customers, whereas citizen electric fights at the level of transmission.[3] As we might remember, transmission denotes the first stage in electricity's transportation where high-voltage transmission lines move electricity from power plants to distribution substations. Distribution, on the other hand, refers to the end stage where the grid's low-voltage wires enter consumption sites like homes. Electricity consumption had not been a source of significant worry for citizen electric; her service had been largely uninterrupted and high-quality, and her bill, although occasionally undesirably high, seldom high enough to ponder the possibility of service interruption. The jolt to her electric consciousness came in the form of an architectural change to the infrastructure that affected her—a change that was a whole level of abstraction removed from her end consumption. This fact has to do with how citizen electric conceives of her infrastructural citizenship as, at least ideally, one of negative rights—one that entitles her to enjoy paid-for services free of violations to her assets. After the jolt had long passed, these groups have also educated themselves on the intricacies of the distribution level, yet their concerns have still evolved along the lines of the protection of the citizen-consumer.

I believe that a techno-economic approach to infrastructure politics offers a way to see citizen political leanings in the US that transcends the "conservative versus progressive" (or "red versus blue") narrative, through which predispositions in the US are all too often understood (for a deconstruction of this binary, see Fraser 2017). According to that narrative, a gun ownership rights supporter and an environmentalist, for instance, might hardly find mutual political ground to support a cause together. StopPATH and Block RICL built coalitions that went against the grain of such received wisdom. Instead of assuming which political stances come bundled together, a techno-economic approach opens the black box of the moments where senses of belonging come to being (Özden-Schilling 2019b). In what follows, we see people in those moments, as they encounter electricity markets in their everyday lives and assemble a classically liberal kind of politics with property at its heart.

## Of Property and Citizenship

Keryn first heard of the Potomac-Appalachian Transmission Highline (PATH) in 2008. PATH was announced to be a joint venture of two corporations, Allegheny Energy and American Electric Power, meant to bring the cheap coal power of West Virginia 275 miles east to demand centers on the Atlantic coast. At the time, Keryn had not given much thought to how electricity reached her. Electricity is, of course, a rare commodity that requires its own dedicated shipping routes: transmission lines, which travel from production sites to distribution nodes, from where it reaches end consumers through the tentacles of the distribution wires. Electricity transmission is undertaken by the electricity industry and often supervised by the same authorities that run markets: ISOs. Transmission lines can cross states, thousands of acres of public and private property, and therefore numerous jurisdictions, which can sometimes be at odds with one other. Who builds transmission lines? Where do they get permission to do so and how do they decide where to build them? Keryn started contemplating these questions a few months after learning about PATH. That is when a neighbor called her to say that the route of the proposed PATH was finally made public; it was to cut through sixteen out of thirty-one houses in their subdivision.

By mid-2008, land agents had started knocking on doors in Jefferson County and asking homeowners if they were willing to sell their property. Through word of mouth, conflicting rumors about PATH were spreading. Keryn and other members of the board of directors in their homeowners' association held a meeting to compare notes and notify everyone of an upcoming "open house" that was going to be held shortly. At the meeting, Keryn noticed that land agents were dispensing inconsistent information. Some were trying to convince homeowners to sell their properties to PATH as quickly as possible by suggesting that their properties were losing value every passing day and soon would be subject to eminent domain. Keryn attended a poorly advertised open house meeting where PATH officials had hung a tentative route for the line on the wall. She recognized one of the houses as her elderly neighbor's, which she then pointed out to the company representative. According to Keryn, the

Figure 4–2. Keryn showing me some of the tiles that the Jefferson County GIS Office made and shared with StopPATH.

representative retorted flippantly that they had planned to buy the property. Keryn told the representative that she would bring Diane, her neighbor, so they could tell her the news themselves. She brought Diane from the other corner of the room, and the representative told Diane the same thing with the same attitude; Diane burst into tears. And "at that point," Keryn told me, "I said, you can pack and go home because this project is not happening."

As she would find out later, companies like PATH hire land agents as contractors, whom they might fire at any time, to "have a layer of separation" as she put it, if the agents' tactics get negative attention (see Wylie 2018 for similar practices in the fracking industry). Their main interaction with the community before they come up with a proposed route consists of taking aerial pictures. At another open house meeting, Keryn studied her town as depicted on PATH's aerial photo tiles. When she could identify some buildings but not others, she realized that there were two problems with the photos. First, they were captured in summertime, when buildings were covered by tree canopy and only partially visible. Second, they were a year old; Keryn could date the photo to

2007 because she saw her house in the photos as it was during the renovation that she and her husband had undertaken the year before. The maps were made before the land agents had appeared.

Keryn approached a routing expert from PATH who was present at the open house and insisted on going over the map with him. She told him that an area that looked like bare dirt in the tiles had now become several rows of new houses. In another tile, the line that denoted PATH came a mere four feet from a lot that looked like a warehouse; PATH would have to purchase the lot and raze it to the ground. But Keryn pointed out that, despite what the visuals may have suggested, the lot was actually the local fire station. To the PATH expert's real or feigned surprise, another seemingly empty lot, Keryn pointed out, had been approved and financed to become an elementary school. In pictures of the unpopulated areas, on the other hand, PATH officials had neglected topography. Keryn told them they probably would have trouble setting up the line on a corridor by the Potomac River, which, despite what the two-dimensional photo might have suggested, was on a steep slope.

During the summer of 2008, the movement swelled from ten neighbors to several thousands. In November, the company announced that it had withdrawn the original proposed route and would be back with a new one within months. Based on the history of transmission lines that they would later come to know, Keryn and Patience would argue to me that companies deliberately propose routes to which they are not completely committed, in an effort to show the state regulation agencies that they have compromised. Working with the Geographical Information Systems (GIS) office of Jefferson County, which had been studying PATH's route at the request of the county commission, Keryn and Patience guessed that the company was likely to move the route to Charles Town, at the other end of the county. Their guess was correct. In a meeting with other neighborhood leaders in Charles Town, Keryn and Patience intended to pass on their knowledge and "bow out gracefully" from the fight. Sharon, a resident of Charles Town with whom I met, reminisced to me about having been given all the information and feeling overwhelmed; she implored Keryn and Patience to stay and lead the fight. To Keryn, who was already motivated, it was a welcome idea: "By this time, we had learned too much about the project and were seriously questioning the need for it."

At the outset, Keryn's case fits comfortably within a familiar narrative of citizen resistance to infrastructure building; in this narrative, citizens contest not the merits of an infrastructure in question or whether it is necessary to society overall, but wish rather that it be built elsewhere, away from their neighborhoods. Since the 1980s, policymakers and journalists often identified citizen discontent in relation to stalemates in infrastructural (often energy-related) projects that entail environmental risk in those terms, pejoratively labeling it "not-in-my-backyard" politics or "NIMBY" (Deshmukh Towery 2014). At the same time, psychologists gave credence to this view by inquiring into how attitudes toward risky technologies may shift in response to their location (cf. Marks and von Winterfeldt 1984). During my fieldwork, I witnessed several economists and engineers belittle citizen discontent by referring to a version of the NIMBY argument. Many would promote providing Federal Energy Regulatory Commission (FERC) with the authority to bypass state and ISO-level jurisdiction to finalize controversial siting decisions if necessary.

In the case of StopPATH, the NIMBY argument is easy to invalidate. Although some members joined the opposition because the transmission lines were announced to affect their property, most participants had never been in danger of being affected. PATH officials changed the proposed route away from Keryn's subdivision only within months of the first announcement, half a year before Keryn registered the group as a grassroots organization. But even when citizens respond to direct threat to their property, the NIMBY argument, as used by policymakers who would like to proceed with infrastructural projects without negotiation or revision, remains a weak one; it limits the discussion of the "rich motivations of the individuals and organizations" engaging in localized activism concerning their environment and fails to capture how they relate themselves to other issues of social justice (Deshmukh Towery 2014, 21). Often presented in pathological terms as the "NIMBY syndrome," this view tends to diminish citizen discontent by ruling out the possibility that citizens may have opinions on the worth of technologies beyond the question of location (Wexler 1996). My interlocutors from StopPATH and Block RICL were very sensitive to the accusation of NIMBYism, since the accusation had been used by companies and authorities to discredit their activism.

What was it that Keryn and her friends had learned about PATH? What made them stay in the fight even though the route was now even further out from their backyard? Reading up comprehensively on the internet—everything from obscure statutes of ISOs to open-access electrical engineering articles—they educated themselves on the history of what I call the "big grid": the twentieth-century history of monopolistic utilities building longer and longer transmission lines to minimize electric generation expenses and maximize the number of consumers (Özden-Schilling 2019a). Where profitable, these utilities built alliances with each other to share their grids, forming what were called "power pools," which are the precursors of today's ISOs. They acquired their monopolistic nature by lobbying for exemption from anti-trust laws using arguments from economics and political economy, such as "economies of scale" and "natural monopoly." They were assisted by states that would grant them the power of eminent domain for the transmission lines they wanted to build. Each state has a regulation agency that supervises the activities of public utilities, providing water, natural gas, and electricity. As Keryn and Patience found out, once the Public Service Commission of West Virginia (i.e., the state regulation agency, as it is called in West Virginia) had approved the PATH project as a public utility, PATH would acquire the prerogative of eminent domain.

Since ISOs were created in the 2000s, transmission has been entrusted to them in about 2 million square miles of territory in the US. In addition to getting approved by the Public Service Commission of West Virginia located in Charleston, West Virginia, PATH officials also wanted to get the approval of PJM, the ISO in parts of thirteen Mid-Atlantic and Midwest states including West Virginia, for approval as a "reliability line." As the name might suggest, a reliability line is a transmission line that is considered necessary to build to keep the lights on in the future. They are announced in ISOs' multiyear expansion plans. Once a line is approved as a reliability line, its cost gets socialized across the ISO, meaning that PATH would look to be financed by hiked-up electricity bills paid by 61 million consumers across PJM's more than 240,000 thousand square miles of territory. After that, utilities that buy electricity on behalf of consumers would pay fixed fees to PATH for usage of the line, which the utilities would then also pass on to consumers' bills.[4] Keryn and Patience took a look at their electricity bills and identified the transmission fees in the breakdown; usually no more than a couple of dollars per year per household amount to, in the aggregate, a risk-free way for utilities to generate a profit of millions of dollars over investment. Patience associated the risk-free devices built into PJM mechanisms with the excesses of "corporate America." She often asked me rhetorically how PJM, which has more than 900 companies as participants and "stakeholders" fully represented in planning meetings, was not a "cartel."

The creation of ISOs has intensified the logic of the "big grid." More and more utilities want to join ISOs' territories for the chance to participate in ISO-run markets, compete with incumbent utilities, and reach larger consumer bases. PJM has more than doubled its territory since its creation in 2001. PATH was a product of this geography and the logic of arbitrage; it was meant to bring the cheap coal-powered electricity from the west corner of West Virginia to Maryland, to be then distributed to the demand centers of the East Coast through lower voltage lines. It was a project of transmitting "coal by wire," as many members of StopPATH put it, to the resource-poor and demand-rich eastern hubs. Such arbitrages bring the nodal prices known as LMPs across PJM's footprint closer together; with PATH, the prices were expected to go up in West Virginia and down in the hubs connected to Maryland, such as Washington, D.C., however minimally. This relative convergence of prices is agreeable to PJM, which is reviewed by an independent monitor (the "market monitor") every year for efficient competition based on tenets of neoclassical economics; a market is a territory where the price for the same good is the same, or more realistically, as similar to each other as possible (Swedberg 1994). It is also agreeable to the hopeful generators and transmission providers who want larger shares in PJM's electricity market.

Keryn and Patience once took me on a drive across Jefferson County. We drove near the Potomac River toward Charles Town on obscure dirt roads. The two women commented on how much they had learned about the back roads in their neighborhood, county, and even the entire state throughout the past five years of driving around, going to meetings, handing out flyers, and interrupting PATH events. We stopped at a soft-serve ice cream stand, the quality of which they both vouched for. Eating at different ice cream stands and refining their taste for soft-serve during long drives had also become an activism tradition. Over raspberry ice cream, Patience explained why she was against the market logic as perpetuated by PJM. The residents of West Virginia's eastern panhandle had made sacrifices to live there. The panhandle was not bustling with cultural activities or employment opportunities, which meant that most people commuted for long hours. Elsewhere, for instance near the coal plants from which PATH was going to get its electricity, people were making other kinds of sacrifices by bearing the costs inflicted by coal on their environment. Why should these people pay the same price for electricity as someone living in Washington, D.C.? After all, they had never voted at any time to be in the same market as the residents of D.C. or anyone else for that matter.

Upon Patience's explanation, I immediately remembered an electricity market class that I had sat in at MIT. One of the instructors had shown a thermal map of prices across PJM, a snapshot taken at a random time, with different colors denoting different ranges of prices, the likes of which I studied often as part of my work at EnTech. Remarking upon the relative smoothness of color transitions, the instructor had marveled with pleasure: "You have no idea how far PJM has come to have a map like this." When I relayed this anecdote to them, Keryn immediately protested the instructor's remark with characteristic fervor: "Maybe he should go out and talk to real people!" The remark also got on the nerves of otherwise self-possessed Patience; why should the homogeneity of prices across demographically and politically heterogenous places be desirable? She gave another example of experts disregarding citizen concern. In 2013, New Jersey, she said, passed a law to subsidize three power plants to meet the generation needs of the state. Subsequently, two utilities participating in PJM sued New Jersey for bypassing PJM's market mechanisms. A federal court found New Jersey's law unconstitutional and revoked it. Patience was outraged; here is an elected government not being allowed by PJM to do its job, she said.

PJM, like other ISOs, is an exclusive private body, closed to public participation or observation. Individual consumers cannot have meaningful access to them, given that even a visit to ISOs require several weeks of notice, security clearance, and most important, a reason for the visit that PJM representatives would approve. State commissions and consumer advocates employed by them, on the other hand, are "barely tolerated" by PJM, as Keryn put it. Keryn and Patience did not have anything positive to say about PJM, which they thought was run by utilities as a cartel since they hold voting majority in planning mechanisms. That left Keryn and Patience looking for other routes of representation and protest. Before PATH announced a changed route, the two started pressuring Joe Manchin, then governor of West Virginia (US senator from West Virginia at the time of writing), who was running for a second term as governor. They selected him to pressure because the governor appoints the members of the commission in Charleston. The fledgling StopPATH staged its first loud, public demonstrations at events where the governor appeared: "We became pests he could not shake." PATH's decision to reroute the line, which came two weeks before the November 2008 gubernatorial elections, might have had to do with StopPATH's activism. PATH might have expected the Shepherdstown-centered opposition to die out, but it did not happen. Having joined forces with the rest of the eastern panhandle, StopPATH started pressuring the commission.

Located a five-hour drive away, Charleston is physically and mentally far away from the panhandle. The residents of the panhandle, I was told repeatedly by former StopPATH members, see themselves as having more in common in terms of education, political choices, and outlook with the residents of

Virginia and Maryland than the blue-collar parts of West Virginia. They also shared grievances with Virginia and Maryland; Keryn and Patience met with groups in those states who had unsuccessfully opposed another transmission line built by AE, called TrAIL (Trans-Allegheny Interstate Line). Sierra Club, EarthJustice, and a Virginia-based group called Piedmont Environmental Council were gearing up to shift their attention to PATH, which was set to also cross through Virginia. While they pressured Virginia's state regulation agency, StopPATH was not exactly welcome in West Virginia's commission. Members of StopPATH signed up as individual intervenors in PATH's permit application case. When the number of individual intervenors hit 150 (about 60 percent of whom were from Jefferson County), the commission referred to the case as a "circus," (which, "I guess, made us the clowns," Keryn commented). Drawing on its experience with TrAIL, PATH launched a campaign of public relations to win the hearts of commissioners in all three states. StopPATH then focused on debunking PATH's statements to make it more difficult for state and PJM officials to eventually endorse the line.

One of the ways in which PJM and, to a lesser extent, state regulation agencies remain unavailable to consumer inclusion is the learning curve of engaging in any conversation about the arcane details of electricity transmission. If PJM declared PATH to be a technical necessity, who was a high school graduate like Keryn to argue that it was not? But one did not need an academic degree to ask questions like "who is the line necessary for?" In 2008, Keryn was transitioning out of the "stay-at-home-mom phase" of her life, and she slipped into a strict eight-hours/day regimen of internet research on everything electric. She started a blog to share what she learned and keep the growing numbers of StopPATH members informed. She studied the obscure rules and regulations of PJM and FERC in addition to internet articles on the mechanics of electricity transmission. Patience, who was taking a year off from a career in journalism in local media, did the same.

Citizen protests in transmission were not common; AEP and AE panicked and blundered. StopPATH members got in the habit of showing up to every PATH event in their StopPATH t-shirts, setting up stands outside, and challenging PATH officials during the events. Returning PATH's belittling treatment of citizens in Jefferson County, they particularly targeted individual officials, like PATH's lawyer, giving him nicknames and watching him lose his temper. PATH's lawyer first declined to respond to some questions, citing to Keryn and Patience the requirement to file discoveries with PJM. Keryn eventually filed three complaints with FERC using the information she obtained, at which time the lawyer challenged Keryn's eligibility to stand as a plaintiff; she was not an electricity consumer and thus not a party to the case, he argued unsuccessfully, because her name was not on the electricity bill (her husband's was). Such discriminatory blunders incensed Keryn. She and Patience went on to create new tactics. Once, realizing that a link on the PATH website—one that read "What the experts say"—was dead, she bought the link's domain and put up a mock website against PATH. In other cases, they doubted the authenticity of some pro-PATH citizen groups showing up to meetings. Looking them up to find out that they were not registered to accept donations, Keryn approached them to ask about their funding sources, which left them visibly in panic.

While having fun with creative opposition tactics, Keryn, Patience, and others developed their opinions on the roots of the problem that faced them. In one, particularly elaborate blog post from 2012, Keryn criticized PJM for running an "artificial market" that does not respect "real economics." According to "real economics" driven by supply and demand, she argued that new generation sources should be created where there is demand that cannot be met by existing generation. Instead, PJM discourages the creation of new generation near demand centers and orders more and more lines cutting across its footprint to manipulate prices without changing supply and demand. If the drive behind PJM's expansion drive was economic, then it was only "artificially" so because it did not reflect supply and demand conditions on the ground. Demand on the East Coast, several studies had shown, had been decreasing in absolute terms thanks to measures of efficiency coming from demand-side management introduced by the smart-grid agenda. If the drive was one of "reliability," as PJM had claimed in its 2005 expansion initiative, then it was at best misguided because demand was not projected to increase, and the huge investment in transmission lines could be instead diverted into efficiency and demand-side management projects that decrease demand. I was struck by how devoted Keryn was to what she perceived as the logic of supply and demand, which she thought the current markets simply did not honor.

Taking this point further, Patience expressed doubts about whether the electric grid was physically a viable venue for a market to begin with. She recommended that I read an academic article titled "What's Wrong with the Electric Grid?" (Lerner 2003), which argues that opening up the electric grid to continuous trade by hundreds of participants had meant forcing the lines to carry electricity in amounts that were too close to their carrying capacity.

Deregulation, the article argued, had discouraged utilities from accomplishing the necessary yet unprofitable tasks of the electric system, such as the production of reactive power—a kind of electric power that is necessary to maintain voltage but cannot be used to power appliances and hence cannot be sold for profit. Especially in systems that have longer-distance transmission lines, reactive power was needed more and supplied less, pushing the transmission lines to their limits. Over soft-serve ice cream, Patience explained that PJM's argument to keep expanding transmission to boost reliability was illogical because, from an engineering standpoint, the most reliable circuit would be the shortest one. Patience's vision for the future entailed a different geography of electricity: one that had shorter circuits of supply, demand, and citizen participation.

Transmission opponents like StopPATH and Block RICL members are aware that the visions they articulate for alternative electricity futures will necessarily respond to environmental issues and signal their environmental convictions. I was always keen to observe how they negotiated their responses to such issues and came up with their own positions. When Keryn held a party for former members of StopPATH in her house so that I might have extended conversations with them, one woman arrived with her newly bought electric car, a Chevy Volt. When she was leaving, everyone got out to observe the car, noticed how quietly it worked, how smooth it looked, complimented it, and expressed interest in getting one in the future (including Keryn who drives an SUV). The woman joked that she felt "environmentally chic" by driving this car, which elicited chuckles from the crowd.

Negotiating where they stand in environmental issues is also important in terms of where they see themselves in relation to larger issues of social injustice. One day on the drive back home, Keryn suggested we stop by a rental store and rent *Promised Land* (2012), a fictional movie revolving around the gas industry's environmentally suspect endeavors of hydraulic fracturing (also known as "fracking"). Keryn had seen the movie before but wanted to see it again. In the movie, a landowner buys a sports car beyond his means after being promised future revenue by a gas company's land agent. Keryn remarked that this was her favorite part of the movie because it encapsulated how citizens were abused at the hands of gas and electricity companies. As the camera panned over the landscape while the land agent drove in search of new deals, Keryn cheerfully noted the prominence of the transmission lines in the landscape.

The next night, Patience joined us in Keryn's basement to watch the second installment of the documentary movie *Gasland* (2010), which had recently come out and also covers fracking. They remarked on the similarities of the tactics deployed by electricity and gas companies' land agents and noted how lucky they were to be living in the only place in West Virginia where there was no shale gas development (i.e., the eastern panhandle). They got incensed over politicians' and CEOs' pro-fracking comments they saw in the documentary. When the voiceover announced that the gas companies went after complainants with the accusation of terrorism, they looked at each other with mock panic, and (only half-) joked that they must be on a list somewhere as well.

Transmission opponents are continuously working out the environmental nuances of their visions for electricity futures. Electricity from solar sources, for instance, was particularly exciting to Patience, for, in addition to being an environmentally responsible choice, it promised to give consumers the capacity of production and consequently alter the dynamics of power that has been central to the development of the "big grid." (Solar electricity, in fact, stimulates excitement for similar reasons among Block RICL members in Illinois.) But it is important to remember that, as we see more concretely in the case of Block RICL, transmission opponents' environmental convictions are neither straightforward nor finalized. Once, Patience remarked to me, "Keryn didn't call herself an environmentalist before [starting StopPATH]," and turning to Keryn, she added provocatively: "she probably still isn't an environmentalist." Keryn retorted self-assuredly: "I'm an environmentalist with things that make sense." PATH just did not make sense to her.

Their indisputable convictions centered, instead, on private property and its inviolability. This became abundantly clear on our long drives across the eastern panhandle, during which we stopped by the houses of former StopPATH supporters, commented on how individual pieces of land were affected by various transmission lines in the past, and just took a moment to appreciate a beautifully maintained lawn. Once, we drove to the house of one of the hardest-working members of the movement (a male member in a fight largely led by women), who raised much-needed money by selling scrap metal. They had met through the movement and had become extremely close friends. He was a self-identified "hillbilly," they remarked to me with a hearty laugh. In his garage, a sign that extolled the right to bear arms was visible along with various StopPATH paraphernalia spread around, which prompted nostalgic commentary from Keryn and Patience. His teenage son, I was told, had grown up with the fight; shyly, he nodded and said, "That was fun." Omitting discussions of other political issues that could have driven a rift between them, Keryn and Patience had become close with the man and his family.

Driving elsewhere, Keryn and Patience pointed at one house after another. Here was someone who had to go back to work after the age of sixty-two because his house, which he was about to sell, had suddenly become unsellable given PATH's impending construction across the property.[5] Here was a seventy-seven-year-old man, whose land had been chopped up over the years by railroads, highways, and transmission lines, who did not believe StopPATH could win but kept on donating money. It is through stories like these that they formed bonds and a sense of ownership that extended beyond the limits of their own properties. "Property is how you become invested as a citizen," Patience remarked. Property, in this case, refers largely to homeownership—labor elsewhere (like in offices in D.C.) transformed into living spaces in the eastern panhandle of West Virginia, which then help citizens take roots in place. For Keryn, who relocated to multiple states as she grew up with her working parents, property is a desired, solid foundation—the kind that underlies motivations for political participation as a citizen. In the Illinoisan case I discuss below, property is also a function of labor *on* the land—labor that underlies claims to the land as well as the political rights to protect it.

Keryn had already been involved in the process of investing as a citizen through property ownership before StopPATH. She had started a fledgling home-owners' association, which she now sat on the board of, when the developer of the subdivision quit prematurely. When I brought up the significance of homeownership for everybody involved in StopPATH, she confirmed to me that property, in fact, was very significant to one's sense of personhood around town, especially for the farmers: "When you say 'That line is going to cross your farm, [farmers] reply, 'That line is going to cross *me*,'" she said thumping her chest. The woman who drove the Chevy Volt was originally from Washington, D.C., and had been farming for twenty years in the eastern panhandle of West Virginia, raising goats and chickens. The land agents, she relayed to me at Keryn's party, would knock on her door to ask how much she would want for her house. When she would reply that the house was not for sale, they would insist: "But, really, how much do you want?" With an indignant expression on her face, she drew an extreme comparison, telling me that this question was tantamount to asking someone to put a price tag on her child. The corporate powers, she thought, as a Christian, violated everything Jesus and his apostles preached. Her father, a developer from D.C. and a "big time Republican and capitalist," had prophesied that the US would be the end of capitalism. Given the corporate excesses she had experienced, she thought, her father might have been right.

Our conversations were permeated by both the calculable (e.g., the loss of property value) and the incalculable (e.g., emotional attachment) forms of value attached to property and the repulsion stirred by its violation. Transmission opponents' arguments resonate heavily with the classical liberal doctrine that originates in philosopher John Locke's writings. Locke wrote widely that holding property was the backbone of citizenship; people entered into society only by generating laws binding for all in order to enjoy their properties in "peace and safety" (1690 [1980], 69). Furthermore, land was the quintessential property; in Locke's figurative reconstruction of the prehistory of wealth, money appears as a way to accumulate wealth without expanding land only when one cannot possibly acquire more land while still being able to put labor into it productively. That, in fact, is the sole criterion of eligibility to property ownership; a citizen needs to make use of the land to continue claiming ownership to it. This should also be the sole criterion of arbitration in property disputes; whoever expands property at others' expense is not only being "dishonest" but also "foolish" (1690 [1980], 28) for making an unproductive investment. According to Locke, then, respecting others' property is also respecting the natural limits of productivity.

One can find strong traces of Lockean beliefs about the distribution of wealth in StopPATH members' line of thought. They are discontented over being excluded from decision-making mechanisms, which, following the Lockean logic, should exist precisely to ensure the safe and peaceful enjoyment of property. In highlighting an overlap between seventeenth-century English philosophy and twenty-first-century infrastructural politics, my goal is not to argue that anti-transmission activists draw on a repository of liberal values available to them. That kind of argument would reproduce the "liberal consensus" paradigm that deals with the question of the pervasiveness of classical liberalism in the American political culture.

"Liberal consensus" refers to a supposed societal agreement over the acceptable limits of politics that cut across all significant fractions of US politics. Policymakers started using the term in the postwar era within a context of rising anti-communist sentiment; historians contributed to this interpretation by arguing that Americans had always been motivated by notions of individual achievement, upward mobility, and material acquisition since the American Revolution, which ruled out the need for any alternative ideology like socialism in the political scene (Hartz 1955; Hofstadter 1948). Other historians have since undermined the consensus interpretation as a version of American exceptionalism neglecting the aristocratic and socialist undercurrents of American history (for a review, see Foner 1984). If liberalism has "triumphed as the dominant rhetoric of American political culture," it was because of the specific histories of the rise and fall of counter-movements, and not an innate American receptiveness for it (Foner 1984, 63).

Anti-transmission activism is not simply another instantiation of Americans' liberal reflexes, but it might illuminate how convictions that resonate with that ideology are arrived at through specific experiences with infrastructures—in this case, the experience of interruption to relatively secure property rights and expectations of fair consumption. The critique that results privileges property as fundamental to politics and is not anti-capitalistic. The denouement of PATH is a case in point that transmission opponents are not necessarily against the capitalistic order of electricity, where one class holds the means of electricity production, and another class simply consumes. Dominion, another electricity corporation that had transmission lines in the area, grew sensitive to the PATH controversy, in the words of StopPATH members, for fear of citizens turning completely against transmission. In early 2011, Dominion proposed rebuilding one of its existing 500 kV lines to increase its thermal capacity by more than half. The line, which was built in the 1960s, was crossing the land of some StopPATH members. Yet StopPATH was receptive to the proposal because it practically obviated PATH's reliability claims. When Dominion started its rebuilding project, Keryn and Patience visited a maintenance site, observing that maintenance staff took care to be considerate in their work practices to the landowners with whom they were working. Robin, whose land was crossed by Dominion's line and also threatened by PATH, reported having a good experience with Dominion to me. When some residents feared that Dominion's upgrading project was another PATH in the making, Keryn calmed them down. With characteristic humor, she once called up Dominion representatives to let them know that she was growing tired of acting as Dominion's public relations representative.

On August 28, 2012, the PJM board of managers met to discuss the recommendation of PJM staff to dismiss PATH with all stakeholders. At the end of the meeting, PJM released a short announcement noting that PATH was removed from its expansion plan due to "analyses showing reliability drivers no longer exist for the project."[6] No further explanation was made. Keryn and Patience guess that the noise that West Virginian citizens made resonated more with the Virginia State Corporation Commission (i.e., Virginia's state regulatory agency) than in West Virginia. And Dominion's announcement to rebuild the

"Mt. Storm-Doubs" transmission line was the tipping point, "where even PJM could no longer support PATH," Keryn said. She threw a funeral party for PATH at her home but did not leave the fight behind. She was getting too many emails for advice from citizens across the country whose communities were threatened by transmission lines, but she was wary of extending her involvement with fights elsewhere beyond advising new transmission opponents—to places where she did not hold property or know the land well. She has been blogging extensively since, finding new electric subjects to examine, including taking a close look at distribution rates. She has thrown her support behind Block RICL by penning opinion pieces widely shared online among electricity activists.

Even though PATH was canceled, the company still charged consumers for the expenses that they had made in the application process. These expenses included the properties that they had bought in the hopes of presenting the project to state regulatory agencies as a fait accompli. She and another woman, an elementary school teacher named Ali, took the matter to FERC. When I visited in 2013, they were in confidential settlement negotiations at FERC. Keryn was going to Washington, D.C., periodically and, after passing through involved steps of security, sitting down with federal regulators. She found FERC, the top authority in the country in all things energy, the fairest and most welcoming venue of all, while acknowledging that no average consumer could be expected to read thousands of pages of legal material to cross-examine corporate lawyers. Later in 2017, FERC ruled that PATH must refund PJM consumers for the $6 million that PJM had charged them for a canceled project. Translating into a nickel per household, it was a huge victory.[7]

## Economics across Farmland

Keryn and Patience thought I should also meet a group in the middle of its fight. They spoke often and dearly of Block RICL and introduced me to Mary, the group's spearhead, over email. Right before I left West Virginia for Illinois, Keryn gave me a book—a present for Mary. The book was about Minnesotan farmers' protest of a transmission line project in the 1970s (Casper and Wellstone 1981). For Keryn, reading up on the history of electricity was both a hobby and a way to make sense of her own activism.

Reading the book on the road was my introduction to the farmers' version of anti-transmission activism. It documented the history of a 430-mile DC line built in the 1970s to bring lignite coal-powered electricity from a plant near Bismarck, North Dakota, to the outskirts of Twin Cities and St. Paul in Minnesota. The line was the product of two historical developments. First, the Rural Electric Administration (REA), originally a creation of the New Deal that provided loans to cooperatives to encourage rural electrification, became co-opted under the Richard Nixon administration; it was now authorized to give loans to cooperative-utility partnerships, which would, in practice, be led by private utilities. Federal money originally intended to subsidize rural electrification became available for the financing of private projects, effectively ridding the REA of its original welfare state functions. Second, projects that used domestic coal reserves had become particularly desirable in response to the 1973 oil crisis, which threatened oil imports. Under these circumstances, in 1973, two cooperative utilities from Minnesota acquired the largest loan in the history of the REA to build a power plant in North Dakota near a mine of lignite coal—a kind of coal previously little esteemed for its modest capacity to generate energy. The companies' consultants generated the line's route by dividing a map of North Dakota and Minnesota into squares and assigning each square a priority number. The route avoided highways, airports, protected areas, and finally urban areas—to affect as few people as possible, the utilities argued—while cutting across most of Minnesota's prized farmland. The utilities expected that they would be authorized by county and state commissions more or less automatically, as had been the case in Minnesota in the past.

"They see the farmers as the path of least resistance," Mary would tell me later about their fight against Rock Island Clean Line, or RICL. However, just like Mary's group of landowners, Minnesotan farmers organized, hired lawyers, and overall made the utilities' job much harder. Governor Rudy Perpich (1977–1979) cited the resistance to the project as the most time-consuming issue of his tenure (Casper and Wellstone 1981, 4). After the line was completed in 1978, farmers began to sabotage the transmission towers. In 1978, Perpich undertook the largest mobilization of state troopers in Minnesota's history to defend the 430-mile line. At times, farmers and troopers entered violent confrontation. Later, the REA took ownership of the line, making the cases of sabotage a federal offense. Between 1976 and 1978, 120 arrests were made in relation to the protests; four people were convicted, one of them of a felony charge (Casper and Wellstone 1981, 286).

One Minnesotan farmer explains: "[A] fundamental issue in human relations is ownership of land. I'm not talking about the economic one your lawyer friends talk about, I'm talking about the land morality, the thing that they are

Figure 4–3. A semi owner shows support for Block RICL. Mary says many of the landowners in rural areas who are elderly "don't do internet." The word travels by the "bush telegraph"—by messages like this one.

the stewards of the land, and that they have assumed the protection of the land, and that they have done it for years of generations or months depending on the farmer, and they are the stewards, and outsiders are desecrating it with this massive thing against their will" (Casper and Wellstone 1981, 46–47). These words anticipated what Susan from Block RICL would tell me later: "Most farmers here, they have tenacity. They're vested in earth!" This is a point of view that should not be regarded as merely sentimental. It hints at a structure of value that does not conform to how a transmission company understands land: a space governed by Euclidian geometry, where transmission lines occupy a calculable and limited amount of space and detract a calculable and limited amount of value from the overall land. In farmers' understanding, on the other hand, the land has the Lockean quality of gaining value through the labor put into it; that labor is shot through with a sense of morality. The land is equally capitalistic for having the potential to yield value exponentially over time—a fact that is not factored into companies' schemes of one-time compensation.

As the Minnesotan history suggests, landowners in the American Midwest are no strangers to right-of-way requests made by infrastructure projects on their land. Scott, a man in his thirties who had been running a blog about RICL, grew up on a farm crossed by two gas pipelines and, most recently, a transmission line built by a corporation called Ameren. Over lunch at a diner in Mendota, Illinois, he told me, only half-jokingly, that he expects to see two more right-of-ways in his lifetime. In the past, his family did not fight these requests; they simply let their attorney negotiate the compensation. Ameren proposed the line that now crosses his land in 2006, arguing that there was need for more electricity service into Chicago. The corporation first proposed three routes, all of which would eventually cross Scott's family farm. His family saw little use in participating in the routing debates. Other residents were not very keen on contesting the line either. "Nobody wants to look NIMBY," Scott said; Ameren lets citizens argue over which route to select and wins at the end of the day anyway. "And you get used to it."

They received a notice from RICL two weeks after they settled on the compensation with Ameren. "We don't panic when we get these notices," he said with a laugh, adding that his family members, all of whom live on adjacent farms, had joked to each other about who would receive their notice last. Perhaps because he was used to right-of-way requests, he could sense RICL's inexperience. In open houses he attended, he observed that RICL officials did not have a clear sense about where the line would be built. This time, Scott felt, the line could be fought. At the same time, he started seeing "Block RICL" signs on the farms he drove by. A quick internet search led him to the force behind Block RICL, Mary.

In the summer of 2013, Mary had only recently returned to her native Illinois from a long stretch abroad due to her husband's work. A professional musician, Mary looked forward to resuming her work as a music teacher and a church choir director soon. But most of all, she was happy that her return to her home state had been timely—a few months after her father received word of RICL. He owned several farms including one with a half-a-mile-long runway on RICL's path, set to be unusable if the line materialized.

RICL was a much more enigmatic project than PATH. It was projected to be a 500-mile DC line bringing electricity from wind power plants in northeast Iowa to the Chicago area. But the wind power plants into which RICL was supposed to plug did not yet exist. Mary also quickly discovered with online self-education that it was technically impossible for a line to carry only wind electricity; wind's intermittent nature would destabilize the line. What is more, a 500-mile DC line is unprecedented in the US. RICL officials had pointed out that DC lines were less prone to electricity losses over long distances, but they had avoided mentioning that electricity loss would be large when DC power was necessarily converted into AC at the end of the line. Because it was a DC line, RICL could not contribute to the grid along its 500-mile trajectory; it would not benefit Iowan and Illinoisan customers along the way in terms of improved reliability or reduced wholesale prices.

Finally, RICL was proposed as a "merchant line" and not a "reliability line" like PATH had been; the investors proposed to assume all costs for the line and undertake the project only for economic gain. Merchant lines are close to nonexistent in the US, which prompted questions about how Clean Line, the company behind RICL, hoped to profit from the line; with its costs not socialized, it was not clear when, if at all, Clean Line would be able to start turning around a profit. Itself based in Houston, Texas, Clean Line had investors in a New York-based private equity firm—a company that regularly invests in oil among other things, but not electricity. Because the company was removed from the Midwest and the electricity industry, citizens expected a surprise. They surmised that Clean Line might eventually apply to Midcontinent Independent System Operator (MISO) for approval as a reliability line to pass the costs onto consumers, or more radically, use the right-of-ways that they acquired for an entirely different purpose, for instance, to build an oil pipeline. Given that right-of-ways can be transferrable, the project might be simply a financial investment, citizens thought.

These irregularities notwithstanding, citizens largely saw their struggle as a corollary to that of StopPATH—as one against unnecessary, market-driven expansion of the electric grid that ultimately threatened their own mode of economics informed by the work of landowning and, for those who owned farmland, the exigencies of farming. If the line was eventually built, it would be in no small amount due to the precedents set by MISO's reliability lines, even if the line's construction ultimately did not go through MISO. And for usage, RICL would seek payment from utilities that are MISO participants, thereby integrating it firmly in the midwestern electricity market.

On my second day as a guest in Mary's house, we drove on Interstate-80 to a law firm. Corn and bean fields, Illinois's lifeline, lay along the interstate as far as the eye could see. Mary said that the governor of Illinois, who was in favor of RICL, had once referred to the I-80 corridor while discussing RICL's route.

Yes, the route paralleled I-80, but it was ten miles away from it. "It's all part of the *cleanlinespeak*," Mary said, as she would often say referring to the selective omissions surrounding RICL. While using the existing right-of-ways would avoid taking more land, she surmised that Clean Energy did not pursue the I-80 right-of-ways because it was cheaper to deal with farmers than the state of Illinois. Mary had been drawn to spearheading the fight precisely as a result of the company's slights—particularly after an incident of a project manager's dismissive reference to affected citizens as "a bunch of farmers."

At the law firm, Mary had a meeting with other members of the Illinois Landowners Alliance (ILA). In May 2011, RICL had filed an application for utility status with Illinois Commerce Commission (ICC, the state regulatory agency as it is called in Illinois). The following year, ILA was born as a statewide coalition to fight the legal battle at the ICC. As a group of landowners, ILA began to serve as an intervenor in RICL's application to become a public utility at the ICC. Outside the law firm, Susan, an effervescent middle-aged woman, pulled into the parking lot, producing from the back of her trunk the Block RICL banners that she had just gotten from the press. "Each for less than 20 bucks!" she exclaimed. While ILA served as the legal face of citizen opposition, Block RICL's Susan shouldered the task of organizing the landowners (including a greater number of farmers than were involved in ILA) while keeping a sense of humor. Mary pointed at one of the old banners in Susan's trunk, which Block RICL supporters had signed: "When all of this is over, I want this one for my house."

At a nearby diner, we gathered for lunch. A businessman—a landowner who was at the ILA meeting beforehand—provided a visual contrast in his business suit to Mary's father, a quick-witted man in his eighties who had just joined us, and a younger farmer in their comfortable attire. The back-and-forth ensued about how everyone's soil was doing—whether they had been happy with the rain they had gotten recently. At one point, Mary's father wrapped up the farm conversation to turn to me and quickly became absorbed by talk about the line. "I don't leave the farm very often and I don't keep up with the news much," he said. One day, his sister-in-law told him about a notice she had received and asked him if he had received one as well. Both of their properties, it would turn out, were on the proposed route, but he had not received a notice. Mary jumped in to add that her aunt holds only four acres as opposed to her father's much larger acreage.

Beginning to talk with other landowners, Mary would realize that the larger one's land was, the less likely it was for them to receive a notice. "[Companies] do that to eliminate resistance," she said. Mary's father was subsequently turned away from a RICL meeting, being told that it was for business purposes only. "I told them, 'Do you think farming is not business?'" He and a few other large landowners had already been motivated to organize because of RICL's initial omissions and mistreatment. Fighting could mean provoking Clean Energy to dump RICL definitively into their territory. "But you had these stubborn men," Mary said. They asked her to organize them. Having been a church choir director for a long time, "I know that if you got talent to sing, you go and sing, and if you got a God-given talent to organize people like me, you do that." In the summer of 2013, one-third of all landowners had already become ILA members, but Mary wanted to enroll all of them.

It became clear during the lunch that the citizen activists had larger questions—maybe too many—about whether the line was needed. That is where Mary's strategizing skills came in. She would agree with most suspicions and complaints aired, but she would gently remind them that battles needed to be picked. Landowners, for instance, were wary of how long-term health effects of stray electricity from transmission lines and towers might affect their families and crops. Mary turned to me to say that a RICL document had cited a 1987 article to shut down this concern. ("Who cites a 1987 article," she asked rhetorically.) But she thought that this concern would make a weak argument to build a case around. She reminded everyone that they had to stick to their point about how the line was not needed. Was Illinois not an exporter of electricity? Did a nuclear plant not just shut down because of decreasing demand? Why did they need Iowan wind power when demand was decreasing already? The landowner in the business suit jumped on this to agree and develop an anti-renewable point; why did they need the unreliable electricity from renewable power plants instead of reliable coal and nuclear-generated electricity from large in-state employers? As I began to see how a more generalized distaste against wind and even renewables writ large was coming alive around RICL, Mary jumped in again; solar electricity was not to be lumped in with wind and, more important, they had to focus on the fact that RICL was an unnecessary venture whose costs exceeded its benefits. Mary always kept a pen and paper out, noting the points and phrases that she thought were effective, to be used later in ILA's testimonies at the state commission.

Mary and Susan cheerfully remarked that their relationship mirrored that of Keryn and Patience. Mary was the "big picture" person who came up with arguments and testimonies; Susan dealt with outreach to Iowa and other states where Clean Line pursued similar projects. They thought of outreach as critical; when a RICL employee told a landowner that other landowners had already agreed to provide right-of-ways or sell their property, Mary and Susan could easily check the veracity of that information. This duo, too, made sure to have fun along the way. They told me about a senior woman in their ranks, who accompanied Mary and Susan to an event where an executive of Clean Line gave a presentation. The woman grilled him in the question-and-answer period; at the end, she was personally approached by him and asked about the then-emerging opposition. He then expressed disappointment that RICL employees were not invited to citizens' meetings. (Mary thought it was ironic that RICL was offended to miss only one Block RICL event, while citizens had been blocked from all RICL events.) But instead, the senior woman, in her soft-spoken voice, joked to him that RICL was very much hated in their county, so the meeting hosts would not be able to guarantee him safe passage were he invited.

At the end of the lunch, Mary's father apologized to me for fear of having complained too much. "It has been really personal for us," he said, before extending an offer to me to visit his farm soon. Over the drive back home with Mary, we passed by tens of Block RICL yard signs, each of which made Mary visibly proud. She remembered the first time when, within the first months of the fight, she saw the signs that she had handed out while driving around the state and felt like the fight could be won. The first Block RICL meeting was attended by 400 landowners instead of the expected 15. The elderly landowners in rural areas "don't do internet," she said, and credited the "bush telegraph" for the speed at which the word for the meeting spread. Upon seeing the signs, some had originally thought "Block Ricl" was the name of a political candidate. They asked each other about it at local diners. Shortly after, LaSalle County, a county that has political weight in Illinois, asked Clean Line not to contact it again before acquiring approval from the state commission. This was Block RICL's first major gain. Then, one by one, even the most cynical landowners were won to the fight. The anti-renewable landowner from the lunch, for instance, was at first only interested in negotiating a good compensation. Now, nothing short of stopping the line would satisfy him.

The conflict between RICL and Block RICL comes down to a fundamental difference in how the parties view the land, economically speaking. The maps that citizens encountered in PATH and RICL's open houses evoked an anchored, stable, and bounded entity (de Certeau 1984, 117–18), which did not account for the topography experienced by farmers and other landowners. Mary, for instance, was told at an open house that RICL's wires would be held up in the air by monopole towers. When RICL's application to the state commission surfaced, it turned out that the proposal had included lattice towers. Standing up on four feet, lattice towers would make a larger area of soil unfarmable. In RICL's interpretation of the land, the towers' impact on the farm would be limited to the area that they would occupy. Limited and calculable, the impact could be compensated for by money. Accordingly, they repeatedly suggested that farmers could continue to farm around the towers—for instance, to aerially spray their crops. A licensed private pilot like many in her family, Mary disagreed; to operate a plane so closely to transmission towers and lines, "you have to take your life in your hands." And without aerial spraying, "you could lose your entire crop." To help people grasp the landscape change at stake, she put up a picture on Block RICL's website: a tower proposed by RICL next to an image of the Statue of Liberty, to scale. The towers, at 200 feet tall, would stand 50 feet taller than Lady Liberty. (The patriotism evoked by the image was a bonus.)

On a breezy Sunday, Mary's father welcomed us to his farm, where he spends most of his days. This was where Mary had grown up. Outside the modest, one-story house where her father lived alone, we picked luscious white transparent apples from trees. When she was growing up, Mary shared a bedroom with two sisters in that house. It was on contiguous farmland that Mary's parents had put together over forty years.

In the tool shed, I marveled at the size of the planter with six rows, the driller, and the wagons that carry a thousand bushels each. Mary noted that another ILA member's equipment was twice as big. I climbed up the 9-foot tall tractor and sat in the comfortable cab, while Mary's father, sitting next to me, told me about all the impressive new digital features meant to assist the driver, including a GPS navigator. Piloting the same tractor around the perimeter of the house, however, I came to agree that narrow turns were not this tractor's strong suit. But piloting was not the only problem. Even if you could successfully operate a sprayer around the 46 by 46 square foot tower, I was told, by the time you backed up, you would have sprayed parts of the crop twice and almost certainly killed them. Furthermore, the lines sag—especially in the summer, from heat—to the point where tractors cannot go underneath. If the lines and towers sustain any damage during farming operations, the liability lies with the farmers.

The size and shape of the land are aspects of farming's economic exigencies that would necessarily escape RICL executives. Farmers upheld a version of

Figure 4–4. Mary's father's tool shed.

the economies of scale—one that was informed by the affordances of farming technology. Mary's father's farm was flat and long, but not quite wide. That is what made it so valuable. The flat and long field was divided into rows for the machines to traverse. Having to operate the machines at an angle, or "kitty cornering," meant that part of the soil would not be worked by the machines to its potential. Expanding contiguous farmland being a prized achievement, having the land chopped up by transmission lines and highways was a most feared outcome. Farmers whose land was crossed by highways experienced a lot of difficulty operating the equipment across; most people eventually gave up on the isolated parts of their property. As to Mary's father, I sensed ambivalence. Having managed the farm alone since Mary's mother's passing, he was weary: "If they came through my land, I would just give it up, retire, rent out the farm," he said early on into our conversation. Later during the day, however, after a long discussion of all the hardship he had endured to put the farm together, he looked me in the eye and said, "If they come and try to get my land, I will fight them."

Taking in the breeze, we walked along rows of sweet corn. Mary's father made me pick a cob and feel the top. The roundness on top meant that it was ready to be picked, so we tossed it onto the pushcart. Fortunately, he said, the machines were doing this now, but it had not been so all along. Mary's family had moved there when she was in fourth grade and started out with very low-tech equipment. They pointed at their old tractor still sitting in the tool shed as a memento. Small and without a cab, it did not look anything like the one that I had just driven. Mary's mother drove the cab-less tractor to the nearby elevator—the proximity of the elevator was another reason why their land was so valuable—all day despite freezing cold temperatures. When they bought their first tractor with a cab, two years before she died, she was over the moon. But despite all the work and good luck, Mary said, the farm remained a gamble for a long time. Her father worked as a commercial pilot for United Airlines and channeled every penny to the farm. In high school, Mary, like most of her peers, worked through summers at Del Monte's nearby canned vegetables factory. She eventually put herself through college. Giving me a quick mathematical account of the equipment, seed, and planting expenses, Mary told me that a few hundred acres less land would be completely impossible to raise a family on. The farm started turning around only when she was already in college. Then, United Airlines filed for bankruptcy in 2002 and defaulted on employees' pension plans. Her father lost his pension. The farm became his only retirement fund.

Seen through this lens, land is not an "inert body" (de Certeau 1984, 118), but a generative space, which has the potential of producing more value than it presently possesses. Contrariwise, when an obstruction is built on it, the land may lose more value than the value of the soil lost to the obstruction. In other words, towers cannot safely extract a limited amount of value from the overall value of the land. Deploying yet another crafty analogy—one they were both proud of—Mary and Susan referred to farms as "nonrenewable" resources, the waste of which must be regarded as severely as the depletion of nonrenewable energy sources. Farmers I talked to pointed out several factors that chip away at the value of farms and squander farmland even beyond the land lost to transmission towers. To build towers, for instance, companies have to build access roads. The vehicles used in construction contribute to soil compaction indefinitely. Soil compaction, many farmers noted from experience, is irreversible.

If gold were discovered underneath your land, Mary asked me rhetorically, would that make your land less valuable and subject to eminent domain? If not, why is that what becomes of the land on the route of a transmission line? The right-of-ways for transmission lines (as opposed to the case with wind turbines) are acquired for perpetuity, and neither the compensation for right-of-ways nor the offers to buy out the land reflect the value that the land may acquire over time. The value that can be added to the land over time, in turn, cannot be calculated using interest rates. It depends on the labor one chooses and is able to put in it. Walking along rows of soybean plants in Mary's father's farm, I heard the constant buzz of bees. Bees pollinate soybean plants and increase yields. But they could abandon the crop if the farm came under transmission lines, Mary's father said to me. "We just don't know." On the way back, Mary and I drove by farm after farm. She often commented on how others took care of their own farms, voicing disapproval over how some farmers let their farms be taken over by weeds.

On my last day in Illinois, Susan took me the Mendota Sweet Corn Festival, where Block RICL would participate in a parade. Walking with the Block RICL car for forty-five minutes, I handed out flyers to Illinoisans who had lined up. While a few times I did get the question of who "Block Ricl" was and what political office he was running for, most people were already aware of the movement and, thinking that I was a part of it, thanked me and asked me to keep up the fight. After I left Illinois, ILA and Block RICL's fight was protracted. The state commission first granted RICL public utility status (which would earn it the power of eminent domain), but the decision was reversed at an appellate court in 2017, and that decision was upheld by the Illinois Supreme Court in the same year, killing the project for good. In the meantime, Block RICL has increased outreach extensively and encouraged the formation of other groups in Missouri, Oklahoma, Kansas, and elsewhere, where Clean Energy has had transmission projects in the works. Many victories for the movement have been won; Iowa, for instance, passed a law generally prohibiting transmission line projects from exercising eminent domain. Mary has continued organizing others through social media, and Susan still periodically undertakes visits across and outside the state. RICL was a gateway to their electric activism.

## The Promise and Peril of Infrastructure

Strong support for each other notwithstanding, StopPATH and Block RICL had been different in certain respects. StopPATH had a generally positive proclivity for environmentalism, while that agenda, at least phrased in that way, took a backseat among Block RICL sympathizers. The leaders of both groups avoided mention of political parties or ideological identification (remember Mary's pleas to stick to the point), although StopPATH hailed from a largely blue-voting area and Block RICL from a largely red one. They knew these things about each other, but somehow that had no effect on how they esteemed each other, even in the political environment in the US that has gotten much more polarized since my original fieldwork. Block RICL members made sure to credit StopPATH for blazing the trail to an electric consciousness. They maintained close contact online, sharing and promoting each other's stories. What to make of a politicization that does not follow apparent nationwide political divides?

I have maintained that, just like experts tracked earlier in this book, citizen activists also have a politics assembled through particular experiences that do not necessarily trickle down from preexisting ideologies or social values. There is a promise in this fact in terms of new kinds of emergent, indeterminate, sometimes surprising politics. Anthropologists Hannah Appel, Nikhil Anand, and Akhil Gupta remind us how infrastructures have "long promised modernity, development, progress, and freedom to people all over the world"—a promise inevitably threatened by the vulnerability of the same infrastructures: "The material and political lives of infrastructure frequently undermine narratives of technological progress, liberal equality, and economic growth, revealing fragile and often violent relations between people, things, and the institutions that govern or provision them" (2018, 5). The promise, I would add, is in the opening of a space that generates new politics and unlikely alliances. The peril is in the ossification of that politics and its fall back onto predictable ideological lines.

Susan spoke of Block RICL's activism proudly as something that gave women who were previously not too vocal in matters of governance a reason to articulate themselves. When I met her husband at the Mendota festival, he was helping the Block RICL car but looked distracted, which prompted Susan to chuckle and emphasize the role of women as the leading force in the fight. Another time, she told me about a senior woman, the "epitome of a farm wife," who had built the drainage tiles for her entire community decades ago and had been told by her husband how important it was to maintain them. When RICL came for the line, she felt stricken for her late husband's memory. Susan drafted her story, she proofed it, and together, they sent it to the local newspaper. Susan told me how proud the woman was of the published piece. "All these years she let the men do everything. Now she had a voice." It was the promise of the infrastructure at work.

There was a peril in how wind electricity made its appearance in the area and how it was received. Many have derived from their anti-RICL activism stances against wind electricity—the kind of energy that RICL was supposed to carry. Their fight was one step removed from electricity markets compared to StopPATH; the critique they developed of transmission lines, on the other hand, more or less applied to wind turbines across the state. For clues into the moments where that attitude was cultivated, let us go back to how Susan found herself doing activist work. Before it all began for her, Susan received a note in the mail about RICL's open house. She went, by her own account, with no expectations. A young woman Susan thought to be a college intern greeted her at the door with an exuberant smile and asked her, "Are you ready to be a part of the clean energy future?" Susan remembered thinking, "I guess." Inside were free food and routing maps. When citizens pointed out anything about the maps, the employees thanked them exaggeratedly for their concern, but did not seem to take notes. Susan thought that the open house was a smokescreen but did not know what could be done. She heard a neighbor angrily walking out shouting, "I'm hiring a lawyer." These stories of slights by infrastructure building companies were a big part of our conversations.

Susan lived on a small farm with her farmer husband and grown children. Her property was next to RICL's route; she would not receive any compensation if RICL was built. She resented having to live under a line and lose her view of clear skies. RICL's proposed towers were tall enough that they would, in all likelihood, be lit up so as to be visible to air traffic. Susan did not enjoy the "light pollution" that the towers would create, as well as the light pollution already created by wind turbines. Driving me around, she repeatedly commented unfavorably on the turbines' red blinking lights, visible from miles away in the flat landscape of Illinois. "At night, they all light up at the same time," she complained. When I asked Susan if RICL caused an anti-wind attitude in Illinois, she said RICL had not *caused* an anti-wind attitude; it had only made *evident* to people the fact that wind farms were inefficient. Referring to the federal tax credits that wind farms received from the federal government, she noted that it was unfair for taxpayers to collectively pay for them. Voicing a concern that others in the movement shared, she added that wind farms were "not designed" to keep jobs in Illinois. The federal support for renewable energy had become a way for outside capital to take advantage of Illinois's resources, be it out of state, as in the case of RICL, or out of country, as others feared.

Like many other states, Illinois enacted a Renewable Portfolio Standard (RPS) Act in 2007. RPS programs require utilities in a state to purchase a set percentage of their electricity from renewable power plants. In Illinois's case, this percentage was set at twenty-five. The Act made Illinois one of the leading hubs in wind energy development in the country, creating the wind turbine landscape that Susan now resents. But recently, the Act has come repeatedly under attack from people on both sides of the environmental spectrum. The Act created the Illinois Power Agency (IPA)—an agency that buys electricity from renewable power plants on behalf of the state's two largest utilities, Ameren and ComEd. The IPA-negotiated long-term contracts with renewable power plants raised the prices for Ameren and ComEd consumers. As a result, many Illinois municipalities, exercising their right guaranteed under another Illinois law, switched to alternative utilities that sell electricity at cheaper prices. These utilities fulfill their RPS requirements by buying renewable energy certificates from out-of-state projects. On the one hand, environmentalists are angry that the Act is no longer providing renewable electricity producers with the long-term contracts that they need to start costly new projects. On the other hand, large energy corporations protest subsidies allocated to wind farms. An effort to fix the Act died in the summer of 2015 after Exelon threatened to shut down two or three of its nuclear plants.[8] In conversations with me, many citizens made a point to voice preference for nuclear power plants over wind farms for providing in-state employment and reliable electricity.

Scott blogged extensively against Illinois's RPS. He wrote unfavorably about Illinois's executive branch for supporting the wind industry, endorsing RICL, and lobbying the IPA for securing long-term contracts with renewable power plants, which raised overall prices but were necessary for increasing the share of renewable electricity in the electricity mix. Politics is the problem, Scott remarked to me during our conversation. The pro-coal presidents of the 1970s expanded the transmission system (to the dismay of Minnesotan farmers), he argued, and now a pro-wind administration (at the time the Barack Obama administration) was encouraging economically unjustifiable wind projects. I pressed Scott as to what should drive electricity decisions if not politics. He answered as promptly as one could: "competitive pricing." Solar-generated electricity, he added with zest, was probably going to become "feasible," which had already scared energy giants like Exelon. As long as different entrepreneurs were allowed to compete to reduce prices, the US would not need further growth of electricity consumption or transmission expansion to drive the growth of the economy, he said referring to a report by the Energy Information Agency.

Just like Keryn who thought that electricity markets were not honoring the basics of supply and demand, Scott believed in competitive pricing, but not in electricity markets as they exist. He admitted that, until a year before (i.e., 2012), when he started educating himself by reading Keryn's blog, he had not even heard of PJM. "Now I know it's a cartel." All enterprises, including solar- and wind-based ones, had to be judged by their capacity to produce affordable electricity. Originally skeptical about solar electricity, Scott was turned on to it after reading a blog post by another blogger from West Virginia—a farmer who also worked for solar cooperatives.

Scott's vision of sound economics made scarce room for climate change. He acknowledged to me the specifics of Block RICL that might distinguish it from other anti-transmission groups. Scott met Keryn and Patience, both of whom he respects immensely, in person at an anti-transmission meeting in Wisconsin. He was surprised to meet activists there from other states who were concerned about fracking and silica sand factories for their effects on human health and the environment. "We have so many of those here," he said referring to the latter, and the only time people protested was when the construction blocked a road. Similarly, when he mentioned the Northern Pass, another transmission line project meant to bring electricity from Quebec to Massachusetts, he noted almost with disbelief that the protesters in New England worried about the line's visual effects on the landscape. He knew of other activists' environmental concerns but could not relate to them. "Here in the Midwest," the only thing that mattered to people was soil, he thought.

Of course, Scott cannot speak for everyone in the Midwest or even Block RICL. Supporters of Block RICL, like all citizens, have a varied set of concerns; as I discussed, Susan was indeed concerned with landscape degradation. But in terms of priorities, his thinking aligned with those of other Block RICL supporters. A concern for land (specifically farmland for those who had it) trumped any other. They challenged not the capitalist order of electricity, but its current incarnation that equates land with money, instantiated in the specific transmission line project that they fought. They argued, in fact, in favor of a capitalist order of electricity driven by what they viewed as the forces of sup- ply and demand—an order that they thought would respect the efficient use of resources whether those resources were used to produce electricity or crops. Still, solar electricity had become legible to Scott through the relationships he cultivated across the country in his anti-transmission fight and reading of his peers. That is the promise of the infrastructure. The peril is in the ossification of that politics—complex matter like wind or electricity becoming stand-ins for other political conversations.

## Conclusion

"When this is all over, I want them [Clean Line] to remember that their project was halted by a church choir director" Mary told me once. She and Susan were laughing at how Clean Line had once referred to them as "radicals" in a press piece. Citizen electric does not uphold radical politics, for certain. Members of StopPATH and Block RICL, as well as the various like-minded groups they have inspired across the country, might have grievances about the regulations that govern electricity and its markets, but they ultimately trust the rule of law. They believe in the morality of licit ways to critique regulations; they hope to transform and enforce regulation as the solution to corporations' wrongdoings. The electricity industry, in its turn, cannot be truly accused of radicalism in terms of the methods it pursues either. Despite all her aggravation with the electricity industry, Keryn once gave in that, had she been going after the coal industry instead, "I would have had an accident by now," putting "accident" in air quotes.

What made the possibility of a classically liberal relationship between consumers and public utilities out of reach for Sowetan water consumers, like a stable monthly income (von Schnitzler 2008), has been within citizen electric's reach. The groups I discussed here consist predominantly of white property owners, although they exhibit variation on income, class, and education. Even though they did not themselves possess legal know-how, engineering expertise, or access to decision-making mechanisms, they did have the know-how to appeal to lawyers and, at least in the case of the movements' leaders, the time to study the regulations of the electric grid. They are surely not the only kind of electricity consumers in the US, but they are unique in the sense of having actively developed a consciousness as electricity consumers and a critique of the current economy through which electricity reaches them. They are, I suggest, that economy's most sustained and substantive critics to date. Their critique is the final building block of the current economy I trace in this book, one with which the experts must contend.

Citizen electric's case is that of a pocket of anti-market organization at home within a capitalist formation. It is a case of an "economic imagination" (Appel 2014) coming to life, not only among the professionals I depicted earlier but also among those who critique those experts' creations and live with them. The purview of techno-economics extends to not only spaces of professional expertise but also everyday encounters with infrastructures. Citizen electric's imagination does not seek to overhaul the current economy as it exists—the economy where electricity has long been a commodity and not a public good or a human right. Instead, she wants electricity flows to be governed with her home, land, and voice in mind. Some of what she wants overlaps with what I called everyday optimizing markets; both the activists and the smart-grid engineers are interested in efficiency measures that will avoid unnecessary infrastructure construction. But those overlaps remain limited as do the conversations between citizen electric and my expert interlocutors.

There is promise embedded in citizen electric's imagination and in her ability to politically recreate herself. There is peril in the lack of communication between electricity's experts and her. If the promise wins out in the future, citizen electric's imagination may translate into political transformations in the grid in subtle ways, for instance, by consumers slowly acquiring production capabilities and launching cooperative arrangements that correspond to smaller representative circuits. Those transformations would reorganize what it means to be a consumer, a producer, and a citizen. The new forms of citizenship and belonging people may develop while inhabiting public infrastructures would also mean a new economy for the fleeting current that is electricity.

# EPILOGUE

## Techno-Economics

Now it is two in the afternoon: still the first day of our electricity market training held by ISO-NE, a nonprofit company that operates New England's electric grid and electricity markets. The participants—traders, analysts, accountants, engineers, regulators, and me—are fidgety and tired from following slide shows and practicing calculating prices and voltages. Most of the presenters have painted a picture of a well-oiled machine—of money and electricity smoothly traveling across the grid. For instance, when I chat during a break with the training coordinator about how I am interested in the intersection of economic knowledge and engineering practice, he lets out an enthusiastic "That's ISO-NE for you!" He jokes that recapping the contents of this weeklong training should be enough for my research publications.

After all this optimism, the afternoon presenter's cynicism comes across as refreshing to my classmates. Larry's[1] first slide is titled "Some economics: the big picture." The subtitle consists of an existential question for the purposes of our training: "Why use a market-based system to price electricity?" Larry lets us ponder the question for a few seconds, then clicks to reveal the answer: "Microeconomic theory says it improves efficiency!" It is more a joke than an answer and Larry makes sure the joke is on the discipline of economics; he says he had an economist from his team put this slide together for him. It appears he is not too interested in winning us over to the raison d'être of electricity markets.

We are made to understand his nonchalance comes from his seniority at ISO-NE. Larry has been at the company for more than twenty years. After having worked in several teams over the years, he has graduated to a small team removed from day-to-day operations, exploring future technological paths for the company. On his consulting-like, low-stress job, he works with nine doctorate holders: engineers and economists. My job, he says drily, is translating what they say to "non-PhD" for the sake of the rest of the company. Larry was there when the company was a voluntary power pool between monopolist utilities in the 1990s. He saw its transition to ISO status legally entitled to run markets at the beginning of the twenty-first century. My long years here, he says, is my job security. "The company wants to keep around somebody who remembers the old days."

Emboldened by Larry's cynicism, the participants keep raising their hands to return to the presentation's opening question. Did markets work? Did overall costs and prices actually go down in the US after markets came along? It is clear that the opening question is motivated by sheer curiosity; no one's professional development will benefit from answering it. And Larry does not try too hard to answer either. Just like economist Richard Schmalensee, to whom I asked the same fateful question, he says market regions and nonmarket regions in the US are too different to isolate the effect of markets in a comparison. Like Schmalensee, he adds cautiously that one could perhaps compare the changes that occurred in the mix of fuel sources before and after markets, but even that is too complex a research question to answer definitively. The question of whether the introduction of markets into electricity's trade has been a good thing at all hangs awkwardly in the ballroom-turned-classroom. We are unable to answer what seems to be a basic question about our joint topic of interest. Whether markets are the fairest organizers of exchange, in electricity or otherwise, will not come up again during the week.

What does it take to build markets in electricity—how do economic ambitions, engineering expertise, and more prosaic know-how come together to make something like electricity, once near-universally thought to be unbefitting of markets, subject to everyday competitive trade? This is the question that this book tackles. I started out by noting something field professionals have repeated to me hundreds of times: Electricity is uniquely quirky as far as commodities go. Except for quantities insignificant for trade, it cannot be stored; except for a few rare and expensive cases, it cannot be shipped to or imported from overseas. The lessons of capitalism learned in other markets cannot be applied to it all too directly. One needs new ways to marry different kinds of expertise and work to allow for competition in electricity. One needs to "glue" Kirchhoff's electricity transmission laws to marginal cost pricing, for instance, to use the language of one of the first market builders in electricity. In that vein, this book charts the specific forms that "gluing" has taken in the past and present of electricity's trade, as well as instances where the glue came off.

But electricity may be less unique than what its experts believe. It is, in fact, quite ordinary that every commodity should have its technical quirks. Every commodity, that is, requires accommodation to be eased into market circulation. Oranges, for instance, require that their storage temperature be adjusted over time so that acidity and flavor are preserved. Natural gas can travel in the ocean, though only in cryogenic temperatures in specialized vessels by way of specialized ports. In that vein, this book has pursued larger questions about market making and maintenance in our moment in capitalism, to which electricity's case is but one answer. With what ambitions do market actors begin to cluster around objects in the economic world? How do they go about building markets-—forms of structured and sustained competition—around them? How do they honor those objects' differences so rules, regulations, and algorithms can be put forth with the expectation that they will work routinely with few exceptions? And equally important, who are these market actors to begin with? Why do they do what they do—why do they contribute to the creation of markets in parts of everyday life where none existed previously?

In the case of electricity, I have found that it takes a number of groups, steeped in particular work cultures, to make, maintain, transform, and populate the current economy where electricity is a tradable commodity—one whose exchange can be trusted to fairly permanent social and technical routines. What I mean here by fairly permanent is that whether the transmission lines can carry all the demand that will incur at a price point, for instance, does not need to be recalculated every day; the market is, in fact, the data-laden and electronic processes that routinize the trade and minimize such physical errors or other exceptions. Electricity's economy continues to be shaped by such groups as electrical engineers in conversations with economists, data workers who create electronic representations of electricity, optimization-minded grid engineers who design future smart grids, and everyday consumers-turned-critics.

Being steeped in work cultures may result in language barriers between different groups. That is what Larry light-heartedly commented on when he defined his job as one of a translator between different groups. Much of this book is set within milieus where translation between vernaculars is not necessary— sometimes work cultures are sequestered and their members interact with only their kindred for long stretches of time with no need for much translation. Let us consider the notion of time, for instance. When the data workers of chapter 2 used the phrase "real time," they referred to not an abstract concept but the specific real-time markets run by ISOs. When the grid engineers of chapter 3 used the same phrase, they referred to an aspirational window of time—much shorter than what the current grid could register—where consumers' smaller actions of consumption could be accounted for. The citizen critics of chapter 4 thought in longer time horizons: equity built through homeownership and contiguous farmland put together in generations' time. A setting like a market training session, on the other hand, brings together people from different work cultures and exposes such differences in understanding and articulation. In such instances, many market actors demonstrate an awareness of themselves as speakers of economic vernaculars, steeped in an agenda sometimes barely intelligible to others. The optimization-minded grid engineers, for instance, joked to me often about how preoccupied they were with optimization in their profession in a way that made them process every single problem they encountered in life as one of optimization.

Such self-teasing commentary reveals both deep immersion in a work culture as well as the ability to step out of it to offer commentary on one's immersion. It also signals a willingness to step out of one's own vernacular, at least every now and then, to begin to entertain counterfactuals and ask existential questions about the work one is engaged in, like the work of electricity markets. The citizen critics, for instance, often insisted that the experts to whose whims they were subjected should "come and talk to real people." They were prepared for such confrontations since they had already mastered their opponents' language and were bent on proving to them the current markets' inefficiencies. For a brief but lively moment, the participants in my market training session were interested in stepping out of their concerns to "match the numbers" or "understand how we make money" to ask what electricity markets had achieved. People develop, as this book maintains, original economic reasonings while engaged in the everyday work of maintaining spreadsheets, running grid scenarios for better algorithms, or harvesting crops from underneath a transmission line, but they also take a moment to consider what lies beyond, however briefly. Work cultures are not static; our everyday toolkits to which we have access give us repertoires of rituals and actions, as sociologist Ann Swidler posits (1986), but they do not necessarily lock us into a particular economic vision forever. It is possible to take a break from work and take a peek outside the office window as I frequently did at EnTech. It is possible to see beyond the current economy while immersed in it.

This is the rich field of techno-economics I want to highlight—the field of visions that emerge both during moments of immersion in one's work culture and moments of stepping out of it. Techno-economics is where the economic is a function of the technological—where the toolkits available to specific work cultures help curate the range of economic actions people can take. Techno-economics is kindred to techno-politics—a field of study through which scholars diagnose how technocrats, technicians, and experts of many kinds undertake profoundly political projects that present an apolitical façade (Barry 2002; Mitchell 2002). In that vein, techno-economics is a study of the many economic projects surrounding us that have limited or no links to an overt agenda of political economy or ideology. These are projects in technological infrastructure building, maintenance, and inhabitancy, and as such, they call for the work of those actors that operate outside the immediate domain of economic theory or explicitly political agenda. The practitioners of techno-economics are all around us building, maintaining, and transforming the economic formations with which we live.

The field of the techno-economic is particularly rife for empirical study in the US, where distinct forms of politics that cannot be easily pinned to ideologies frequently emerge and take root in technological workspaces. Critics observing Silicon Valley tech-entrepreneurs' beliefs, for instance, have referred to a certain "techno-liberalism," marked by progress by way of technological innovation in an otherwise conflict-free society (Kelkar 2018; Kelty 2014; Malaby 2012). Despite those entrepreneurs' more or less consistent voting behavior (Ferenstein 2015), their particular brand of politics is too specific to be explained away by party affiliation. Much remains to be done to unearth what pockets of economics and politics exist in contemporary spaces of everyday work and life—what technological pedagogies and toolkits sustain them—in the US as elsewhere. Similarly, much remains to be done to extend our critical eye to spaces of work less associated with professional expertise, like activities of householding, landowning, and farming; we need to see those places for the technological and economically generative spaces they are. Anthropological studies of the techno-economic promise to make timely connections in ethnographic representation between otherwise disparate nodes of social life, like expertise and wires, law and steel, and, economics and electricity.

There is a path for anthropological responsibility in the study of techno-economics. While studying as extensive an object as the electric grid, one notices the disconnects between different nodes, not only due to language barriers but also due to the pressing nature of work and life in the everyday. It is all too easy for an expert of electricity market expert, for instance, to never find a way to go and "talk to real people" as citizen critics had asked. The anthropologist's role, then, is to connect the dots between the different nodes in ethnographic representation. It is also our role to sustain those fleeting questions that come up in moments of cross-communication. During the market training session, those kinds of questions—whether markets, in their current or future forms, have been the fairest or most efficient methods of exchange—came up only briefly. After all, the accountant, by her own account, had simply shown up to learn how to match the numbers and the executive had simply shown up to learn how his company made money. Despite their run-of-the-mill reasons to be there, in that brief moment, I could observe the invigorating energy of those questions going around in the room. I could see how people suddenly sat up in their seats and how even the trader glued to his phone finally lifted his eyes. These questions may be as easy to table as they are invigorating, for the everyday work of necessities never ends. For anthropology, there is an opportunity to make note of these questions and carry them forward.

During my research, I attempted such connections by reporting on my fieldwork from one node to interlocutors in another, either in formal presentations or during chats. I observed how, for instance, many of my expert interlocutors were sympathetic to the travails of citizen activists (the experts were, after all, everyday electricity consumers themselves). But beyond a listening ear, I also observed how they could not envision their work as in the same field as that of the citizen activists' problems. Their sympathies, in other words, were constrained by the range of actions afforded to them by their toolkits. This is why there is work ahead for anthropologists beyond collecting and sustaining our interlocutors' questions. If economic formations emerge in the techno-economic territory, what does that mean for methods to alter them? How does one go about building different, better formations—better, more just economic worlds?

The answer is not categorically different from what might apply to my interlocutors who are engineers, data workers, optimizers, psychologists, and citizen activists. The answer has to do with building new techno-economic cultures, complete with toolkits that will help redistribute resources. Building techno-economic cultures requires being at peace with inhabiting a technological milieu, being ensconced in particular technological toolkits, and engaging with vernacular economics rampant in these milieus—and not operating from a place of mere rejection or refusal. What interventions redistribute resources or wealth better across specific communities? What toolkits best support our economic visions for the future? What economic imaginations do we need to marshal to assemble a better economic order? Those are the hard questions that face us in the current economy—of electricity or otherwise.

# NOTES

## INTRODUCTION

1. While this book is set in the fully electrified context of the US, an estimated 1.1 billion people remain without electricity access according to the World Bank's most recent data. Out of the 217 countries and territories tracked, 95 have electrification rates below 100 percent (see data.worldbank.org). Electricity remains far from taken for granted for everyday consumers in contexts of electrification—it is, instead, an object of humanitarianism, ingenuity, or improvisation (Cross 2013; Degani 2018).

2. Interview with Richard Schmalensee, 23 May 2013.

3. Alternating current became the industry standard in the US in the late nineteenth century after what became known as the "war of currents" between Thomas Edison, who built a direct current–based grid in New York, and George Westinghouse, who, with help from Nikola Tesla, built an AC-based grid in the American Midwest (T. Hughes 1993). Transporting electricity via AC causes fewer losses during transportation than DC. Although the majority of transmission lines across the world are AC lines, DC is still used, for instance, to create weak, emergency-only connections between otherwise separate grids because DC, as opposed to AC, does not create or require synchrony between the grids it connects.

4. According to the *Oxford English Dictionary*, the term "grid" was applied to a number of assemblages that involved lines and connected objects. The dictionary cites US and UK publications from the 1920s and 1930s that refer to an "electric grid"—roughly the period when connections between individual nodes, or producers of electricity, started to increase in both countries, resulting in the emergence of "interconnected grids" (see oed.com).

5. See *https://www.iso-ne.com/about/key-stats/*.

6. "EnTech" and the names of EnTech employees used in this book are pseudonyms. EnTech generously allowed me to learn by doing as an intern on a mapping project and write about how the firm operates.

## CHAPTER 1

1. This chapter reports from three interviews: with Richard Schmalensee (23 May 2013), Richard Tabors (22 January 2015), and Ignacio Pérez-Arriaga (9 May 2013).

2. "Liberal" denoting "left-wing" is a phenomenon quite particular to the US (Conover and Feldman 1981).

3. As used as US audiences are to the current color coding of electoral maps, red and blue denoting Republican and Democratic voting tendencies has a relatively recent history, going back only to the 2000 presidential elections (Battaglio 2016).

4. As opposed to futures transactions, where the price is established for the exchange of a commodity on a set date in the future, in spot transactions, the exchange is to be settled immediately following the transaction, the meaning of "immediately" depending on the specific market. The meanings of spot prices change by the commodity, but for the purposes of Schweppe and his group, the essential purpose of the term was to distinguish it from regulated prices—prices set by utilities and vetted by state regulators in infrequent intervals such as once or twice a year. Schweppe and his coauthors often qualify the term in the book as in "hourly spot prices." Today, the Locational Marginal Prices that electricity markets deploy are a form of spot pricing.

5. Schweppe wrote, "Today the relationship between customer and utility is one of master to slave. The customer is the master who demands power from the utility, his slave. The slave is expected to provide as much power as the master wants, any time the master wants it. The control systems reflect this relationship because they are designed to help the slave do everything possible to meet the master's demands. When control systems push the slave beyond its limits, the slave collapses and the master is left on his own" (Schweppe 1978, 44). It must be noted that, in using such a disturbing analogy while discussing engineering concepts, Schweppe was unfortunately not alone. Across different kinds of engineering, the master/slave metaphor has been used into the present century to denote arrangements where one component follows the signals from the other component, like synchronizing clocks (Eglash 2007). It is possible that Schweppe was encouraged to use such language by the relative ubiquity of this metaphor in engineering. The metaphor caught on in the 1960s, a long time after slavery ended in the US, potentially as a result of the emergence of mechanisms with a subservient yet relatively autonomous component, such as robotic systems (Eglash 2007). According to Ron Eglash, the concept's disturbing popularization might be explained by a number of things in addition to ill intent. Perhaps it is "because [the metaphor] ameliorates a tension between a desire for more autonomous machines and a desire to retain human mastery. By referring to a master/slave relation in devices, professionals may reassure themselves that they will remain masters of machines" (2007, 366). Schweppe seems to have used the unfortunate metaphor to refute this professional desire and to foreground his description of a harmonious grid.

6. Tabors credited too many contributors to mention here. Among them are MIT professor James Kirtley, MIT visiting professor on leave from University of South Wales Hugh Outhred, and Frederick Pickel, then an MIT graduate student who went on to become the chief regulator of the Los Angeles Department of Water and Power. The 1980 article does not credit Roger Bohn and Michael Caramanis, the two members in addition to Tabors and Schweppe, who would go on to author *The Spot Pricing of Electricity*.

7. Citizenship is usually a requirement to serve on electric regulatory commis-

sions of Europe, except for the occasional independent member. Pérez-Arriaga (who does not hold Irish citizenship) served as the independent member on Ireland's commission.

8. "Enron Traders Caught on Tape," *CBS News*, 1 June 2004, *http://www.cbsnews.com/news/enron-traders-caught-on-tape*.

## CHAPTER 2

1. Google Earth is a computer program that draws on satellite imagery to represent Earth in three dimensions.

2. For scale, PJM Interconnection, one of the seven ISOs in the US, reported that in 2018, the average megawatt/hour price had been in the $35 to $40 range, with more than 90,000 megawatt/hours sold to be consumed every hour. See *pjm.com* for updated statistics.

3. Weather is a key determinant of demand for electricity. Employing in-house meteorologists as opposed to relying on outside weather reports is an example of EnTech's ambition to increase "granularity."

4. In this chapter, I use the word "data" in the singular in keeping with my interlocutors' general practice. For a discussion on the grammar and punctuation of "data," see Boellstroff 2013; Gitelman and Jackson 2013.

5. As Tom Boellstroff notes, the term "scrape" is an extension of the acceptance of rawness, as it denotes "scraping flesh from bone"—an existence prior to human contact (2013).

6. The establishment of OASIS was a key FERC measure that has allowed competition on a daily basis. Prior to deregulation, monopolists with exclusive rights of operation in demarcated territories did not have to communicate with each other because they did not share the transmission infrastructure; and they did not have a use for a shared information environment like OASIS.

## CHAPTER 3

1. After the computer revolution, academic electrical engineering found itself a new purpose by entering into a tacit division of labor with computer science. While the latter would focus on the study of algorithms, the former would engineer the circuits that powered those algorithms—in other words, electrical engineering would provide the hardware of the digital computation revolution and computer science its software (Ceruzzi 1996). While electronics became the talent-attracting subfield within electrical engineering, grid engineers remained a respectable community within the larger electrical engineering scene, albeit a small and relatively insular one, as my interlocutors view it.

2. In this chapter, names that are only first names are pseudonyms.

3. This vision did not necessarily rule out cooperation with ISOs—it encompassed them. Joo, the group's demand-side management expert, thought the ISOs were in a key role; they were to initiate a spiral of conversation by forwarding prices, based on

which utilities would solve their own optimization problems, based on which end users would also solve their own optimization problems, at which point the direction of the interaction would reverse; the process would continue until the mismatch between supply and demand dropped below a certain preset level, at which point the prices were set. This method internalized the complexities, as Joo put it; the ISOs were relieved from the burden of knowing all the relevant details about ramp-up and -down times, and the utilities did not have to encroach on users' privacy to calculate their optimum. About her method, Joo wrote, "it requires the least amount of information from the local entities to solve the global system problem" (2013, 45).

4. Wholesale prices, as we know from chapter 2, change every day, which is still too long an interval for the optimizing engineers who want to turn the grid into an everyday optimizing market.

5. Feminist scholars would agree that *homo economicus* is a "man"—a figure with "androcentric bias" (for an overview, see Ferber and Nelson 1993). The discipline's tendency to prioritize choice, sociologist Paula England argues, promotes a "separative model of human nature," where humans and their decisions were modeled as "radically separated from physical and social constraints" (1993, 32), "autonomous, impervious to social influences, and lack[ing] sufficient emotional connection to each other to make empathy possible" (1993, 37).

## CHAPTER 4

1. In this chapter, only first names are used.

2. A consumer who does not worry about her electricity bill is not representative of how electricity use is experienced by all Americans. In the US, poorer households spend more of their income on electricity bills than higher-income households. Due to a variety of factors, like energy-saving measures being more accessible to homeowners and those who have the finances to spare, the electricity bill is also higher per square footage for poorer families (Spector 2016).

3. I thank Antina von Schnitzler for bringing this point to my attention in a personal communication.

4. The dumping of many investor-incurred costs onto consumers' bills was a much-repeated refrain during my market training with ISO-NE. When we went over various pricing mechanisms, participants would often wonder how some items of auxiliary cost would be covered. The instructors said, "Load pays" (i.e., "Consumers pay") so often that the line became laughingstock, with participants randomly shouting "Load pays" during the week to elicit a chuckle from others. The joke reflected a sense of shared despondency; all the professionals in the room were, after all, consumers of electricity themselves.

5. In West Virginia, property owners need to disclose existing or impending right-of-way arrangements in their property when the property is put up for sale.

6. The announcement can be found on PJM's website: *https://www.pjm.com/~/media/committees-groups/committees/teac/20120913/20120913-srh-letter-to-teac-re-mapp-and-path.ashx*.

7. However, in 2020, new commissioners reversed the decision of their predecessors and ordered PATH to recollect its previous refunds to consumers. Keryn and Ali have since filed an appeal of this decision with the D.C. Circuit of the US Court of Appeals.

8. For coverage of this issue, see Tony Reid, "Illinois Nuclear Shutdown Threatened," *Herald-Review*, 1 February 2015, *http://herald-review.com/news/local/illinois-nuclear-shutdown-threatened/article_79b16ed2-b365-5f6f-9512-fdd1d40c4bc3.html.*

## EPILOGUE

1. A pseudonym.

# BIBLIOGRAPHY

Almklov, Petter. 2008. "Standardized Data and Singular Situations." *Social Studies of Science* 38 (6): 873–97.

Anand, Nikhil. 2011. "Pressure: The Polytechnics of Water Supply in Mumbai." *Cultural Anthropology* 26 (4): 542–64.

Appel, Hannah. 2012. "Offshore Work: Oil, Modularity, and the How of Capitalism in Equatorial Guinea." *American Ethnologist* 39 (4): 692–709.

———. 2014. "Occupy Wall Street and the Economic Imagination." *Cultural Anthropology* 29 (2): 602–25.

Appel, Hannah, Nikhil Anand, and Akhil Gupta. 2018. "Introduction: Temporality, Politics, and the Promise of Infrastructure." In *The Promise of Infrastructure*, edited by Hannah Appel, Nikhil Anand, and Akhil Gupta, 41–61. Durham, NC: Duke University Press.

Austin, J. L. 1962. *How to Do Things with Words*. Oxford: Clarendon Press.

Barad, Karen. 2007. *Meeting the Universe Halfway: Quantum Physics and the Entanglement of Matter and Meaning*. Durham, NC: Duke University Press.

Barnes, Jessica. 2016. "Uncertainty in the Signal: Modelling Egypt's Water Futures." *Journal of the Royal Anthropological Institute* 22 (S1): 46–66.

Barnet, Belinda. 2013. *Memory Machines: The Evolution of Hypertext*. New York: Anthem Press.

Barry, Andrew. 2002. "The Anti-Political Economy." *Economy and Society* 31 (2): 268–84.

Bateson, Gregory. 1971. "The Cybernetics of 'Self': A Theory of Alcoholism." *Psychiatry* 34 (1): 1–18.

———. 2000. *Steps to an Ecology of Mind*. Chicago: University of Chicago Press.

Battaglio, Stephen. 2016. "When Red Meant Democratic and Blue Was Republican: A Brief History of TV Electoral Maps." *Los Angeles Times*, 3 November 2016. *https://www.latimes.com/entertainment/tv/la-et-st-electoral-map-20161102-htmlstory.html*.

Baudrillard, Jean. 1988. *Simulacra and Simulation*. Stanford, CA: Stanford University Press.

Bell, Genevieve. 2015. "The Secret Life of Big Data." In *Data: Now Bigger and Better!*, edited by Tom Boellstorff and Bill Maurer, 7–26. Chicago: Prickly Paradigm Press.

Bernstein, Sebastian, and Renato Agurto. 1992. "Use of Outage Cost for Electricity Pricing in Chile." Special issue, *Utilities Policy* 2 (4): 299–302.

Besky, Sarah. 2014. *The Darjeeling Distinction: Labor and Justice on Fair-Trade Tea Plantations in India*. Berkeley: University of California Press.

Bestor, Theodor. 2004. *Tsukiji: The Fish Market at the Center of the World*. Berkeley: University of California Press.

Beunza, Daniel, and David Stark. 2004. "Tools of the Trade: The Socio-Technology of Arbitrage in a Wall Street Trading Room." *Industrial and Corporate Change* 13 (2): 369–400.

Biglaiser, Glen. 2002. "The Internationalization of Chicago's Economics in Latin America." *Economic Development and Cultural Change* 50 (2): 269–86.

Blanchette, Alex. 2020. *Porkopolis: American Animality, Standardized Life, and the Factory Farm*. Durham, NC: Duke University Press.

Bockman, Johanna. 2011. *Markets in the Name of Socialism: The Left-Wing Origins of Neoliberalism*. Stanford, CA: Stanford University Press.

Boellstroff, Tom. 2013. "Making Big Data, in Theory." *First Monday* 18 (10). *https://firstmonday.org/ojs/index.php/fm/article/view/4869/3750*.

Bohannan, Paul. 1959. "The Impact of Money on an African Subsistence Economy." *Journal of Economic History* 19 (14): 491–503.

Borges, Jorge Luis. 1999 [1946]. "On Exactitude in Science." In *Collected Fictions*, translated by Andrew Hurley, 325. New York: Penguin.

Boucher, Marie-Pier, Stefan Helmreich, Leila W. Kinney, Skylar Tibbits, Rebecca Uchill, and Evan Zeporyn. 2019. "Being Material: An Introduction." In *Being Material*, edited by Marie-Pier Boucher, Stefan Helmreich, Leila W. Kinney, Skylar Tibbits, Rebecca Uchill, and Evan Zeporyn, 11–12. Cambridge, MA: MIT Press.

Bowker, Geoffrey. 1993. "How to Be Universal: Some Cybernetic Strategies, 1943–70." *Social Studies of Science* 23 (1): 107–27.

———. 2005. *Memory Practices in the Sciences*. Cambridge, MA: MIT Press.

Bowker, Geoffrey, and Susan Leigh Star. 2000. *Sorting Things Out: Classification and Its Consequences*. Cambridge, MA: MIT Press.

Boyer, Dominic. 2008. "Thinking Through the Anthropology of Experts." *Anthropology in Action* 15 (2): 38–46.

———. 2013. *The Life Informatic: Newsmaking in the Digital Era*. Ithaca, NY: Cornell University Press.

———. 2014. "Energopower: An Introduction." *Anthropological Quarterly* 87 (2): 309–33.

Çalışkan, Koray. 2010. *Market Threads: How Cotton Farmers and Traders Create a Global Commodity*. Princeton, NJ: Princeton University Press.

Çalışkan, Koray, and Michel Callon. 2010. "Economization, Part 1: Shifting Attention from the Economy Towards Processes of Economization." *Economy and Society* 38 (3): 369–98.

Callon, Michel. 1998. *The Laws of the Markets*. Malden, MA: John Wiley.

———. 2005. "Why Virtualism Paves the Way to Political Impotence: A Reply to Daniel Miller's Critique of 'The Laws of the Market,'" *Economic Sociology: European Electronic Newsletter* 6 (2): 3–20.

Carr, Summerson. 2010. "Enactments of Expertise." *Annual Review of Anthropology* 39:17–32.

Carse, Ashley. 2012. "Nature as Infrastructure: Making and Managing the Panama Canal Watershed." *Social Studies of Science* 42 (4): 539–63.

Casper, Barry, and Paul D. Wellstone. 1981. *Powerline: The First Battle of America's Energy War*. Amherst: University of Massachusetts Press.

Cattelino, Jessica. 2008. *High Stakes: Florida Seminole Gaming and Sovereignty*. Durham, NC: Duke University Press.

Ceruzzi, Paul. 1996. "From Scientific Instrument to Everyday Appliance: The Emergence of Personal Computers, 1970–77." *History and Technology* 13 (1): 1–31.

Chandler, Alfred. 1977. *The Visible Hand: The Managerial Revolution in American Business*. Cambridge, MA: Belknap Press.

Clifford, James. 1988. *The Predicament of Culture: Twentieth-Century Ethnography, Literature, and Art*. Cambridge, MA: Harvard University Press.

Collier, Stephen. 2011. *Post-Soviet Social: Neoliberalism, Social Modernity, Biopolitics*. Princeton, NJ: Princeton University Press.

Collins, Harry. 1985. *Changing Order: Replication and Induction in Scientific Practice*. London: Sage.

Conover, Pamela Johnston, and Stanley Feldman. 1981. "The Origins and Meaning of Liberal/Conservative Self-Identifications." *American Journal of Political Science* 25 (4): 617–45.

Cowan, Ruth Schwartz. 1983. *More Work for Mother: The Ironies of Household Technology from the Open Hearth to the Microwave*. New York: Basic Books.

Cowen, Deborah. 2014. *The Deadly Life of Logistics: Mapping Violence in Global Trade*. St. Paul: University of Minnesota Press.

Cross, Jamie. 2013. "The 100th Object: Solar Lighting Technology and Humanitarian Goods." *Journal of Material Culture* 18 (4): 367–87.

Dalton, George. 1965. "Primitive Money." *American Anthropologist* 67 (1): 44–65.

Das, Veena. 2006. *Life and Words: Violence and the Descent into the Ordinary*. Berkeley: University of California Press.

De Certeau, Michel. 1984. *The Practice of Everyday Life*. Berkeley: University of California Press.

Degani, Michael. 2018. "Shock Humor: Zaniness and the Freedom of Permanent Improvisation in Urban Tanzania." *Cultural Anthropology* 33 (3): 473–98.

Deshmukh Towery, Nathaniel. 2014. "Changed Climate: Networking, Professionalization, and Grassroots Organizing in U.S. Environmental Organizations." PhD diss., Massachusetts Institute of Technology.

Dudley, Susan. 2011. "Remembering Kahn, 1917–2010: The Father of Airlines Deregulation." *Regulation Magazine*, Spring 2011. *http://object.cato.org/sites/cato.org/files/serials/files/regulation/2011/4/regv34n1-2.pdf*.

Edwards, Paul, Matthew Mayernik, Archer Batcheller, Geoffrey Bowker, and Christine Borgman. 2011. "Science Friction: Data, Metadata, and Collaboration." *Social Studies of Science* 41 (5): 667–90.

Eglash, Ron. 2007. "Broken Metaphor: The Master-Slave Analogy in Technical Literature." *Technology and Culture* 48 (2): 360–69.

England, Paula. 1993. "The Separative Self: Androcentric Bias in Neoclassical Assumptions." In *Feminist Economics Today: Beyond Economic Man*, edited by Marianne Ferber and Julie Nelson, 37–50. Chicago: University of Chicago Press.

Eriksen, Thomas, James Laidlaw, Jonathan Mair, Keer Martin, and Soumhya Venkatesan. 2015. "The Concept of Neoliberalism Has Become an Obstacle to the Anthropological Understanding of the Twenty-First Century." *Journal of the Royal Anthropological Institute* 21 (4): 911–23.

Eriksson, Maria. 2103. "Close Reading Big Data: The Echo Nest and the Production of (Rotten) Music Metadata." *First Monday* 21 (7). *https://firstmonday.org/ojs/index.php/fm/article/view/6303*.

Espeland, Wendy, and Mitchell Stevens. 1998. "Commensuration as a Social Process." *Annual Review of Sociology* 24 (1): 313–43.

Ferber, Marianne, and Julie Nelson, eds. 1993. *Feminist Economics Today: Beyond Economic Man.* Chicago: University of Chicago Press.

Ferenstein, Gregory. 2015. "The Unusual Politics of Silicon Valley, Explained." *Vox*, 6 November 2015. *https://www.vox.com/2015/9/29/9411117/silicon-valley-politics-charts*.

Fischer, Michael M. J. 2007. "Culture and Cultural Analysis as Experimental Systems." *Cultural Anthropology* 22 (1): 1–65.

Fleming, Peter. 2017. "The Human Capital Hoax: Work, Debt and Insecurity in the Era of Uberization." *Organization Studies* 39 (5): 691–709.

Floridi, Luciano. 2004. "Open Problems in the Philosophy of Information." *Metaphilosophy* 35 (4): 554–82.

Foner, Eric. 1984. "Why Is There No Socialism in America?" *History Workshop* 17:57–80.

Fraser, Nancy. 2017. "From Progressive Neoliberalism to Trump—and Beyond." *American Affairs*, 1 (4): 46–64.

Galison, Peter. 1994. "The Ontology of the Enemy: Norbert Wiener and the Cybernetic Vision." *Critical Inquiry* 21 (1): 228–66.

———. 1997. *Image and Logic: A Material Culture of Metaphysics*. Chicago: University of Chicago Press.

Ganti, Tejaswini. 2014. "Neoliberalism." *Annual Review of Anthropology* 43:89–104.

*Gasland*. Dir. Josh Fox. 2010.

Gitelman, Lisa, and Virginia Jackson. 2013. "Introduction." In *Raw Data Is an Oxymoron*, edited by Lisa Gitelman, 1–14. Cambridge, MA: MIT Press.

Glabau, Danya. 2019. "Food Allergies and the Hygienic Sublime." *Catalyst* 5 (2): 1–26.

Goldstein, Carolyn. 1997. "From Service to Sales: Home Economics in Light and Power, 1920–1940." *Technology and Culture* 38 (1): 121–52.

Granovetter, Mark. 1985. "Economic Action and Social Structure: The Problem of Embeddedness." *American Journal of Sociology* 91 (3): 481–510.

Granovetter, Mark, and Patrick McGuire. 1998. "The Making of an Industry: Electricity in the United States." *Sociological Review* 46 (1_suppl): 147–73.

Hall, Jonathan, and Alan Krueger. 2018. "An Analysis of the Labor Market for Uber's Driver Partners in the United States." *ILR Review* 71 (3): 705–32.

Halperin, Rhoda. 1977. "Introduction: The Substantive Economy in Peasant Societies." In *Peasant Livelihood: Studies in Economic Anthropology and Cultural Ecology*, edited by Rhoda Halperin and James Dow, 1–16. New York: St. Martin's Press.

Harcourt, Bernard. 2011. *The Illusion of Free Markets: Punishment and the Myth of the Natural Order*. Cambridge, MA: Harvard University Press.

Hartz, Louis. 1955. *The Liberal Tradition in America: An Interpretation of American Political Thought Since the Revolution*. New York: Harcourt.

Harvey, David. 2005. *A Brief History of Neoliberalism*. Oxford, UK: Oxford University Press.

Hayek, Friedrich. 1945. "The Use of Knowledge in Society." *American Economic Review* 35 (4): 519–30.

———. 1948. "The Meaning of Competition." *Individualism and Economic Order* 13 (2): 360–72.

Hershey, Robert, Jr. 2010. "Alfred Kahn, Chief Architect of Airline Deregulation, Dies at 93." *New York Times*, 29 December 2010. *https://www.nytimes.com/2010/12/29/business/29kahn.html*.

Hirschman, Daniel, and Elizabeth Popp Berman. 2014. "Do Economists Make Policies? On the Political Effect of Economics." *Socio-Economic Review* 12:779–811.

Ho, Karen. 2009. "Disciplining Investment Bankers, Disciplining the Economy: Wall Street's Institutional Culture of Crisis and the Downsizing of 'Corporate America.'" *American Anthropologist* 111 (2): 177–89.

———. 2012. "Finance and Morality." In *A Companion to Moral Anthropology*, edited by Didier Fassin, 413–32. Hoboken, NJ: Blackwell.

Hofstadter, Richard. 1948. *The American Political Tradition and the Men Who Made It*. New York: A. A. Knopf.

Hogan, Bill. 1995. "Electricity Transmission and Emerging Competition." *Public Utilities Fortnightly* 133 (13): 32–36.

Horan, Hubert. 2019. "Uber's Path of Destruction." *American Affairs Journal* 3 (2): 108–33. *https://americanaffairsjournal.org/2019/05/ubers-path-of-destruction/*.

Hughes, David McDermott. 2017. *Energy Without Conscience: Oil, Climate Change, and Complicity*. Durham, NC: Duke University Press.

Hughes, Thomas. 1993. *Networks of Power: Electrification in Western Society, 1880–1930*. Baltimore: Johns Hopkins University Press.

Ilić, Marija, Francisco Galiana, and Lester Fink, eds. 1993. *Power Systems Restructuring: Engineering and Economics*. New York: Springer.

Ilić, Marija, Le Xie, and Qixing Liu, eds. 2013. *Engineering It-Enabled Sustainable Electricity Services: The Tale of Two Low-Cost Green Azores Islands*. New York: Springer.

Irani, Lilly. 2015. "Justice for 'Data Janitors.'" *Public Books*, 15 January 2015. *https://www.publicbooks.org/justice-for-data-janitors/*.

Isaacson, Walter. 2004. *Benjamin Franklin: An American Life*. New York: Simon and Schuster.

Jones, Christopher. 2016. "Petromyopia: Oil and the Energy Humanities." *Humanities* 5 (2): 1–10.

Joo, Jhi-Young. 2013. "Adaptive Load Management: Multi-layered and Multi-temporal Optimization of the Demand Side in Electric Energy Systems." PhD diss., Carnegie Mellon University.

Joskow, Paul, and Richard Schmalensee. 1983. *Markets for Power: An Analysis of Electric Utility Deregulation*. Cambridge, MA: MIT Press.

Kahn, Alfred. 1988. *The Economics of Regulation: Principles and Institutions*. Cambridge, MA: MIT Press.

Kearney, Joseph, and Thomas Merrill. 1998. "The Great Transformation of Regulated Industries Law." *Columbia Law Review* 98 (6): 1323–1409.

Kelkar, Shreeharsh. 2018. "Engineering a Platform: The Construction of Interfaces, Users, Organizational Roles and the Division of Labor." *New Media and Society* 20 (7): 2629–46.

Kelty, Chris. 2014. "The Fog of Freedom." In *Media Technologies: Essays on Communication, Materiality, and Society*, edited by Tarleton Gillespie, Pablo Boczkowski, and Kirsten Foot, 195–220. Cambridge, MA: MIT Press.

Khan, Shamus Rahman. 2012. *Privilege: The Making of an Adolescent Elite at St. Paul's School*. Princeton, NJ: Princeton University Press.

Kirzner, Israel. 1960. *The Economic Point of View: An Essay in the History of Economic Thought*. New York: New York University Press.

Knafo, Samuel, Sahil Jai Dutta, Richard Lane, and Steffan Wyn-Jones. 2019. "The Managerial Lineages of Neoliberalism." *New Political Economy* 24 (2): 235–51.

Krippner, Greta. 2001. "The Elusive Market: Embeddedness and the Paradigm of Economic Sociology." *Theory and Society* 30 (6): 775–810.

Landsberger, Henry. 1958. *Hawthorne Revisited*. Ithaca, NY: Cornell University Press.

Larkin, Brian. 2008. *Signal and Noise: Media, Infrastructure, and Urban Culture in Nigeria*. Durham, NC: Duke University Press.

———. 2013. "The Politics and Poetics of Infrastructure." *Annual Review of Anthropology* 42:327–43.

Latour, Bruno. 1990. "Drawing Things Together." In *Representation in Scientific Practice*, edited by Michael Lynch and Steve Woolgar, 19–68. Cambridge, MA: MIT Press.

Law, John. 1987. "Technology and Heterogeneous Engineering: The Case of Portuguese Expansion." In *The Social Construction of Technological Systems: New Directions in the Sociology and History of Technology*, edited by Wiebe Bijker, Thomas Hughes, and Trevor Pinch, 111–134. Cambridge, MA: MIT Press.

Lépinay, Vincent. 2011. *Codes of Finance: Engineering Derivatives in a Global Bank*. Princeton, NJ: Princeton University Press.

Lerner, Eric. 2003. "What's Wrong with the Electric Grid?" *Industrial Physicist* 9 (5): 8–13.

Lévi-Strauss, Claude. 1969. *The Raw and the Cooked*. Chicago: University of Chicago Press.

———. 1997. "The Culinary Triangle." In *Food and Culture: A Reader*, edited by Carole Counihan and Penny Van Esterik, 28–35. London: Routledge.

Lippert, Ingmar. 2015. "Environment as Datascape: Enacting Emission Realities in Corporate Carbon Accounting." *Geoforum* 66:126–35.

Locke, John. 1690 [1980]. *Second Treatise of Government*. Indianapolis: Hackett.

MacKenzie, Donald. 2006. *An Engine Not a Camera: How Financial Models Shape Markets*. Cambridge, MA: MIT Press.

MacKenzie, Donald, Fabian Muniesa, and Lucia Siu, eds. 2008. *Do Economists Make Markets? On the Performativity of Economics*. Princeton, NJ: Princeton University Press.

Malaby, Thomas. 2012. "Digital Gaming, Game Design, and Its Precursors." In *Digital Anthropology*, edited by Heather Horst and Daniel Miller, 288–305. New York: Bloomsbury.

Malm, Andreas. 2016. *Fossil Capital*. New York: Verso.

Marcus, George. 1995. "Ethnography in/of the World System." *Annual Review of Anthropology* 24:95–127.

Marcus, George, and Michael M. J. Fischer. 1986. *Anthropology and Cultural Critique: An Experimental Moment in the Human Sciences*. Chicago: University of Chicago Press.

Marks, Gary, and Detlof von Winterfeldt. 1984. "Not in My Backyard: Influence of Motivational Concerns on Judgments About a Risky Technology." *Journal of Applied Psychology* 69 (3): 408–15.

Marshall, Alfred. 1890. *The Principles of Economics: Volume One*. New York: MacMillan.

Martin, Emily. 1994. *Flexible Bodies: The Role of Immunity in American Culture from the Days of Polio to the Age of AIDS*. Boston: Beacon Press.

Martinez-Gallardo, Cecilia, and Maria Victoria Murillo. 2011. "Agency under Constraint: Ideological Preferences and the Politics of Electricity Regulation in Latin America." *Regulation & Governance* 5 (3): 350–67.

Marx, Karl. 1977 [1867]. *Capital*. Vol. 1. New York: Random House.

Maurer, Bill. 2006a. "The Anthropology of Money." *Annual Review of Anthropology* 35 (1): 15–36.

———. 2006b. *Pious Property: Islamic Mortgages in the United States*. New York: Russell Sage Foundation.

Mayer-Schönberger, Viktor, and Kenneth Cukier. 2013. *Big Data: A Revolution That Will Transform How We Live, Work, and Think*. New York: Houghton Mifflin Harcourt.

McCloskey, Deirdre. 1998. *The Rhetoric of Economics*. Madison: University of Wisconsin Press.

McConnell, C. R. 1960. *Elements of Economic Analysis*. New York: McGraw-Hill.

McDonald, Forrest. 1958. "Samuel Insull and the Movement for State Regulatory Commissions." *Business History Review* 32 (3): 241–54.

McLean, Bethany, and Paul Elkind. 2004. *The Smartest Guys in the Room: The Amazing Rise and Scandalous Fall of Enron*. New York: Penguin Books.

McMahon, Michal. 1984. *The Making of a Profession: A Century of Electrical Engineering in America*. New York: IEEE Press.

Medina, Eden. 2011. *Cybernetic Revolutionaries: Technology and Politics in Allende's Chile*. Cambridge, MA: MIT Press.

Miller, Daniel. 2005a. *Materiality*. Durham, NC: Duke University Press.

———. 2005b. "Reply to Michel Callon." *Economic Sociology: European Electronic Newsletter* 6 (3): 3–13.

Mindell, David. 2004. *Between Human and Machine: Feedback, Control, and Computing Before Cybernetics*. Baltimore: Johns Hopkins University Press.

Mirowski, Philip. 1989. *More Heat Than Light: Economics as Social Physics, Physics as Nature's Economics*. Cambridge, UK: Cambridge University Press.

———. 2002. *Machine Dreams: Economics Becomes a Cyborg Science*. New York: Cambridge University Press.

Mitchell, Timothy. 2002. *Rule of Experts: Egypt, Techno-Politics, Modernity*. Berkeley: University of California Press.

———. 2008. "Rethinking Economy." *Geoforum* 39 (3): 1116–21.

———. 2011. *Carbon Democracy: Political Power in the Age of Oil*. London: Verso.

Miyazaki, Hirokazu. 2003. "The Temporalities of the Market." *American Anthropologist* 105 (2): 255–65.

Monticelli, A. 2000. "Electric Power System State Estimation." *Proceedings of the IEEE* 88 (2): 262–82.

Mosca, Manuela. 2008. "On the Origins of the Concept of Natural Monopoly: Economies of Scale and Competition." *European Journal of the History of Economic Thought* 15 (2): 317–53.

Negroponte, Nicholas. 1995. *Being Digital*. New York: Vintage.

Nye, David. 1992. *Electrifying America: Social Meanings of a New Technology: 1880–1940*. Cambridge, MA: MIT Press.

———. 2010. *When the Lights Went Out: A History of Blackouts in America*. Cambridge, MA: MIT Press.

Oka, Rahul, and Ian Kujit, 2014. "Introducing an Inquiry into the Social Economies of Greed and Excess." *Economic Anthropology* 1:1–16.

Ostrom, Elinor. 2009. "A General Framework for Analyzing Sustainability of Social-Ecological Systems." *Science* 325 (5939): 419–22.

Özden-Schilling, Canay. 2015."Economy Electric." *Cultural Anthropology* 30 (4): 578–88.

———. 2018. "Why the Lights Went Out in Puerto Rico." *Public Books*, 20 September 2018. *http://www.publicbooks.org/why-the-lights-went-out-in-puerto-rico/*.

———. 2019a. "Big Grid: The Computing Beast That Preceded Big Data." In *Current Thinking: Electricity and Anthropology*, edited by Simone Abram, Brit Ross Winthereik, and Thomas Yarrow, 161–99. New York: Bloomsbury Press.

———. 2019b. "Grid Country," *Journal of North American Anthropology* 22 (2): 118–20.

Patterson, Scott. 2012. *Dark Pools: High-Speed Traders, AI Bandits, and the Threat to the Global Financial System*. New York: Crown.

Paxson, Heather. 2008. "Post-pasteurian cultures: The Microbiopolitics of Raw-Milk Cheese in the United States." *Cultural Anthropology* 23 (1): 15–47.

Persky, Joseph. 1995. "Retrospectives: The Ethology of Homo Economicus." *Journal of Economic Perspectives* 9 (2): 221–31.

Pickering, Andrew. 1995. "Cyborg History and the World War 2 Regime." *Perspectives on Science* 3 (1): 1–48.

Plehwe, Dieter. 2009. "Introduction." In *The Road from Mont Pelerin: The Making of the Neoliberal Thought Collective*, edited by Philip Mirowski and Dieter Plehwe, 1–44. Cambridge, MA: Harvard University Press.

Polanyi, Karl. 1944. *The Great Transformation: The Political and Economic Origins of Our Time*. Boston: Beacon Press.

———. 1947. "Our Obsolete Market Mentality" *Commentary* 3 (1): 109–17.

Polanyi, Michael. 1966. *The Tacit Dimension*. Chicago: University of Chicago Press.

*Promised Land*. Dir. Gus van Sant. 2012.

Puchta, Susann. 1996. "On the Role of Mathematics and Mathematical Knowledge in the Invention of Vannevar Bush's Early Analog Computers." *IEEE Annals of the History of Computing* 18 (4): 49–59.

Rampell, Catherine. 2012. "Elinor Ostrom, Winner of Nobel in Economics, Dies at 78." *New York Times*, 12 June 2012. *https://www.latimes.com/local/obituaries/la-xpm-2012-jun-13-la-me-elinor-ostrom-20120613-story.html.*

Riles, Annelise. 2004. "Real Time: Unwinding Technocratic and Anthropological Knowledge." *American Ethnologist* 31 (3): 392–405.

Rodolfo, Kelvin. 2000. "What is Homeostasis?" *Scientific American* 282.

Rosenberg, Daniel. 2013. "Data Before the Fact." In *Raw Data is an Oxymoron*, edited by Lisa Gitelman, 15–40. Cambridge, MA: MIT Press.

Roth, Alvin. 1986. "On the Allocation of Residents to Rural Hospitals: A General Property of Two-Sided Matching Markets." *Econometrica* 54 (2): 425–27.

Rudolph, Richard, and Scott Ridley. 1986. *Power Struggle: The Hundred-Year War over Electricity*. New York: Harper and Row.

Samuelson, Paul. 1958. *Economics: An Introductory Analysis*. New York: McGraw-Hill.

Schwartz, Daniel, Baruch Fischhoff, Tamar Krishnamurti, and Fallaw Sowell. 2013. "The Hawthorne Effect and Energy Awareness." *Proceedings of the National Academy of Sciences* 110 (38): 15242–46.

Schweppe, Fred. 1969. "Power System Static State Estimation, Part III: Implementation." *Power Apparatus and Systems* 89 (1): 130–35.

———. 1978. "Power Systems 2000: Hierarchical Control Strategies." *IEEE Spectrum* 15 (7): 42–47.

Schweppe, Fred, Michael C. Caramanis, Richard D. Tabors, and Roger E. Bohn. 1988. *Spot Pricing of Electricity*. New York: Springer.

Schweppe, Fred, Richard Tabors, and James Kirtley. 1982. "Homeostatic Control for Electric Power Usage." *IEEE Spectrum* 19 (7): 44–48.

Schweppe, Fred, Richard Tabors, James Kirtley, Hugh Outhred, Frederick Pickel, and Alan Cox. 1980. "Homeostatic Utility Control." *IEEE Transactions on Power Apparatus and Systems* 99 (3): 1151–63.

Seavoy, Richard. 2006. *An Economic History of the United States: From 1607 to Present*. New York: Routledge.

Shurkin, Joel. 1996. *Engines of the Mind: The Evolution of the Computer from Mainframes to Microprocessors*. New York: W. W Norton.

Simmel, George. 1907. *The Philosophy of Money*. New York: Routledge.

Simon, Herbert. 2004. *Models of Man: Essays in Memory of Herbert A. Simon*. Edited by Mie Augier and James March. Cambridge, MA: MIT Press.

Smith, Adam. 2003 [1776]. *The Wealth of Nations*. New York: Oxford University Press.

Spector, Julian (and the City Lab). 2016. "Why Poor Americans Have Some of the Highest Electricity Bills." *Atlantic*, 18 April 2016. *https://www.theatlantic.com/*

*business/archive/2016/04/why-poor-americans-have-some-of-the-highest-electricity-bills/478551/.*

Star, Susan Leigh. 1999. "The Ethnography of Infrastructure." *American Behavioral Scientist* 43 (3): 377–91.

Stigler, George. 1971. "The Theory of Regulation." *Bell Journal of Economics and Management* 2:3–21.

Stigler, George, and Claire Friedland. 1962. "What Can Regulators Regulate? The Case of Electricity. *Journal of Law and Economics* 5:1–16.

Strathern, Marilyn. 1992. *Reproducing the Future: Anthropology, Kinship, and the New Reproductive Technologies.* Manchester, UK: Manchester University Press.

Swedberg, Richard. 1994. "Markets as Social Structures." In *Handbook of Economic Sociology*, edited by Neil Smelser and Richard Swedberg, 255–82. Princeton, NJ: Princeton University Press.

Swidler, Ann. 1986. "Culture in Action: Symbols and Strategies." *American Sociological Review* 51:273–86.

Taussig, Michael. 1980. *The Devil and Commodity Fetishism in South America.* Chapel Hill: University of North Carolina Press.

Tett, Gillian. 2009. *Fool's Gold: The Inside Story of J. P. Morgan and How Wall St. Greed Corrupted Its Bold Dream and Created a Financial Catastrophe.* New York: Free Press.

Ulbrich, Holley. 1991. "Natural Monopoly in Principles Textbooks: A Pedagogical Note." *Journal of Economic Education* 22 (2): 179–82.

Von Schnitzler, Antina. 2008. "Citizenship Pre-paid: Water, Calculability, and Politics in South Africa." *Journal of South African Studies* 34 (4): 899–917.

Walford, Antonia. 2017. "Raw Data: Making Relations Matter." *Social Analysis* 61 (2): 65–80.

Walley, Christine. 2013. *Exit Zero: Family and Class in Postindustrial Chicago.* Chicago: University of Chicago Press.

Weiser, Marc. 1993. "Some Computer Science Issues in Ubiquitous Computing." *Communications of the ACM* 36 (7): 75–84.

Welles, Orson, and Peter Bogdanovich. 1998. *This is Orson Welles.* New York: Da Capo Press.

Wexler, Marc. 1996. "A Sociological Framing of the NIMBY (Not-In-My-Backyard) Syndrome." *International Review of Modern Sociology* 26 (1): 91–110.

Wiener, Norbert. 1948. *Cybernetics or Control and Communication in the Animal and the Machine.* New York: Wiley.

Winner, Langdon. 1980. "Do Artifacts Have Politics?" *Daedalus* 109 (1): 121–36.

Wylie, Sara. 2018. *Fracktivism: Corporate Bodies and Chemical Bonds.* Durham, NC: Duke University Press.

Zaloom, Caitlin. 2003. "Ambiguous Numbers: Trading Technologies and Interpretation in Financial Markets." *American Ethnologist* 30 (2): 258–72.

———. 2006. *Out of the Pits: Traders and Technology from Chicago to London*. Chicago: University of Chicago Press.

———. 2012. "Traders and Market Morality." In *The Oxford Handbook of the Sociology of Finance*, edited by Karin Knorr Cetina and Alex Preda, 169–86. Oxford, UK: Oxford University Press.

# INDEX

accountants, 5, 6, 169, 174
agency and materiality, 10–11, 14
Agurto, Renato, 49
Allegheny Energy (AE), 137, 144
Almklov, Petter, 63, 72, 73
alternating current (AC), 15, 16, 103, 155,
177n3
Ameren, 153, 165
American Electric Power (AEP), 42–43,
137, 144
American Recovery and Reinvestment Act
of 2009, 126
Anand, Nikhil: on hydraulic citizenship,
135, 136; on infrastructure, 163
anthropology: and big data, 67; culture
in, 8; economic anthropology, 11, 12,
22, 23, 29, 62, 79, 81, 87, 89, 94, 101;
ethnographic research, 4, 5, 9–10, 23,
63, 66, 91, 105, 174–75; information as
anthropological object, 66–67, 87; and
infrastructure, 14–15, 135; and market
actors, 89; multisited research in, 23; and
neoliberalism, 29, 105; and raw data,
70; substantivist school, 11; technology
in, 11
Appel, Hannah, 101; on economic imaginations, 13, 55, 167; on infrastructure, 163
appliances, electric, 3, 6, 17–18, 97, 99, 107,
113, 119, 127
arbitrage, 20, 63, 69, 79, 85, 142
Argentina: deregulation in, 50, 51
Austin, J. L., 12
Azores: electricity consumption in, 22, 96,
114, 115, 119, 122

Barad, Karen: on agency and materiality,
10, 11
Barnes, Jessica, 72
Barnet, Belinda, 104
Barry, Andrew: on techno-politics, 173
Bateson, Gregory: on information bits, 66
Battaglio, Stephen, 178n3
Baudrillard, Jean: on simulacra, 82
Beer, Stafford, 108
behavioral researchers, 4, 15, 120, 126
Bell, Genevieve: on big data and truth, 67,
70
*Bell Journal/Rand Journal*, 33–34
Berman, Elizabeth Popp, 36, 37
Bernstein, Sebastian, 50
Besky, Sarah, 10
Bestor, Theodor, 89
Beunza, Daniel, 11, 77; on economies of
information, 79, 81, 86
big data, 65, 67–70
Biglaiser, Glen, 50
blackouts, 1, 16, 19, 21, 52, 89, 104, 105,
111
Blanchette, Alex, 10
Block RICL, 133, 134, 136, 140, 146, 151–
66, 167–68
Bockman, Johanna, 108
Boellstroff, Tom, 179n5; on raw data, 70,
179n5
Bogdanovich, Peter, 32
Bohannan, Paul, 11
Bohn, Roger, 39, 44, 45, 178n6
Borges, Jorge Luis: imperial cartography in
"On Exactitude in Science", 82, 83, 85, 91

Granovetter, Mark: on social networks and
electricity industry, 11
granularity, 19, 21, 117, 118, 128; and information workers, 83–84, 85, 86, 94, 179n3
Great Depression, 31
Gulf Oil, 42
Gupta, Akhil: on infrastructure, 163

Hall, Jonathan, 101
Halperin, Rhoda, 11
Harcourt, Bernard, 27
Hartz, Louis, 149
Harvey, David, 96
Hawaii: electricity market in, 26
Hawthorne Effect, 125–26
Hayek, Friedrich: on competition, 115; as
cyborg economist, 107; on information,
66–67, 115; "The Use of Knowledge in
Society", 115
Hershey, Robert, Jr., 33
Hirschman, Daniel, 36, 37
history of science, 47, 102
Ho, Karen, 12, 13, 55
Hofstadter, Richard, 149
Hogan, Bill: and Locational Marginal Prices
(LMPs), 45–46, 56
homeostasis for utilities, 39–40, 41, 46, 48
Horan, Hubert, 129
Hughes, David McDermott, 13
Hughes, Thomas, 16, 18, 103, 177n3

ideology, 23, 25, 26, 100, 173; and citizen
activists, 133, 134, 162–63; relationship
to deregulation, 4, 7, 9–10, 35, 49–50,
108, 112; relationship to market building, 4, 7, 9–10, 13, 27, 30, 108–9, 112–13.
See also neoliberalism
Ilić, Marija: and optimization lab at
Carnegie Mellon, 47, 95–96, 97, 98, 99,
101, 104–5, 107, 108, 109, 114, 117–18,
127, 128; and optimization lab at MIT,
127–28; and Ostrom, 113–14; relationship with Schweppe, 46–47, 51, 98; and
smart grids, 46–47, 97, 104–5, 109–19,
121, 122–23, 127, 128; views on competition, 98, 115; views on costs, 110, 112,

114, 115; views on ISOs, 110, 112, 118;
views on markets, 98, 108, 112, 113, 114,
115; views on neoclassical economics,
12, 113, 115, 116, 118–19; in Yugoslavia,
110–11
Illinois: Commerce Commission (ICC),
156, 162; Illinois Power Agency (IPA),
165; Renewable Portfolio Standard (RPS)
Act, 164–65; Supreme Court, 162
Illinois Landowners Alliance (ILA), 156,
157, 162
Independent System Operators (ISOs)/
Regional Transmission Organizations
(RTOs), 22, 34, 38, 48, 57–59, 97, 99,
172; bids and offers accepted by, 3, 19,
58, 61, 64–65, 68, 74, 75, 92, 112, 114,
115, 116, 118; boards of, 59; and capacity
markets, 55–56; consultants to, 58–59;
creation of, 19, 141–42; daily operations,
57–58; Ilić's views on, 110, 112, 118;
information from, 81, 87–88; Locational
Marginal Prices (LMPs) in, 45–46, 56,
83, 91, 142, 178n4; location of, 7, 74; as
private nonprofit entities, 58–59, 143;
and reliability lines, 141, 150; and smart
grids, 98, 179n3; and transmission of
electricity, 84–85, 137. See also ISO-NE;
PJM Interconnection
India: electricity in, 14; water in Mumbai,
135, 136
information: as anthropological object,
66–67, 87; big data, 65, 67–70; as bits of
data, 62–63, 67, 72, 81, 88–89, 90; data
proliferation, 63, 67–71, 86, 89–90; data
standardization, 62, 63, 64, 72–73, 89;
defined, 62, 66; economies of, 81; Hayek
on, 66–67, 115; interpretation of data,
79, 81, 86; from ISOs, 81; as reality, 66,
83; relationship to economics, 66; relationship to profit, 21, 62, 63–64, 66, 69,
85, 86, 90, 94
information workers: and computer
monitors, 61, 66, 75; database workers,
4, 8, 21, 59, 62, 63, 65, 70, 72–73, 75,
79, 80, 82–83, 84–85, 87–88, 91, 92,
105, 171–72, 175; data experts, 4, 5, 15,

CPSIA information can be obtained
at www.ICGtesting.com
Printed in the USA
JSHW020020210821
18042JS00002B/113